BREXIT AND LITERATURE

Brexit is a political, economic and administrative event: and it is a cultural one, too. In *Brexit and Literature*, Robert Eaglestone brings together a diverse range of literary scholars, writers and poets to respond to this aspect of Brexit. The discipline of 'English', as the very name suggests, is concerned with cultural and national identity: Literary studies has always addressed ideas of nationalism and the wider political process. With the ramifications of Brexit expected to last for decades to come, *Brexit and Literature* offers the first academic study of its impact on and through the humanities. Including a preface from Baroness Young of Hornsey, *Brexit and Literature* is a bold and unapologetic volume, focusing on the immediate effects of the divisive referendum while meditating on its long-term impact.

Robert Eaglestone is Professor of Contemporary Literature and Thought at Royal Holloway, University of London. He has published widely on contemporary fiction and philosophy and on the Holocaust and other genocides. He is the author of the best-selling textbook *Doing English*, 4th edn (Routledge, 2017), *The Broken Voice* (2017) and in 2014 was awarded a National Teaching Fellowship.

BREXIT AND LITERATURE

Critical and Cultural Responses

Edited by Robert Eaglestone

Routledge
Taylor & Francis Group

LONDON AND NEW YORK

First published 2018
by Routledge
2 Park Square, Milton Park, Abingdon, Oxon OX14 4RN

and by Routledge
711 Third Avenue, New York, NY 10017

Routledge is an imprint of the Taylor & Francis Group, an informa business

British Library Cataloguing-in-Publication Data
A catalogue record for this book is available from the
British Library

Library of Congress Cataloging-in-Publication Data
A catalog record has been requested for this book

ISBN: 978-0-8153-7668-2 (hbk)
ISBN: 978-0-8153-7669-9 (pbk)
ISBN: 978-1-351-20319-7 (ebk)

Typeset in Bembo
by Apex CoVantage, LLC

The editor and contributors dedicate this book to the memory of *Jo Cox, MP*. As a consequence, their royalties from this publication have been donated to the Jo Cox Foundation to support the continuation of her work.

CONTENTS

CONTRIBUTORS

Eva Aldea is a Polish-Romanian Swede based in London. She is a lecturer and writer, teaching literature and critical theory for the University of London, and has just finished her first novel. She enjoys interdisciplinary work and has spoken on nomadism and Europe at the LSE's Forum for European Philosophy and published on the topic on openDemocracy.net. She is author of *Magical Realism and Gilles Deleuze: The Indiscernibility of Difference in Postcolonial Literature* (Continuum 2010). Her first work of fiction to be published is featured in the *Best New Singaporean Short Stories: Volume Three* (Epigram 2017).

Bryan Cheyette is Chair in Modern Literature and Culture at the University of Reading and a Fellow of the English Association. He has authored or edited ten books, most recently *Diasporas of the Mind* (Yale UP, 2013), which was a 2013 *Times Higher* Book of the Year, and, as co-editor, a definitive history of the post-war novel (Oxford UP, 2016). He is also a Series Editor for Bloomsbury (*New Horizons in Contemporary Writing*) and has published more than sixty chapters in books from T. S. Eliot to Bob Dylan and from *Schindler's List* to Muriel Spark. He has lectured widely throughout the United States and Europe and has held visiting positions at Dartmouth College, the University of Michigan, and the University of

Pennsylvania. He also holds fellowships at the universities of Leeds, Southampton and Birkbeck College, London. He reviews fiction for several British newspapers and has published nearly one hundred essays on film, theatre and fiction for the *Times Literary Supplement*. He is currently working on a short book on the Ghetto for Oxford University Press.

Thomas Docherty studied in Glasgow, Paris and Oxford. He graduated with his MA in English and French language and literature from Glasgow, where he also studied mathematics and philosophy. He then took a DPhil and MA in Oxford. After five years teaching in Oxford, he moved to University College Dublin and then on to Trinity College Dublin, where he held the Chair of English (1867) – sometimes called the 'Dowden Chair', and one of the earliest Chairs of English in the world – between 1990–95. He was then elected as Fellow of Trinity College Dublin. In 1995, he returned to the UK, taking the Chair of English and Directorship of Research in the University of Kent. He moved to Warwick in 2004, where he headed the department until 2009 before again becoming Director of Research until 2013. Under his leadership as Director of Research, Warwick English was rated as the top department in the UK in the Research Excellence Framework. In 2016, he was awarded an honorary D.Litt. from the University of Kent in recognition of his academic achievements and commitment to higher education. He is the author of seventeen books, including, most recently: *Complicity*; *Universities at War*; *Confessions*; *For the University*. Two new books – *Literature and Capital* and *The New Treason of the Intellectuals* – will both appear in 2018, as will *Mood*, a volume of essays co-edited with Birgit Breidenbach. Another new book, *Political English*, will also appear shortly.

Robert Eaglestone is Professor of Contemporary Literature and Thought at Royal Holloway, University of London. He works on contemporary literature and literary theory, contemporary philosophy and on Holocaust and Genocide studies. He is the author of six books, including *Ethical Criticism: Reading after Levinas* (1997), *The Holocaust and the Postmodern* (2004), *The Broken Voice* (2017) and *Doing English* (4th edition 2017) and the editor or co-editor of seven more including *Derrida's Legacies* (2008) and *The Future of Trauma Theory* (2013). In 2014 he won a National Teaching Fellowship.

Ann-Marie Einhaus is Senior Lecturer in Modern & Contemporary Literature at Northumbria University, Newcastle-upon-Tyne. Her research centres on the literary and cultural legacy of the First World War, particularly in the medium of the short story, and her monograph, *The Short Story and the First World War*, was published by Cambridge University Press in 2013. She has since edited a new *Cambridge Companion to the English Short Story* (2016) and, most recently, the twenty-six chapter *Edinburgh Companion to the First World War and the Arts* (EUP, 2017). Her current research stretches from the immediate pre-war years to the Second World War and examines the contribution of literary and cultural magazines to discourses around European identity.

Michael Gardiner is Professor in the Department of English and Comparative Literary Studies at the University of Warwick. His books include *The Cultural Roots of British Devolution* (2006), *The Return of England in English Literature* (2012), *The Constitution of English Literature* (2013) and *Time and Action in the Scottish Independence Referendum* (2015).

Simon Glendinning is Professor of European Philosophy in the European Institute at the London School of Economics and Political Science. Having worked for a long time in European philosophy he is now attempting to develop an approach to the philosophy of Europe. Along with a number of articles and chapters on this theme, he is currently completing a two-volume study on the relationship between philosophical history (universal history) and the idea of Europe, entitled *Europe: A Philosophical History*.

Gabriel Josipovici was born in Nice, France, in 1940, of Russo-Italian, Romano-Levantine Jewish parents. He lived out the war years in a village in the Massif Central with his mother. He studied for four years in Egypt at Victoria College, Cairo, from 1952–56, before coming to England and finishing his high school education at Cheltenham College, Gloucestershire. He read English at St Edmund Hall, Oxford, graduating with a First in 1961. Gabriel Josipovici taught at the University of Sussex from 1963 until 1998, where he is Research Professor in the Graduate School of Humanities. He gave the Northclffe Lectures at the University of London in 1981, and in 1996 he was Weidenfeld Professor of Comparative Literature at the University of Oxford. Josipovici has published more than a dozen novels, three volumes of short stories and a number of critical books. Carcanet Press have published his work since his novel *Contre Jour* in 1986. His plays have been performed throughout Britain and on radio in Britain, France and Germany, and his work has been translated into the major European languages and Arabic. In 2001 he published *A Life*, a biographical memoir of his mother, the translator and poet Sacha Rabinovitch. In 2007, Gabriel Josipovici gave the University of London Coffin Lecture on Literature; the lecture was entitled "What ever happened to Modernism?" and was subsequently expanded into a book and published by Yale University Press. He is a frequent contributor to the *Times Literary Supplement*.

Anshuman A. Mondal is Professor of Modern Literature at the University of East Anglia. His research is principally concerned with the ways in which religious and cultural identities have been shaped and reshaped by social and political rhetorics within the frames of colonial modernity, nation-state formation and capitalist globalisation. He is the author of four books and numerous essays in the field of postcolonial studies, including *Nationalism and Post-Colonial Identity* (2003), *Amitav Ghosh* (2007), *Young British Muslim Voices* (2008) and *Islam and Controversy: The Politics of Free Speech after Rushdie* (2014). He is currently Chair of the Postcolonial Studies Association.

Ankhi Mukherjee is Professor of English and World Literatures at the University of Oxford. She is the author of *Aesthetic Hysteria: The Great Neurosis in Victorian Melodrama and Contemporary Literature* (Routledge, 2007) and *What Is a Classic? Postcolonial Rewriting and Invention of the Canon* (Stanford, 2014), which won the British Academy Rose Mary

Crawshay Prize for English Literature in 2015. Mukherjee has edited two volumes: *The Concise Companion to Psychoanalysis, Literature, and Culture* (Wiley-Blackwell, 2015) and *After Lacan* (Cambridge, 2018). Her current book project, funded by the Wellcome Trust and the AHRC, is titled *Unseen City: The Psychic Life of the Poor in Mumbai, London, and New York* and examines psychoanalysis in an international frame, and at the intersection of race and class. Mukherjee is on the editorial board of several journals and has been awarded visiting fellowships/professorships at the Australian National University (2014) and Johns Hopkins University (2019).

Martin Murray is the Head of Creative Technologies and Digital Media at London Metropolitan University. He teaches in the areas of modern and contemporary US and UK literature, continental philosophy, psychoanalytic theory and media and cultural studies. His offline and online publications – which are in academic journals, blogs and magazines – are also in these areas. He is the author of *Jacques Lacan: A Critical Introduction* (Pluto, 2016). In descending order of ability, he listens to, writes about and plays popular music of as many sorts as possible. He is currently writing a book about the psychodynamics of learning and teaching.

Petra Rau is a Senior Lecturer in Modern Literature at UEA. Her research areas are literature and film about war, fascism and expulsion as well as travel writing and Anglo-German relations. She is the author of *Our Nazis: Representations of Fascism in Contemporary Fiction and Film* (2013) and *English Modernism, National Identity and the Germans* (2009) and editor of *Conflict, Nationhood and Corporeality in Modern Literature* (2010) and *Long Shadows: The Second World War in British Fiction and Film* (2016). Her current monograph, *The Aesthetics of Loss: Flight and Expulsion in Postwar German Literature and Film*, is supported by a British Academy mid-career fellowship. She is also writing a family memoir entitled *A Journey of Giraffes*. She is (and will remain) a German citizen and has been living in the UK since 1997 but finds herself unsettled.

Kristian Shaw is Senior Lecturer in Contemporary and Postcolonial Literature at the University of Lincoln. He is the author of

Cosmopolitanism in Twenty-First Century Fiction (2017), was funded by the AHRC, and has recently completed a chapter in The Cambridge Companion to British Postmodern Fiction (forthcoming). He is currently starting his second monograph entitled *BrexLit* and is working on a Leverhulme-funded project on the causes and aftermath of the referendum result. He serves as a reader and editor for *C21 Literature: Journal of 21st-Century Writings*.

J.A. Smith is Lecturer in English Literature, 1660–1780, at Royal Holloway, University of London. His books are *Samuel Richardson and the Theory of Tragedy: Clarissa's Caesuras* and *Other People's Politics: Corbyn and the New Populism*.

Lyndsey Stonebridge is Professor of Modern Literature and History at the University of East Anglia. Her latest book is *The Judicial Imagination: Writing after Nuremberg* (2011/2014), winner of the British Academy Rose Mary Crawshay Prize. *Placeless People: Rights, Writing, and Refugees* is forthcoming with Oxford University Press (2018). Her other books include *The Destructive Element* (1998), *Reading Melanie Klein* (with John Phillips, 1998), *The Writing of Anxiety* (2007) and *British Fiction after Modernism* (with Marina MacKay, 2007). She is currently writing a short book on literature and human rights for OUP's *Literary Agendas* series, and collaborating on a large interdisciplinary project, *Refugee Hosts* (https://refugeehosts.org/).

George Szirtes was born in Hungary in 1948 and came to England as a refugee in 1956. He published his first book of poems, *The Slant Door*, in 1979. It won the Faber Memorial Prize. He has published several others since including *Reel* (2004), which was awarded the T. S. Eliot Prize, and for which *The Burning of the Books* (2009) and *Bad Machine* (2013) were also shortlisted. He has won various prizes for his translations from the Hungarian, including the Man Booker International translator's prize for his work on László Krasznahorkai. His latest book is *Mapping the Delta* (2016). His *New and Collected Poems* appeared in 2008.

Sara Upstone is Associate Professor of English Literature at Kingston University, London and Head of Humanities, where she specialises in contemporary literatures and critical theory, with particular interests in racial and gender politics, music philosophy and representations of desire. She is the author of three monographs: *Rethinking Race and Identity in Contemporary British Fiction*; *British Asian Voices: Twenty-first-century Fiction* and *Spatial Politics in the Postcolonial Novel*, as well as *Literary Theory: A Complete Introduction*. She is also co-editor of *Postmodern Literature and Race* (with Len Platt); *Researching and Representing Mobilities* (with Lesley Murray) and *Postcolonial Spaces: The Politics of Place in Contemporary Culture* (with Andrew Teverson).

Anne Varty is Professor of English at Royal Holloway, University of London. Her research interests are in contemporary and modern poetry, Victorian, British and European drama, Women's poetry and autobiographies of the First World War and Victorian literature. Amongst her publications are the edited collection *The Edinburgh Companion to Liz Lochhead* (2013), and with Robert Crawford, *Liz Lochhead's Voices* (1993). Her monographs are *A Preface to Oscar Wilde* (1997) and *Children and Theatre in Victorian Britain* (2007).

Lola Young, Baroness Young of Hornsey, OBE, is a Professor of Cultural Studies and Crossbench peer. Her publications include *Fear of the Dark: Race, Gender and Sexuality in Cinema* (1995). From 2001 to 2004 she was head of culture at the Greater London Authority and was created a life peer on 22 June 2004, taking the title Baroness Young of Hornsey in the London Borough of Haringey. Young's other public appointments include membership of the board of the Royal National Theatre, the South Bank Centre and the board of Governors of Middlesex University, chairing the Arts Council's Cultural Diversity Panel, and membership of the board of the Council of Museums, Archives and Libraries, and a commissioner on the Royal Commission on Historical Manuscripts. She has also chaired the judging panel of the Orange Prize for Fiction and was Chair of the 2017 Booker Prize jury. She takes an active interest in ethical issues in international trade, in Europe and in matters of culture.

PREFACE

Baroness Young of Hornsey

Several of the publications submitted to the 2017 Man Booker Prize attempted to describe the mood of the post-Brexit moment or offer explanations or went into a full apocalyptic lament, some with greater effectiveness and subtlety than others. In fact, as Chair of the judging panel, I was surprised that so many writers were so quick to incorporate or even focus on the recent shifts in global geo-politics, led by the tragedies unfolding in Iraq and Syria, the subsequent mass migrations, refugees dispersed across different parts of the world, as well as the tumult caused by the referendum and the election of Donald Trump as US president.

Books such as *Brave New World* and *Nineteen Eighty-Four* were meant to alert us to the dangers of the authoritarian, totalitarian state, but it turns out they've been adopted as the playbook of both elected and unelected dictatorships across the globe. Arguably, although the sales of both these books were hugely boosted by the outcome of the US presidential election, they don't seem to have made enough people aware of just how complicit we've become in extending the reach of purposeful electoral manipulation, big data and global capital. We noted the similarities between these twentieth-century, ugly dystopian visions but didn't act with sufficient robustness to address the situation. There's a role for literature, so adept at humanising big questions and creating emotional and cultural landscapes, in metaphorically poking us all in the ribs and urging us to start thinking critically and becoming politically active again.

Assuming we haven't yet reached the end of history and the writing of it really is still shaped by the victors, then what kind of historical narrative will eventually emerge from our current and future predicaments as exposed by Brexit? Given that, in any case a) there were no winners in that referendum and b) there aren't enough people dedicated to writing a factual, rational account of what happened in the summer of 2016, I would suggest that the answer to that question is anyone's guess.

All of which raises more questions than can be sensibly addressed in a substantial novel, let alone a preface to an intriguing collection of essays.

People working in the creative industries were overwhelmingly in favour of remaining in the EU and voted accordingly. Quite how creative minds in the sector will work through this political and existential mire remains to be seen in spite of the insightful, valiant efforts already published. It's clearly early days and I expect to see many more literary works at the very least alluding to the ramifications of Brexit in every aspect of our lives. Boldly stepping up to try and tease out and interpret some initial thinking about Brexit – and how I hate that we've all adopted that ugly word – and its impact on literature, the writers in this book deploy a mixture of critical strategies to interrogate what we've seen and heard so far.

ACKNOWLEDGEMENTS

At Routledge, I'm grateful to Polly Dodson for her initiative and support and to Zoe Meyer for her work on this book. Also to Kerry Boettcher, Project Manager from Apex CoVantage. I'd also like to thank Iona Lawrence, the Director of the Jo Cox Foundation; all in the Department of English at Royal Holloway, University of London; Gail Marshall for her support; Alan White; Nick Hoare; Alex Eaglestone; Bella Eaglestone; and finally, I'm especially grateful to Poppy Corbett for her support, ideas and conversations about Brexit, and love.

INTRODUCTION

Brexit and literature

Robert Eaglestone

An island, entire of itself?

Brexit is not only political, economic and administrative: perhaps most significantly it is an event in culture, too. Brexit grew from cultural beliefs, real or imaginary, about Europe and the UK; the arguments before, during and after the referendum were – and are – arguments about culture; its impact on the cultural life of these islands may last for generations.

Culture is the heart of national identity, as Benedict Anderson's *Imagined Communities* showed. A nation is too huge to be a real community in which everyone actually knows each other. Instead, nations are produced in the imagination by concepts, narratives, memories and traditions: that is, through the work of culture. One aspect of culture especially closely linked to national identity is literature: this is evident in the name of the subject that studies it, 'English'. English specializes in profounder understanding and thought about ideas, stories, feelings, language and so, in this context, supplements and deepens the social sciences. And so literature is an especially useful and appropriate way to address the political arguments about national identity which lie at the heart of Brexit.

More, brexit inescapably concerns emotions and community. Aristotle's *Rhetoric*, his model for public deliberation, describes three aspects to political argument: *logos* (akin to our word 'logic' but meaning here something like 'evidence-based argument'), *pathos* (from which come our words empathy and sympathy, using feeling) and *ethos* (our shared values, our sense of community). Literature and the study of literature encompass reason but also take emotions (personal, communal, subjective, in all their complexity) and ideas about value seriously as forms of knowledge and meaning.

Literature and its study play a crucial role in our thought about how we live as individuals and as communities because of its deep involvement with personal and communal identity and because it broadens and reflects on our ability to think, feel and argue. These are the reasons for this book.

Involved in mankind

With this in mind, *Brexit and Literature* is a little different from most academic collections of essays. Brexit is unavoidably to do with identity as well as analysis, 'who we are' as well as 'what we do', and demands thoughtful out-of-the-ordinary critical and cultural responses of all kinds, as the subtitle indicates. So, in addition to more conventional academic criticism and theory, this book includes personal reflection, memoir, polemic and poetry. I've also tried to make the book accessible to the general reader.

The first five chapters circle around Brexit and what literature can tell us. Lyndsey Stonebridge, facing what she names the banality of Brexit, discusses Hannah Arendt's account of the significance of thinking to argue that literature is a natural enemy of thoughtlessness but that we will need more than the "literary liberalism bequeathed to us at the end of the Cold War", to help restore political judgement in the contemporary politics of Brexit. Kristian Shaw notes a rash of new fiction – he coins the term 'BrexLit' – including cash-in pot boilers, dystopias, crime and literary fiction. However, it is Ali Smith's *Autumn* (2016), "arguably the first significant post-Brexit novel" which most attracts his attention, while Anthony Cartwright's *The Cut* (2017) and Mohsin Hamid's *Exit West* (2017) also have much to say about the crisis of cosmopolitanism. Petra Rau draws on her own life experience and her experience of teaching fiction to discuss Brexit, and she again turns to Ali Smith's *Autumn*, focussing on its understanding of time. Sara Upstone analyses the role literature plays in Brexit politics by looking at Luton as a microcosm of the UK in contemporary writing: the town appears in the fiction of Nicola Barker and the memoir of Sarfraz Manzoor, for example. Upstone suggests that how we imagine a place shapes our cultural imaginary and so our sense of identity and that this, too, sets a challenge to writers. Anne Varty gives an account of Carol Ann Duffy's 'Shore to Shore' poetry tour, which featured several poets and took place during and after the referendum campaign in June 2016. As the events unfolded, the poems acquired new and important resonances. Varty cites the poet Gillian Clarke: "words speak to the heart, the hurt, the anxiety of a nation in crisis. We see it, and hear it, in every audience, every town, every stopping-place on this journey".

Reflecting on the powers of literature, closing this passage of chapters and beginning the next, Bryan Cheyette offers an autobiographical reflection on a kind of migrancy into literature and literary studies and the role of a migrant's perspective for writers and critics. He argues that Brexit "means that our national straightjacket – Englishness, not even Britishness – becomes much tighter and the value of a migrant's perspective becomes increasingly discounted and devalued". Ankhi Mukherjee's personal account uses Rawi Hage's novel *Cockroach* (2008) for a discussion of the complex ways migrancy shapes the psyche. She notes how "Hage's *Cockroach* makes its leading character, an active, not passive subject, a migrant who refuses to be read, neutralised, or immobilised" and then excoriates the dangerous words on migrants from the 'Leave' campaign and the British right. What connects the two parts is the "swarm" of Cameron's and Farage's phobic imagination and the avenging insect of Hage's novel. Following on from this, Anshuman Mondal's 'Scratching the Post-Imperial Itch' shows how the "structures of feeling" produced by legacy of Imperialism, in which the "principal ingredient" is race and racism, has "still not fully wound . . . through the digestive tracts of the United Kingdom's body politic" and lies behind Brexit. Moving from the 'structures of feeling' inherited from Empire to those bestowed by the Second World War, I examine the affective memory of the War in Brexit as a form of 'cruel nostalgia' and analyse its wider consequences. Focusing again on the relation of past and present, Michael Gardiner argues that the neo-liberal present can be interrupted by texts which use 'anachronism as a weapon' through which the past haunts and disrupts the current moment. He argues that the Brexit vote was a "vast repository of such untimely traces" which allowed the upsurge of what neo-liberalism had repressed. J.A. Smith revaluates the great and controversial critic F.R. Leavis, and finds in his work not only an analysis of the broader context but also a vocabulary for encountering cultural and communal worth. This, he argues, might be of more long-term importance than the "reactive inoculation against fake news that we have for a long time reassured ourselves is one of more robust by-products of trained 'close reading'". Academics are, too, central to Murray's account of the psychopolitics of Brexit, in which he turns to psychoanalysis to understand how the psychic nature of conflict, as much as the content, shapes ourselves and the outcome. Writer and academic Gabriel Josipovici, too, is concerned with cultural worth, past and present. He offers his brief autography in order to outline the "vision of other possibilities" of the imagination which are "embedded in our universities" and presses our need to go on "articulating them". Josipovici's elegiac view is echoed in Eva Aldea's description of the nomad, inspired by Rosi Braidotti. Aldea's autobiographical reflection on those for whom land is a "route rather than a root" explores, like Cheyette, Josipovici and Smith, the significance of education and literature.

Moving, in a way, from teaching to research, Ann-Marie Einhaus draws on her own work on British and German periodicals from the first half of the twentieth century. She reflects on the parallels between British engagement with European cultural identity, then and now, to argue that literature is "a negotiator between peoples and cultures even in times of extreme crisis". Simon Glendinning too, turns to Germany and, reading Nietzsche, contrasts the French and German philosophical visions of Europe's past and future with what is taken to be a more 'English' view. He proposes not a European supra-national government but instead a recognition that Europe is not unified but a place in which differences are celebrated: not a united states of

Europe but a united Europe of states. This book began with Arendt and the importance of thought. Thomas Docherty's polemic, 'Thinking and Resistance', brings it full circle. Brexit, he writes, is

> an assault upon the intellect, which, by definition, cannot be 'national'. The intellect – thinking – is what takes us beyond our own body, our own physical self. It is the intellect that opens us to foreignness, to things previously undreamt of in our philosophies. Brexit is a steely closing of that and every other door.

That is, to think is to resist.

The epilogue is an autobiographical lecture and reflection on Brexit, interspersed with poems, from George Szirtes. Edward Thomas's 1917 poem 'Adlestrop' describes a moment of beauty at the tiny railway station there: suddenly the poet hears "all the birds of Oxfordshire and Gloucestershire". Szirtes's closing poem, 'The Immigrant at Port Selda', literally reverses Adlestrop. Here, the pastoral "beauty of the country" does not open up "to all the birds" but is the location for a faceless nationalistic rejection of those "who will never be/our collective unconscious nor of our race". Szirtes speaks for many of us, born in the UK or abroad, who find ourselves now at Port Selda.

It tolls for thee

In the days after the referendum, a fragment from John Donne's Meditation XVII was widely cited (for example, by P.J. Harvey during her Glastonbury performance) and circulated on social media.

> No man is an island, entire of itself; every man is a piece of the continent, a part of the main. If a clod be washed away by the sea, Europe is the less, as well as if a promontory were, as well as if a manor of thy friend's or of thine own were: any man's death diminishes me, because I am involved in mankind, and therefore never send to know for whom the bell tolls; it tolls for thee.

The sentiment, that no one is an island, that if "a part of the main" is washed away "Europe is the less" and that any one's "death diminishes me, because I am involved in mankind", seems very apt. Many, if not quite all, writers and literary scholars have always felt "a part of the main" in the sense that they feel attached to intellectual work and culture from the wider world, cosmopolitan.

However, many in the UK now feel apart *from* the main. Brexit has stirred up a terrifying political discourse in which opponents of Brexit are described as 'saboteurs' or 'enemies of the people': and 'I think people in this country have had enough of experts'. Prime Minister May herself declared that she is 'putting … on warning' those who think they are 'a citizen of the world' because they are, she said, 'a citizen of nowhere' who doesn't 'understand what the very word "citizenship" means'. In October 2017, Tory whip Chris Heaton-Harris wrote to all Vice-Chancellors asking for the 'names of professors at your establishment who are involved in the teaching of European affairs, with particular reference to Brexit'. The same week, the *Daily Mail* launched an attack on "Our Remainer Universities" complete with an email address for anyone who has 'experienced anti-Brexit bias at university' to tell all. This Brexit discourse is no friend to creative, cosmopolitan literature nor to attentive and responsive literary scholarship: we oppose it.

That said, an academic book of literary essays isn't much and, as Donne points out, a little 'clod' is easily 'washed away by the sea'. But a seawall set against a rising storm tide is not made of one single titanic rock but of very many small stones, deliberately and thoughtfully placed and firmly set together.

1

THE BANALITY OF BREXIT

Lyndsey Stonebridge

1

Stupid. Men too stupid to think about the consequences of their actions tricked the British into making a fatally stupid decision. This is how Brexit is most commonly described. In the UK our stupid politicians tend to actually look stupid. It's a clever but dangerous deception. Boris Johnson, the boy with the flyaway hair and the love of a doting mother in his eyes, roaring and thumping the pride of Britain throughout the campaign, was left mouthing bland nothings the day after his success. On the same morning, buffoon-in-chief Nigel Farage, he of the marionette jaw and the patent shoes patterned with the Union Jack flag, exulted: "And we'll have won it, without a single bullet being fired." Barely 24 hours earlier the body of Jo Cox MP had been released to her family; the coroner recorded that she had died of 'multiple stab and gunshot wounds'.

This is a dark and dangerous stupidity, all the more pernicious for the way it is worn so lightly by its perpetrators and tolerated, sometimes even indulged, by the rest of us. Bereft educated remainers have taken to consoling themselves with their cleverness, collectively rolling their eyes at the stupidity of others. This is not only arrogant;

it is also stupid in its own way. The stupidity that is leading the UK out of the EU, the easy idiocy that has unleashed hate and intolerance, economic and political instability, is in fact a banality that we need to take very seriously.

Weightless, rootless, banality creeps like fungus, sticking to everything. Often you don't know it's there until the furniture of politics goes clammy and starts to rot.

Johnson and Farage take evident pleasure in performing their twitfuckery. By contrast, Adolf Eichmann thought of himself as a serious, even profound man. This was why when the political philosopher Hannah Arendt travelled to Jerusalem to confront the Nazi specialist face to face, she burst out laughing. The man was a buffoon, a vain cardboard cut-out of a person, unable to account for himself in anything other than clichés. Eichmann wasn't banal because he was stupid, he was banal because he was radically thoughtless. The longer you listened to him, Arendt said, the more obvious it became that he was incapable of thinking from the standpoint of anyone else. He lacked the two-in-one dialogue with oneself, the classical Socratic definition of thought itself. It is thoughtlessness, not mere twittery, that is banal.

"Remember thinking?" asked a despairing former archbishop of England, Rowan Williams, at a meeting on antisemitism in Westminster days after the Brexit vote. Arendt thought that thinking was the precondition of political judgment. Thinking is not politics, but politics needs thinking if it is to thrive. Without thought there can be no moral responsibility. This is an old Athenian idea, another piece of European heritage that Britain appears to have turned its back on.

Banality is not just being wrong, it is being radically indifferent to the world. The point when many people think the Leave campaign finally crossed the line was when Boris Johnson attempted to justify President Obama's opposition to Brexit by reference to a 'part-Kenyan ancestral dislike of the British empire.' This was a stupid thing to say. It was also a defining moment of banality. Johnson couldn't understand the offence because he is incapable of thinking of a world where other lives, or views, really exist. Thoughtlessness like this is contagious. It was not only the casual racism of the remark that was shocking but the fact that so many people failed to understand – to think – that it was racist at all.

These are the people Arendt called the "nonwicked everybody" who, having "no special motives" are "capable of infinite evil" (Arendt, 1994). But it is the politicians whose thoughtlessness abrogates responsibility, the properly wicked, who in the end make evil possible. Philippe Sands QC, author of *Lawless World* (2005) the definitive takedown of Bush and Blair's assault on international law, has argued that the path to Brexit began with Iraq (Sands, 2016). Another bad decision made by men who could not think out of their own prejudices. There has always been lying in politics, but the insouciant disregard for either process or reality then marked the beginning of the end of political trust for an entire generation.

And so it has continued. After Brexit came Trump, more bling than banal, perhaps, more of an idiot than Boris Johnson, probably, but the flatus of POTUS is similarly insidious. Across the West we are experiencing the zero-gravity political cultures that only two years ago we assumed belonged to other times and other places. The moral obscenities continue to mount up. In the spring of 2017 the UK Home Office reneged on its promise to take children from Calais (the Dubs' Agreement) on the grounds that to do so would be encourage children to put their lives in danger. In the summer, the elected representatives of Kensington and Chelsea Council faced the survivors of the Grenfell Tower fire and rolled their eyes.

2

Literature, writing, poems, songs, and plays are the natural enemies of banality. Writing is the staging of two-in-one thinking. Novels, Bakhtin taught us, are dialogic. Poems remind us that language is a rich, complex, and surprising place to live in. Literature is where meanings and morals are put in place and put on trial. Literature is "world making" in Gayatri Spivak's sense (Spivak, 1985). At times, those worlds collude with cruelly insouciant barbarism. Sometimes literature opens up new worlds, offering avenues of liberty. At first glance, at least, literary studies presents itself as an attractive alternative to the banality of Brexit. Here is where we do the thinking it seems that our political culture can no longer support.

All this is true – so true, perhaps, that in the long history of the relationship of literature to political culture, it almost seems banal to point it out just now. Is this really the moment to inflate the cultural, let alone political, power of literature?

This question was eloquently raised by a student at a meeting arranged by the alternative media organisation *Norwich Radical* in March 2017. The student was observing that in bestseller lists you have to go quite a long way down before you find a literary fiction title. The implication was that if literary fiction was more widely read, our political culture might be less banal. But then she smartly checked herself. Literariness might be an antidote to thoughtlessness; but might thoughtless assumptions about the value of some books over others, some ways of thinking over others, also be part of the problem, she wondered? Her family did not read literary fiction but were no less thoughtful for not having Ian McEwan on their shelves.

We are missing something important about what has happened over the past two years if we assume that literary liberalism is a plausible response to our current predicament. It was certainly not the debate on sovereignty that its good-faith supporters intended, and the lies told make its mandate precarious, but what is certain is that, at least in part, Brexit was a protest against some people assuming that other people were stupid. Eye rolling is not only the vice of the pantomime villains of neo-liberalism.

Although she was clear that thinking was the precondition of politics, Arendt too worried about the role of reflection in dark times. True, to think is to make words mean again – which is why literature has a special affinity with critical thinking; but thinking can also be a kind of retreat, an 'inner emigration,' perversely, a way of not taking moral responsibility for the world you live in. Rather than allowing escape, for Arendt thinking should lead to an unmediated comprehension of reality, however much – and especially when – we are revolted by that reality.

The revolting reality of Brexit Britain today is that the buffoons of ethno-nationalism have been allowed to crowd out the spaces where debates about inequality, disenfranchisement, fairness, participation, community, political facts, hopes, and histories should have taken place. That happened partly because some of us who like to think of ourselves as very thoughtful indeed were not thinking hard or widely enough. The consequence is that many of the most culturally enfranchised people in the country are currently, and unusually, experiencing what it feels like to be politically disenfranchised. That is an uncomfortable reality but a good starting point for reflection.

Before we offer literature as the antidote to banality, we need to think harder about the history of cultural and political belonging. In her early study of Rahel Varnhagen, the eighteenth-century Jewish salonnière, Arendt wrote of Varnhagen's desire for "a new language where all the words have lost their banality" (Arendt-Stern, 1934). A woman and a Jew, Varnhagen believed that the universalism proposed by Goethe's World Literature could make good the promise of equality for all offered by the European dream. She was wrong. By the time Arendt was finishing her reflections on Varnhagen's life in the mid-1930s, by then a refugee in Paris about to be deported to Gurs detention camp, the eighteenth-century iteration of European universalism had crashed. Arendt never stopped believing that poetic language offered a means of creative being; but henceforth she would stake out a place for the tradition of pariahs – Jews, refugees, the others of European citizenry.

The task Arendt and others of her generation confronted at the end of the Second World War was to invent a humanism that could be universal and particular, collective and specific. This task required much more than tolerance, empathy, or being 'mindful' about difference. Imperialism, colonialism, racism, rapid economic expansionism, and the collapse of the state into nationalism had all created the conditions for totalitarianism. No humanism, literary or otherwise, could re-invent itself without at the same time reckoning with those histories which may, indeed, be why no Western humanism really bothered to try that hard; the humanism of anti- and post-colonial thinking is another matter (Gilroy, 2014). Nor can we confront the banality of Brexit today without acknowledging the realities of political and cultural dispossession.

As many of us have done over the past year, Arendt took Orwell into the classroom to help her and her students think about these matters. *Nineteen Eighty-Four* was on the syllabus of a course she taught at Berkeley in 1955 (she later taught *Down and Out* and *Homage to Catalonia* to students at the New School and Cornell). This was at the beginning of the Cold War and, like Orwell, Arendt was keen to understand the function of the political lie. Arendt thought Orwell was half right. Two plus two would never make five, she pointed out in *Origins of Totalitarianism*, mathematical reason will always be mathematical reason; the real point wasn't the evident stupidity of totalitarian ideology but the way its banality created the loneliness that allowed totalitarianism to thrive. The original title of Orwell's novel was *The Last Man in Europe*.

Much of this is newly resonant. But to turn to *Nineteen Eighty-Four* today without reckoning with the book's own political and historical journey through and beyond the Cold War is to risk, once again, confusing the antidote with the symptom. For generations of Western schoolchildren who grew up during the Cold War, *Nineteen Eighty-Four* became the touch-text for liberal values, particularly those of compassion and emotional engagement with the suffering of others. That ideological legacy continued into the late twentieth and early twenty-first centuries, providing the basis for a liberalism based on pragmatism and humanitarian values. Martha Nussbaum described the novel as detailing the "death of pity" under a political regime, arguing that Orwell showed how human empathy was essential to the functioning of liberal democracies (Nussbaum, 2005). Similarly, Richard Rorty, writing just at the end of the Cold War, claimed the novel's continued relevance lay in Orwell's rejection of political reason as a means to a just end and his promotion, instead, of the intolerance of cruelty which marked postwar liberal thought (Rorty, 1993).

We hear less from these authors of Orwell's intolerance of poverty, his contempt for colonialism, of the enraged critic of the faux humanism of the so-called liberal democracies who argued, as far back as 1939, that a democratic union of countries that refused to count the lives of those who made its wealth and privilege possible had no real moral grounds to deplore tyranny in such smugly shrill tones (Orwell, 2001). We need to hear more of this Orwell now.

Arendt did not ask her students to read Orwell so they could learn about how to pity those less fortunate than themselves. Thoughtfulness did not mean continuing to reap moral capital whilst brushing political reality to one side. She wanted them to read him in order to better understand what she called 'Political Experience in the Twentieth-Century' (the title of one of her most popular courses). The task, she noted in one of her introductory seminars, was not to empathise but to think, to use political judgment to comprehend a reality that was not their own (but "partly mine," she also noted wryly).

In her essay on *Nineteen Eighty-Four*, Elaine Scarry describes thinking as follows:

> The human ability to think freely – or, simply, to think – is premised on an ability to carry out two distinguishable mental practices, the practice of accurately identifying what is the case and the practice of entering mentally into what is not the case. The two familiar names for these practices are history and literature.
>
> (Scarry, 2005)

Arendt would have approved of this description. Poetic language – and *Nineteen Eighty-Four*, so often read as a political text, is without doubt the most literary of Orwell's writings – makes thinking possible. But without accurately identifying reality, without doing history too, contemplation can easily turn solipsistic. The 'self-thinking' that Varnhagen attempted in her misidentification with European literary life, Arendt argued, was an evasion of the reality of her situation. "Introspection and its hybrids engender *mendacity*," she snapped (Arendt, 1997).

There's nothing more mendacious on these islands just now than the contemporary politics of Brexit. But if we are to successfully teach 'Political Experience in the Twenty-First Century' – assuming that there is a 'we' who might want to do this – we are going to need something better than the literary liberalism bequeathed to us at the end of the Cold War. Encouraging people to read more literary fiction will not defeat the banality of Brexit. Creating the conditions for the return of political judgement, however, might help.

Norwich, June 2016/September 2017

The first part of this essay was written in June 2016 and published on the *DiEM25* blog, with an introduction by Yanis Varoufakis: https://diem25.org/the-banality-of-leaving-the-eu/.

Bibliography

Arendt, Hannah. (1994). *Eichmann in Jerusalem: A Report on the Banality of Evil (1963).* Harmondsworth: Penguin.

———. (1997). *Rahel Varnhagen: Life of a Jewess* (1957), trans. Richard and Clara Winston. Baltimore: Johns Hopkins University Press.

Arendt-Stern, Hannah. (1934). Rahel Varnhagen et Goethe. *Cahiers Juifs,* 11–12 (October–December 1934), quoted and translated by Haun Saussy. The Refugee Speaks of Parvenus and Their Beautiful Illusions: A Rediscovered 1934 Text by Hannah Arendt. *Critical Inquiry,* 40.1 (Autumn 2013).

Gilroy, Paul. (2014). Race and the Value of the Human. In: *The Meanings of Rights: The Philosophy and Social Theory of Human Rights,* eds. Costas Douzinas and Conor Gearty. Cambridge: Cambridge University Press.

Nussbaum, Martha C. (2005). The Death of Pity: Orwell and American Political Life. In: *On Nineteen Eighty-Four: Orwell and Our Future,* eds. Abott Gleason, Jack Goldsmith and Martha C. Nussbaum. New York: Princeton University Press.

Orwell, George. (2001). Review: Clarence K. Streit, *Union Now,* July 1939. In: *Orwell and Politics,* ed. Peter Davison. Harmondsworth: Penguin.

Rorty, Richard. (1993). *Contingency, Irony and Solidarity.* Cambridge: Cambridge University Press.

Sands, Philippe. (2016). A Grand and Disastrous Deceit. *London Review of Books,* 38, p. 15, 28 July 2016.

Scarry, Elaine. (2005). A Defense of Poesy (The Treatise of Julia). In: *On Nineteen Eighty-Four: Orwell and Our Future,* eds. Abott Gleason, Jack Goldsmith and Martha C. Nussbaum. New York: Princeton University Press.

Spivak, Gayatri. (1958). Three Women's Texts and a Critique of Imperialism, 'Identities'. Kwame Appiah and Henry Louis Gates, Jr. eds., special issue, *Critical Inquiry* 12 (1).

2

BREXLIT

Kristian Shaw

> In novel, perhaps in redemptive, forms, new kinds of art and
> thought [could] contribute to a revised and properly cosmopoli-
> tan definition of what Europe was and what its values would need
> to be in the future. Culture could reacquaint Europe with the
> humanity from which it had been comprehensively estranged.
>
> (Gilroy, 2013: 123)

Britain's recent exit from the European Union on 23 June 2016
signalled an unprecedented historic moment for the nation and has
resulted in a form of political isolationism unthinkable at the turn
of the millennium. The years leading up to the EU referendum witnessed a sudden and violent shift towards right-wing populism, hostility towards supranational forms of cosmopolitical democracy and
global interdependence, extensive opposition to open border policies,
discontent with the cultural implications of globalisation, and a xenophobic resistance to both immigrants and transnational mobility in
general. This chapter will consider the response of contemporary literature in an increasingly fragile and uncertain political climate, arguing that the referendum debate entailed a broader struggle between

the forces of cosmopolitanism and nationalism (represented by the contradictory narratives woven by the Remain and Leave camps, respectively). Beginning with a brief analysis of Brexit and its immediate consequences, the chapter will then provide a timely and original close reading of post-Brexit fictions (forming a genre which I am naming 'BrexLit'), demonstrating literature's potential to engage with emergent political realities.

Brexit did not divide the nation, it merely revealed the inherent divisions within society. The referendum was the manifestation of more than three decades of Euroscepticism, resistance to mass migration from Eastern Europe and the Middle East, impotent rage regarding the eurozone crisis, and the corresponding failures of the left to either endorse European integration or acknowledge the values of modern patriotism. Nonetheless, the campaign did play a vital role in shaping the narrative. (In the run-up to the 2015 UK general election, the market research organisation Ipsos MORI found that fewer than 10% of British voters named the EU as a 'top three' issue affecting their decision (2015: n.p.)

Members of the left shared UKIP's fears of an 'ever closer union' with the EU but for differing reasons, perceiving the organisation not as a progressive forum for cosmopolitical debate but an exclusive, injurious, and undemocratic capitalist club. Nevertheless, the EU has been championed as a valid attempt to reconcile existing tensions between national and cosmopolitan forms of belonging and identification. Daniele Archibugi goes so far as to hail the EU as 'the first international model which begins to resemble the cosmopolitan model' (1998: 219). The supranational polity arguably translates cosmopolitanism's universal abstractions into pragmatic practices, evident in the legislative frameworks, transnational projects, and trade agreements established between nations. However, as Chris Rumford has persuasively argued, EU policy makers 'almost never refer to cosmopolitanism', its politicians 'tend not to allude to Europeans as cosmopolitans', and its reports in general 'eschew the language of cosmopolitanism' (2007: 4). The top-down bureaucratic mechanisms of the EU lead Ulrich Beck and Edgar Grande to suggest that a 'deformed cosmopolitanism' emerges, produced by 'egoism of the member states, economic self-interest and the asymmetries in influence on political decisions' (2007: 20).

The Remain camp advocated the benefits of an interconnected Europe but, for floating voters, failed to acknowledge the disruptive realities of cross-border relationships and the bureaucratic nature of the EU in general. At the core of the Brexit debate was the question of national borders: how should they be controlled? In a globalised world of transnational mobilities are porous borders an inevitability? Or is the maintenance of existing borders a form of defence from acts of global terrorism and undocumented immigration? For many British citizens the ongoing Syrian refugee crisis encapsulated these concerns and fuelled nationalist rhetoric. Angela Merkel described the crisis as one critical element of 'our rendezvous with globalisation' and acknowledged the importance of this battle (reflected in her subsequent forthright refusal for a post-Brexit Britain to opt out of freedom of movement): 'we will have to take on more responsibility in an open world for what happens outside our European borders' (2016: n.p.). Nonetheless, the perceived spread of Islamic ideology beyond the nation's perimeter and the growing demands for devolution and independence within provoked populist responses and a renewed effort to preserve established national traditions and values. Brexiteers maintained that the nation-state could become a 'Global Britain' without relying on restrictive regulatory obligations to the EU or suffering further cultural influence detrimental to British ways of life. Theresa May's blueprints for a so-called Global Britain, predicated on these suggested trading ties outside Europe's domain, intimated an inherent opposition to cosmopolitan ideology: 'If you believe you're a citizen of the world, you're a citizen of nowhere' (May, 2016: n.p.). Britain was not alone in experiencing this wave of populist thought: strong parallels have been drawn between Brexit and Donald Trump's shocking victory in the US presidential election. In France, the leader of the Front National, Marine le Pen, ran a racist and divisive campaign based on the politics of fear; while in Hungary, the prime minister Viktor Orban advocated an 'illiberal democracy' involving the widespread construction of substantial fences as a direct solution to the refugee crisis.

Post-Brexit fiction

What role, if any, does literary studies have to play in responding to such cosmopolitical events? What is the purpose of 'national' literature in a divided cultural landscape? Literature has always been a significant influence on the perception of Britishness (or a narrower Englishness), shaping the identifiers of national identity in the popular cultural imagination. As Martha Nussbaum emphasises, it is only by 'looking at ourselves through the lens of the other, [that] we come to see what in our practices is local and nonessential, what is more broadly or deeply shared' (2010: 159). There is a history of Eurosceptic British fiction (relating specifically to the EU) dating back to the United Kingdom's first attempt at joining the European Economic Community (EEC), as authors addressed Britain's loss of political sovereignty and diminished post-war role on the world stage from a dominant player to a disempowered European member state. In a post-Brexit landscape, novels are already appearing that could claim the tag of Brexit fiction, or 'BrexLit', reflecting the divided nature of the UK and the ramifications of the referendum. The term BrexLit concerns fictions that either directly respond or imaginatively allude to Britain's exit from the EU, or engage with the subsequent socio-cultural, economic, racial or cosmopolitical consequences of Britain's withdrawal. However, many pre-Brexit Europhobic fictions anticipate the thematic concerns encapsulated by this proposed literary term, including the nostalgic appetite for (an admittedly false) national heritage, anxieties surrounding cultural infiltration, and a mourning for the imperial past. The chapter will now examine novels which provide an immediate response to the referendum, confronting legitimate grievances such as radical inequalities of access and socioeconomic imbalance, as well as addressing fears surrounding national identity and cultural change in post-Brexit Britain.

Both the run-up to and immediate aftermath of the vote witnessed the first forays into fiction by numerous mainstream political commentators. Andrew Marr and Stanley Johnson (father of Boris) followed Edwina Currie's example by penning overwrought political thrillers occupied with the fallout of the referendum result. While Currie's *The Ambassador* (1999) continued a Eurosceptic trend within

British fiction by imagining a dystopian future ruled by the EU, Marr's *Head of State* (2015) and Johnson's *Kompromat* (2017) offer satirical glimpses of the inner workings of pre- and post-Brexit dealings. The referendum has also contributed to a resurgence in speculative political-dystopia novels (continuing the trend established in British Eurosceptic fiction) which imagine potential futures for a Britain cut off from its continental European counterparts and thus offer an escape from the bleak realities of cultural isolationism. Heinz Helle's *Euphoria* (2017) is an early effort at depicting what a post-apocalyptic, post-Europe future may resemble, while Mark Billingham's crime novel *Love Like Blood* (2017) envisions a disproportionate rise in racial attacks and xenophobic hate crimes as a wave of nationalist triumphalism follows the referendum vote. *Time of Lies* (2017) by Douglas Board emerges as one of the first post-truth novels, in which an ex-football hooligan, Bob Grant, arises from the ashes of a post-Brexit landscape to run on a Trumpesque platform opposed to both the EU's bureaucratic machinations and the sickly influence of generic foreigners. The darkly comic, dystopian novel charts Grant's path to success as he rides the populist tide to become leader of Britain's Great party and subsequently Prime Minister (much to the chagrin of his *Guardian*-reading, left-leaning brother Zack).

Established literary figures such as Ian McEwan, Hilary Mantel, Philip Pullman, and Zadie Smith have all immediately engaged with these charged political events, speaking out on this apparently troubling act of national self-harm. Smith's 'Fences: A Brexit Diary' offers a levelled and vigorous response to Britain's sudden and unexpected political isolationism. The article acknowledges London's unique role as a model for cross-cultural conviviality – an 'outward-looking city [. . .] so different from these narrow xenophobic places up north':

> around here change is the rule. The old grammar school up the hill became one of the largest Muslim schools in Europe; the old synagogue became a mosque; the old church is now a private apartment building. Waves of immigration and gentrification pass through these streets like buses.

> (Smith, 2016: n.p.)

Smith concedes that for too long an affluent London has chosen to 'lecture the rest of the country on its narrow-mindedness while simultaneously fencing off its own discreet advantages', engendering a 'London vs. the rest' attitude which merely serves to deepen existing class divisions (ibid). Yet the referendum revealed the 'painful truth [...] that fences are [also] being raised everywhere in London', exposing the existing inequalities within the capital.

The political shift in the nation following Brexit exemplifies the socioeconomic and racial tensions evident in Smith's *Swing Time* (2016), as well as her earlier works such as *NW* (2012) and *The Embassy of Cambodia* (2013), and influences subsequent readings of these novels. *NW*'s opening scene, concerning the protagonist Leah Hanwell's decision to answer her front door rather than remain in her fenced-off garden, evokes the necessity for Britain to maintain cultural ties and avoid becoming 'fenced off' from its continental counterparts. By allowing otherness to pass over the threshold of Leah's doorway in an act of cosmopolitan hospitality, Smith is indicating her desire for British society to reject narrow self-interest in favour of ethical engagement and remain open-minded to more cosmopolitan modes of belonging. The cultural encounters in Smith's fictions reflect Paul Gilroy's notion of 'a "vulgar" or "demotic" cosmopolitanism', which 'glories in the ordinary virtues [...] that can be cultivated when mundane encounters with difference become rewarding' (2004: 75). A.L. Kennedy's *Serious Sweet* (2016) and Jonathan Coe's *Number 11* (2015), both published in the run-up to the referendum, echo the work of Smith in diagnosing the pre-existing ailments of contemporary London, interrogating Tory spending cuts and prevailing fiscal attitudes within the capital, while Jon McGregor's *Reservoir 13* (2017) and Amanda Craig's *The Lie of the Land* (2017) tackle the impact of Brexit on more parochial English locales. McGregor's effort, set in Lincolnshire (which witnessed the highest percentage of Leave votes in the UK), is a rejuvenated state-of-the-nation novel narrated by local inhabitants and foreign visitors, revealing the breakdown in communication that led to an emergent 'Little Englander' mentality.

The construction of fences (both physical and psychological) is central to Ali Smith's *Autumn* (2016), arguably the first significant post-Brexit novel. *Autumn*, the first of a planned 'seasonal' quartet by Smith, offers a sustained meditation on the anus mirabilis that changed the political and cultural landscape of twenty-first-century society, embedding the contemporaneous events of the EU referendum within a wider cyclical process of British history and natural decline. In directly referencing a range of recent events from the murder of the Batley MP Jo Cox to the refugee crisis (with tourists 'holidaying up the shore from the dead'), Smith immediately places the reader in a post-Brexit landscape where 'a new kind of detachment' dictates social interactions (2016: 12, 54). Even the celebratory memory of the London 2012 Olympics has been eroded and betrays the inward-looking melancholia behind the outward-facing façade: 'now you couldn't tell that any of these summer things had ever happened. There was just empty field. The sports track had faded and gone' (2016: 115). Smith's own festering authorial anger at the political elite is evident throughout *Autumn* as she looks ahead to a forthcoming 'winter' of discontent: 'I'm tired of having to wonder whether they did it out of stupidity or did it on purpose' (2016: 57). Indeed, *Autumn* may also claim the title of the first British 'post-truth' novel. Characters are aware that '[f]acts don't work', positioning right-wing nationalistic propaganda as a contributing factor in the demise of democracy as a pragmatic form of political governance (yet could equally serve as a rebuke of the left's failure to foster a dialogic and collaborative tone during the campaign): 'It has become a time of people saying stuff to each other and none of it actually ever becoming dialogue. It is the end of dialogue' (2016: 137, 112). This is a Britain in less splendid isolation.

The narrative begins with the fallout of the Brexit vote – the opening lines serving as a riff on Charles Dickens' *A Tale of Two Cities* ('It was the worst of times, it was the worst of times') – following the lives of Elisabeth Demand, an art history lecturer in London, and Daniel Gluck, an older neighbour from her childhood (2016: 3). (Elisabeth's surname comes from the French – de and monde – alluding to the notion of being a cosmopolitan citizen 'of the world' [2016: 50]; 'Gluck' means happiness in German). The divisive consequences of the referendum are complemented by the collage-like, disjointed temporality of the narrative structure, with brief, fragmentary chapters shifting from Daniel's youth in 1930s Europe to

Elisabeth's childhood in 1990s England, emphasising that their relationship '[is] about history, and being neighbours' (2016: 45). These memoryscapes enforce a backward-looking focus on the narrative, interrogating the national pathology that resulted in the referendum campaign and subsequent fracturing of the populace:

> All across the country, there was misery and rejoicing [. . .] All across the country, people felt it was the wrong thing. All across the country, people felt it was the right thing. All across the country, people felt they'd really lost. All across the country, people felt they'd really won [. . .] All across the country, people looked up Google: *what is EU?*' [. . .] All across the country, people said it wasn't that they didn't like immigrants. All across the country, people said it was about control.
>
> (2016: 60–1)

The tense parochial interactions of Elisabeth's village serve as a microcosm for the UK's deteriorating relationship with the ethical values of the EU (and cultural relationships more widely), revealing a community split between hospitality and hostility. The words 'GO and HOME' are daubed over a cottage in the village, under which someone later adds 'in varying bright colours' representative of a resistant multiculture: 'WE ARE ALREADY HOME THANK YOU' (2016: 53, 138). While the 'wild joyful brightness painted on the front of that house in a dire time' suggests a resistance to such nationalistic fervour and the possibility of communal empathy in the aftermath of such a divisive political campaign, moments of cultural conviviality are punctuated by the frenzied invective of angry nativists long after the referendum has passed: 'Rule Britannia [. . .] Britannia rules the waves. First we'll get the Poles. And then we'll get the Muslims. Then we'll get the gyppos, then the gays' (2016: 197).

The erection of an electrified chain-link fence on common land near the village, topped by razor wire and security cameras, operates both as a territorial reminder of a nation divided and as an allusion to the enforcement of toxic anti-immigration policies on the horizon. Enclosing 'a piece of land that's got nothing in it', the fence soon doubles in size and is patrolled by a security agency named S4FA who are unable to adequately explain the fence's purpose (2016: 55). The decision by Elisabeth's mother, Wendy, to defy its presence by throwing a stockpile of antiques at the fence in the closing scenes – 'bombarding that fence with people's histories and with the artefacts of less cruel and more philanthropic times' – symbolises a resistance to borders both figurative and corporeal, both internal and external to the nation (2016: 255). Smith has spoken at length elsewhere of the writer's responsibility to practice a form of narrative hospitality. She reiterates this outlook through Daniel's neighbourly guidance of Elisabeth: 'always try to welcome people into the home of your story' (2016: 119). As Smith's polemical stance makes clear, if good fences make good neighbours, then the need for cosmopolitan hospitality becomes an urgent necessity in a post-Brexit world.

Anthony Cartwright's *The Cut* (2017) is a unique post-Brexit novel in that it was specifically commissioned by Peirene Press to provide a direct response to the result and construct 'a fictional bridge between the two Britains that have opposed each other since the referendum day' (2017: n.p.). Cartwright dramatises the divide between nationalist and cosmopolitan forms of identification within his native Black Country landscape, demonstrating how class inequality continues to run deep and informs the public mood towards European integration. Cairo Jukes, a labourer on a zero-hours contract in Dudley, and Grace Trevithick, a documentary filmmaker (and personification of an elite British media) from Hampstead in London, represent the two sides of this disconnected post-Brexit nation. The novel encapsulates how geography emerged as a crucial factor in the referendum result, echoing John Lanchester's insightful remark in his article 'Brexit Blues' that 'the primary reality of modern Britain is not so much class as geography. Geography is destiny. And for much of the country, not a happy destiny' (2016: n.p.). In post-industrial edgelands of the north, Midlands, and Wales – areas which had failed to recover from Thatcherite policies – a sense of powerlessness and impotent rage fuelled unexpectedly high turnouts. By charting the daily lives of those citizens 'left behind' by globalisation, Cartwright exposes just how easily a destructive nostalgia can stimulate a belligerent national autarchism as a psychological defiance to socioeconomic disparities. As Craig Calhoun identifies, nationalism is often 'denigrated by proponents of transnational society who see the national and many other local solidarities as backward or outmoded, impositions of the past on the present' (2007: 170). And yet, nationalism itself operates as a source of social integration 'insofar as it structures collective identities and solidarities' and should not be treated as 'a sort of error smart people will readily move beyond – or an evil good people must reject' (ibid: 152, 7). For many undecided voters it was difficult to perceive the benefits of a vague supranational identity when their national identity was much more tangible and intrinsically tied to their cultural memory and day-to-day lives. Such cosmopolitan citizenship seemed to be the purview of privileged elites alone.

Working amidst the canals of Dudley – open scars of a battered post-industrial landscape – Cairo is unable to relate to either metropolitan Grace or a wider world that has ignored and forgotten the presence of his community: 'here were the ruins, and here were the ghost people among them, lost tribes' (2017: 100). Cairo bemoans the decline of industry in the Black Country, echoing Gilroy's diagnosis of a resurgent 'postimperial melancholia' ingrained in the national psyche and its influence in shaping a political narrative: 'A lot of it is gone, erased. The industrial past [. . .] Now you act – we act – like there's some sort of shame to it all. The rest of the country is ashamed of us. You want us gone' (2004: 109, 2017: 111). His involvement in Grace's documentary and assertion that the approaching EU referendum signifies 'the weight of the past on the present [. . .] of retribution on some grand, futile scale' is a desperate attempt to justify both his own life choices and a passionate defence of his abandoned community: 'He wanted to say something, about the sense of his world being made invisible, mute' (2017: 24; 30). Grace's initial repudiation of Cairo's concerns symbolises the Remain camp's dismissal of nationalist rhetoric as simply 'bigotry' or evidence of 'Little Englander' syndrome, thus ignoring the fears of many undecided voters and appearing out of touch to those outside the London Bubble or Westminster circles. Recounted in alternating chapters, entitled 'Before' and 'After', *The Cut* emphasises the severity and momentous consequences of the referendum, deepening the already fractious fissures within contemporary society. The title itself not only alludes to the post-Brexit divide but echoes the sentiments of Zadie Smith,

A.L. Kennedy, and Jonathan Coe in blaming Tory austerity for both the abandonment of the industrial order (the open 'cuts' of the canals signifying that 'this place used to be somewhere') and the subsequent neglect of the working class in the north and the Midlands (2017: 44). However, rather than play to established stereotypes, the novel challenges expectations surrounding class-based politics and forces characters to re-evaluate their cultural prejudices, opening a space for dialogue and thus offering a modicum of hope for cultural recuperation and regeneration.

The post-Brexit literary landscape has also witnessed fictions by non-British authors tackling the broader ethno-political and cultural issues that impacted the referendum campaign. Immigration was widely heralded as the most critical issue for undecided voters – even those gravitating towards a vote for Remain – and exposed the resounding symbolic sensitivity to politico-cultural borders. The publication of the latest immigration figures on 26 May 2016 – revealing that net migration had risen from 177,000 in 2012 to 330,000 in 2015 (with EU countries contributing to approximately half that number) – gave greater momentum to the Vote Leave campaign. The figures torpedoed David Cameron's empty pledge to reduce immigration to 'tens of thousands' and suggested quotas were easily dismissed as meaningless rhetoric. Following the Maastricht Treaty in 1993, free movement had been reinforced as a central principle of the single market and non-negotiable factor in membership, leading to EU expansion. As a result, during the campaign EU membership was positioned as a direct catalyst for rising immigration and its erosion of parliamentary sovereignty, while borders were utilised as polysemic political resources and instruments of control: from London's 'ring of steel' to the territorial boundaries of the nation-state to the (expanding) perimeter of the EU and the Schengen immigration zone. The Leave campaign insinuated that borders should operate asymmetrically, permitting the flow of transnational mobilities and goods and services required for global trade while blocking the passage of demonised 'others' (invariably Muslims and Eastern Europeans). Unfortunately for Vote Remain, these geo-political tensions, fears surrounding securitisation, and a resilient politics of self-determination ensured that a noxious brand of atavistic nationalism, rather than a debate concerning the merits of institutional cosmopolitanism, came to define the referendum.

Mohsin Hamid's geopolitical novel *Exit West* (2017) follows a young Muslim couple, Saaed and Nadia, in an unnamed Middle Eastern country suffering under Islamic insurgency. Fleeing their city – 'swollen with refugees' – they join the wave of displaced migrants attempting to enter European nation-states, initially running up against the implacability of border controls (2016: 1). The presence of coast guard agencies in the novel reflects the practices of Frontex, the EU's border management agency, which patrols the Mediterranean and prevents asylum seekers and refugees from infiltrating or even reaching the secure borders of EU member states. By sneaking through a series of mysterious black 'doors', the couple first arrive at a migrant camp on the Greek island of Mykonos before eventually gaining passage to London. The post-Brexit 'dark London' the couple encounter is peopled by angry nativist mobs aiming to 'reclaim Britain for Britain' and anxious migrants scrutinised by surveillance and securitisation measures: 'between Westminster and Hammersmith legal residents were in a minority, and native-born ones vanishingly few, with local newspapers referring to the area as the worst of the black holes in the fabric of the nation' (2016: 142, 132, 126). The black door portals utilised by the migrants are a useful stylistic device in gesturing towards new forms of connectivity that transform existing transnational relations: 'they had grasped that the doors could not be closed, and new doors would continue to open' (2016: 164). The magical realist nature of their construction, however, exposes the idealistic and hopeful sentiments (as opposed to analytical value) of cosmopolitanism in formulating a borderless world – a position Hamid purposely assumes: 'having a sense of hope for me is a direct political response to [. . .] Brexit' (2017: n.p.). Cosmopolitan hospitality retains a contemporary resonance when addressing this issue of asylum. Asylum seekers and refugees complicate (and force a reconceptualisation of) unconditional hospitality, revealing the stark limitations of cosmopolitan discourses when discussing issues of national belonging, humanitarian intervention, and openness to otherness. The novel's engagement with the Syrian refugee crisis (partly responsible for provoking the resurgence in populist, xenophobic responses to immigration) underscores the desired maintenance of a fortress Europe to guard against undesirable cultural influence and suggests that EU policy merely reinforces Europe's external borders and weakens internal ones, ensuring that an embrace of alterity remains ultimately deferred.

The study of contemporary fiction, rather like the immediate analysis of a political climate, is inevitably vulnerable to hindsight. If Brexit has effectively eroded the meta-narratives of European cooperation, centralisation, and supranationalism, what forms of new narrative will emerge to legitimise the relevance of cultural inter-dependence? Sunjeev Sahota, author of Booker-shortlisted *Year of the Runaways* (2015), perceives Brexit to be 'a stain on our national identity, our sense of ourselves and our place in the world', but gestures towards literature's capacity to interrogate how we relate to one another across national and cultural boundaries, offering an imaginative space for the envisioning of political futures: 'I think writers will continue to write globally and won't be hemmed in by these boundaries that politicians try to impose on our minds. I think writers will write truth to power' (Shaw, 2017: n.p.). Indeed, it is not altogether surprising that the longlist for the Man Booker Prize 2017 contains several novels which immediately engage with a post-Brexit world. One would expect that planetary challenges requiring the mobilisation of a global citizenry (or at least a re-embrace of a European demos), such as climatological risk, will undoubtedly stimulate this form of literary response, as well as the inevitable emergence of Scottish, Northern Irish, and Welsh Brexit fictions that forge new dialogues with the question of British cultural identity. (According to official European Commission statistics, 'more than two-thirds' of EU citizens consider climate change 'a very serious problem', despite the survey being conducted during the 'overshadowing' Eurozone debt crisis of 2008 [2009: 16]). And yet the risk remains that the literary discussion of such critical national and global concerns will simply create another leftist echo chamber that neither heals nor speaks to an already fractious nation.

Rather than engaging with the larger realities of European life, the first wave of post-Brexit fiction largely seems to be detailing the specific frailties and parochial trivialities of an insular and diminished small island – updated forms of state-of-the-nation novels that retain a narrow focus on British society and its isolation from the continent. However, as opposed to late twentieth-century works of British Euroscepticism, certain BrexLit fictions betray a further purpose, gesturing towards more inclusive and diverse forms of public culture, identifying the social divisions affecting the nation, and engaging in a struggle with British society and its prevailing political climate. In this way, they espouse an outward-looking cosmopolitan engagement as a form of resistance to an increasingly nationalistic and inward-looking cultural landscape. Universities also have a crucial pedagogical role to play in shaping forthcoming narratives regarding life 'after' Europe (despite Michael Gove's remarks that British society has had enough of 'experts'). As Pippa Norris identifies, 'Western universities are generally cosmopolitan institutions that thrive on the international movement of researchers and students, and on the flow of ideas that movement can bring'; thus the rise in nationalist populism and its effect on migration and international student numbers poses 'a direct threat to the university culture' (2016: n.p.). If, as Rumford suggests, cosmopolitanism is 'a political strategy which draws upon resources of the imagination in order to constitute an alternative social connection' between global citizens, then the teaching of literature offers the means to inspire and reinvigorate cultural imaginaries of national and transnational identity (2007: 107).

More than a year after the referendum, British society remains deeply divided over both the vote and the subsequent process of leaving the EU. There remains widespread uncertainty regarding the reasons behind the result as well as anxiety over the consequences. One thing is clear: Brexit marks a profound change in the political landscape of the nation – one that could lead to the eventual dissolution of the UK and a reshaping of our national culture. Whether Brexit will initiate a 'domino effect' on other EU member-states and lead to the breakup of Europe's political organisation (Emmanuel Macron's recent electoral landslide over Le Pen in 2017 makes a 'Frexit' unlikely), or whether such disintegration will result in new forms of European collaboration oriented to global challenges, untethered by the EU's more neoliberal and bureaucratic tendencies, remains to be seen. As Will Kymlicka identifies, the boundaries of a political 'community of fate' are not determined by 'the forces people are subjected to, but rather how they respond to those forces, and, in particular, what sorts of collectivities they identify with when responding to those forces' (2010: 437). If Brexit does mark the re-emergence of socio-political anti-cosmopolitan ideology that will define international relations in the twenty-first century, then the role of literature as a bastion of cultural cosmopolitanism becomes all the more significant.

Bibliography

Archibugi, D. (1998). Principles of Cosmopolitan Democracy. In: *Re-imagining Political Community: Studies in Cosmopolitan Democracy*, eds. D. Archibugi, D. Held and M. Kohler. Cambridge: Polity Press, pp. 198–228.

Beck, U. and Grande, E. (2007). *Cosmopolitan Europe*. Cambridge: Polity Press.

Calhoun, C. (2007). *Nations Matter: Culture, History, and the Cosmopolitan Dream*. London: Routledge.

Cartwright, A. (2017). *The Cut*. London: Peirene Press.

Clark, T. and Gibson, O. (2012). *London 2012's Team GB Success Sparks Feel-good Factor*. [online] *The Guardian*. Available at: www.theguardian.com/sport/2012/aug/10/london-2012-team-gb-success-feelgood-factor [Accessed 4 June 2017].

Eurobarometer. (2009). *European's Attitude Towards Climate Change*. Brussels: European Commission.

Gilroy, P. (2004). *After Empire: Melancholia or Convivial Culture?* London: Routledge.

———. (2013). Postcolonialism and Cosmopolitanism: Towards a Worldly Understanding of Fascism and Europe's Colonial Crimes. In: *After Cosmopolitanism*, eds. R. Braidotti, P. Hanafin and B. Blaagaard. Oxford: Routledge, pp. 111–31.

Hamid, M. (2016). *Exit West*. London: Hamish Hamilton.

———. (2017). Mohsin Hamid: There's a Real Fear of the Future Right Now [online]. *The Irish Times*. Available at: www.irishtimes.com/culture/books/mohsin-hamid-there-s-a-real-fear-of-the-future-right-now-1.3002735 [Accessed 14 July 2017].

Ipsos MORI. (2015). April 2015 Issues Index [online]. *Ipsos MORI*. Available at: www.ipsos.com/ipsos-mori/en-uk/economistipsos-mori-april-2015-issues-index.aspx [Accessed 23 June 2017].

Kymlicka, W. (2010). Citizenship in an Era of Globalization. In: *The Cosmopolitan Reader*, eds. G. Wallace Brown and D. Held. Cambridge: Polity Press, pp. 435–43.

Lanchester, J. (2016). Brexit Blues [online]. *London Review of Books*. Available at: www.lrb.co.uk/v38/n15/john-lanchester/brexit-blues [Accessed 12 June 2017].

May, T. (2016). Keynote Address. Conservative Party Conference, The ICC Birmingham. 5 (October 2016).

Merkel, A. (2016). Merkel: Germany Should Play Bigger Role on World Stage [online]. *DW*. Available at: www.dw.com/en/merkel-germany-should-play-bigger-role-on-world-stage/a-19088542 [Accessed 2 June 2017].

Norris, P. (2016). The Problems of Populism: Tactics for Western Universities [online]. *Times Higher Education*. Available at: www.timeshighereducation.com/features/the-problems-of-populism-tactics-for-western-universities [Accessed 17 June 2017].

Nussbaum, M.C. (2010). Patriotism and Cosmopolitanism. In: *The Cosmopolitan Reader*, eds. G. Wallace Brown and D. Held. Cambridge: Polity Press, pp. 155–62.

Rumford, C. (2007). Introduction. In: *Cosmopolitanism and Europe*, ed. C. Rumford. Liverpool: Liverpool University Press, pp. 1–15.

Shaw, K., and Sahota, S. (2017) Living by the Pen: In Conversation with Sunjeev Sahota.

Smith, A. (2016). *Autumn*. London: Hamish Hamilton.

Smith, Z. (2016). Fences: A Brexit Diary [online]. *The New York Review of Books*. Available at: www.nybooks.com/articles/2016/08/18/fences-brexit-diary/ [Accessed 1 May 2017].

3

AUTUMN AFTER THE REFERENDUM

Petra Rau

In the spring of 2017 I was due to co-teach a new module on contemporary fiction for one of the School's MA courses. Needless to
say, compiling a remotely satisfactory reading list for such a module
would normally be challenging enough. We pondered our criteria
at length: how to weight aesthetics and innovation against politics
and topicality; whether to accord significance to literary prizes and
account for publishing trends; the need to balance literary debuts
with already more established texts and authors; to give equal space to
authors who were not white, male, middle-class, straight and English;
to reflect on globalisation alongside listening to regional and local
voices; the list could go on. It did go on. But above all, we needed
to circle around the notion of the contemporary and how the novel
tackled the 'now'.

As if the pedagogical quandaries attendant upon course design
were not tricky enough, that 'now' proved hard to grasp for me, not
least because of the breath-taking pace of political developments
in 2016. My own 'now' – and quite a few plans for the future –
fell through the floor in the wake of the referendum's outcome.
I have no recollection of what I read or wrote or even did in the
weeks after the vote to leave the EU. I seem to have spent much

of the summer in a paralysed state of fury and disbelief. Aware of entrenched ideological Euroscepticism and the flaws of the EU, I had expected a narrow vote but hoped that the UK would come down on the side of pragmatism and the status quo. 'You are disappointed', a friend in Germany said to me. In German, to be disappointed – *enttäuscht sein* – literally means to be rid of a delusion, disillusioned. Disappointment, being disillusioned, makes you face the reality of things. I was not just disappointed: I was radically disorientated by the new 'now' and the impending 'soon'. An EU citizen in an EU country, I had been at home – or close enough. On June 24, I felt like a migrant worker in a foreign country. It dawned on me that I did not really know the country in which I had lived and worked for the past twenty years; at least not much beyond the academic bubble and a self-elected family of international(ist) friends. I had had no idea that my existence, as part of the three million or so EU citizens in the UK, was such a source of anxiety and resentment for so many. It was unsettling, and it indeed shook my emigrant roots even looser.

Autumn did little to relieve this peculiar feeling of unmoored irreality. Certainly my students were still reeling from the referendum result, although in a different way. They felt increasingly determined by elders who could not be trusted with their future while at the same time lumbered with mountains of debt and ever-decreasing prospects. The election of Donald Trump as the forty-fifth US president in November appeared to continue a surreal trajectory of deeply implausible political nightmares. I say implausible because the crude rhetoric, deep ignorance, overt racism, flagrant incompetence and, above all, the brazen lies of both these campaigns would once have sunk a candidate or an agenda. Now politicians, politics and political language seemed to suffer from such wholesale accumulated discreditation that a large part of the electorate either believed nothing that came out of a politician's (or expert's) mouth or everything, no matter how risible or mendacious, as long as it was clad in paratactical sound bites, wrapped in nostalgia and finished with an exclamation mark: '£350 million a week for the NHS!' 'Make America great again!' 'Control our borders!' 'Build that wall!' How did we get here, to this historic 'now' in which such phrases were shoutable, and what could the generally softly spoken literary novel say about this moment and its 'structure of feeling'?

Homeopathic archeologies

These questions would ultimately determine the vacillating chronology of our reading list, and they would extend any narrow definition of the contemporary by digging up some of its seedlings much earlier. John Lanchester's *Capital* (2012), for instance, made the credit crunch feel Balzacian and the threat of terrorism Conradian. This wasn't the first financial crash that had furnished the plot of a novel; so had Trollope, Zola, Dreiser or Fallada. Had nothing changed? Beholden to conspicuous consumption and endless upgrading but largely financially illiterate, we are encouraged to embrace debt, and our economy depends on it. Many students felt they had been socialised into it. 'I was told that going to university was an investment in my future', a student said in a tutorial. 'A different option wasn't really up for discussion. I wake up at night worrying about the debt and never getting on the property ladder. What kind of job is reading novels and writing essays going to get me? It feels more like a gamble to me'. But not all accepted their debt, moral or financial, noted a Greek visiting student: while Greece was on its knees under the EU's severe austerity mandate, in the US a multiple bankruptee could furnish his cabinet with billionaires whose businesses would profit from the policies they passed or abolished. And the cabinet of Eton boys that had gambled with the UK's future appeared to walk away from the responsibility into lucrative jobs and positions. Another student noted that all the skills and services available in Lanchester's Pepys Street had to be imported (the nanny from Hungary, the builder from Poland, the Premier-league footballer from Senegal and the traffic warden from Zimbabwe). 'Do we only do banking and art now? What are we still good at? Do people resent immigrants because we are so obviously dependent on foreign labour?'

In many ways, the novels worked as a (homeopathic) archaeology aimed at retrieving a measure of complexity from the banality of populist arguments and rash commentaries: this debacular 'now' has had a long run-up and a number of equally catastrophic predecessors.

As Julian Barnes realised about his own reading of George Simenon's *Chez Krull* in the months after the referendum, our books too were 'picking up an extra charge and weight from the circumstances in which they [were] read' (2017: 41). Unsurprisingly, then, our discussions regularly returned to the referendum; or rather, the students identified the issues several of the novels grappled with as ones that also featured in voters' decision making and politicians' rhetoric: social inequality; the effects of technology, terrorism and religious extremism, immigration and displacement, globalisation. Andrea Levy's *Small Island* led to an angry indictment of the national curriculum and the yawning chasms it had left in students' knowledge about empire. Why had no one told them about colonial troops' contribution to the British war effort? Why had the war been so mythologised into a collective heroism when it had divided and traumatised so many as well? Why had no one spoken about the everyday racism black Jamaicans faced in the 'mother country' that had invited them, as if such attitudes were long obsolete when all it took was a slim majority in a referendum to license vandals to spray paint the Polish Cultural Centre in London or yell abuse at random passers-by just because they spoke a foreign language?

Kamila Shamsie's *Burnt Shadows* imagined how different forms of political violence fan out across the globe, affecting different generations in different ways: nuclear war, Indian partition and sectarian violence, the Cold War and its proxy wars, the Russian invasion of Afghanistan and growing religious fundamentalism as a form of resistance, and the war on terror with its 'extraordinary rendition' and Guantanamo Bay. With its hybrid families scattered across five countries, it seemed indicative of the new international Anglophone writing. Did this mean that 'English literature' was now an outdated subcategory with fairly parochial concerns? What might be the flip side of globalisation? Many of Shamsie's characters were displaced or had fled their home country; how did this affect their cultural identity? What and where was 'home'? Was there a link between displacement, community and terrorism? What kinds of anxieties and tensions, we wondered again, are produced by the global, the cosmopolitan, the hybrid and hyphenated, the free flow of goods and people? Hard not to think of the Leave vote here as one of the symptoms of anxiety about one's place in the world. Hard to forget Theresa May's rejection of cosmopolitanism and corporate or political elites at the Conservative Party conference in 2016, where she professed to be in touch with 'the people down the road', presumably not those living and working in the real-world equivalent of Pepys Street but the patriotic provinces of England: 'If you believe you're a citizen of the world you're a citizen of nowhere. You don't understand what the word citizenship means'. 'She clearly hasn't read Goethe', one of the Swiss students pondered, 'but maybe this flies in Maidenhead'. The British students remembered her infamous, ignorant remark; they would remember it once more in the general election.

Gary Shteyngart's *The Super Sad True Love Story* got short shrift for its *de-haut-en-bas* attitude towards a younger techno-savvy generation, but students fully recognised the tyranny of being hardwired into social media and its impact on mental health and self-esteem. "I don't know who or what I'm curating anymore, and I want to stop, but all this stuff, these versions of me are out there now and it's like servicing some avatar or other me's that is eating my life and my time'. Being 'liked' as some sort of vampiric need, filling a monstrous narcissistic deficit, created and fed by technology, brought us back to politics. Shteyngart's dystopia had already been overtaken by reality. In our 'now' you could win an election by attention-seeking unfettered tweets and reach millions of followers who preferred your 'news' in 140 characters to sober reportage or nuanced analysis. The less coherent and accountable, the more 'relatable' such a figure seemed to be to his 'base' (as if this were a prime qualification for leadership of any kind).

Old stories, circular time

If the pace of political developments exhausted commentariat and electorate alike, how on earth could fiction keep step with, let alone digest, the contemporary? In a recent interview in *The Guardian*, Claire Messud felt overwhelmed by the egomaniac spectacle of the US presidency and its daily fireworks: 'the pace of the madness seems so intense. We are all like Linus and Snoopy in front of the TV with our hair blowing back. It is somewhat sapping' (in Adams, 2017). The same could be said for news relating to Brexit, a process whose deadline dictates a tempo hardly suited to measured debate, detailed analysis and careful consultation. Hardly a week has gone by without what Angela Merkel once called a 'shitstorm' of leaks, pronouncements and speculations. The literary novel seemed far too finely woven a cloth for such precipitation. Was this climate best viewed in hindsight, once the pace had slackened, and meanwhile left to journalism, cabaret and satire? Would such delay not forfeit the novelist's ability to intervene and take a stance? And yet there was a notable exception wrestled from the dog days of 2016 which launched us into the spring semester – Ali Smith's *Autumn*, the first instalment of a quartet of seasonal novels. Written and produced with extraordinary speed, Smith couldn't really be more bravely 'now': 'I knew the book had to (and I had to, too) square up to what was happening if the notions of contemporaneousness if it were to mean anything at all' (in Anderson, 2017). Squaring up is an interesting phrase here. As if the now were a bill to be settled, an account to be closed; certainly a squall to face rather than to wait out in some sheltered Ivory Tower. Reviewers quickly hailed *Autumn* as the first Brexit novel. One US critic even called it a 'post-Brexit masterpiece' (Gilbert, 2017) although it is clearly set post-referendum and Article 50 had not even been triggered, consequently nothing had happened at all to legally initiate the Brexit process let alone catapult us into the post-Brexit era. This conflation of the referendum as a democratic iteration with its – then still debated – consequence (exit from the European Union) was not uncommon, a time lapse particularly favoured by those who felt the referendum result licensed them to freely express racism and xenophobia.

If the book resonated so powerfully with the students it was because one of its protagonists was reasonably close to the readers' position: a female academic in her early thirties on a lousy temporary contract and still in student digs, passionate about her subject (art history: what kind of job can you get with that?) but far too intelligent and sensitive to brace the current political weather without serious bouts of depression or bewilderment. Elizabeth Demand's own vote in the referendum is never mentioned, but her reflections and her disorientation at the country's climate change suggest she is a

Remainer. The novel's loose form, its reliance on interior monologue and its nimble segueing between Elizabeth's embattled present and her friend the centenarian Daniel Gluck's memories of the thirties and sixties do not attempt to wrench meaning from the turmoil of 'now'. Sure, it mentions the murder of MP Jo Cox in Birstall and Arkadiusz Jóżwik in Harlow, but these are examples of a time out of joint, in which no event is accorded proper attention: 'Once it would have been a year's worth of news. But news now is like a flock of speeded-up sheep running off the side of a cliff. [. . .] Thomas Hardy on speed' (38–9). Or Linus and Snoopy in front of the TV with their hair blowing back.

Time is at the heart of *Autumn*: its perception, its pace, its peculiar loops and cycles, its relativising quality, its ideological uses as 'the past', its waste as an abuse of power. The novel's literary allusiveness – most obviously to the famous opening chapter of Dickens' *A Tale of Two Cities* – suggests that this 'now', however strange it may feel to us, may only be yet another crisis in a long human history of conflicts and cataclysms: 'the worst of times. Again'. (1) This was not the first time a nation found itself divided. 'Here's an old story so new that it's still in the middle of happening, writing itself right now with no knowledge of where or how it'll end' (181). And even the crises had to jostle with each other for attention. While Britain was reeling from the referendum result, thousands of refugees were still fetching up on Mediterranean beaches – an emergency so uncharitably ongoing that it was no longer newsworthy, just another 'old story'. The subjective experience of time and its unknowable import feature repeatedly. In the first chapter of *Autumn*, Daniel Gluck is drifting in and out of consciousness, mingling scenes from *The Tempest* with his memories of romance and images of corpses on a tourist beach. Later in the book it is clear how such blending comes about as we realise that Elizabeth visits Daniel in his care home, telling him of recent events and reading to him. Fiction blurs with facts, news with classic tales.

Much of such nimble temporal juxtaposition accounts for the form of *Autumn*, its quasi-paratactical and/and/and that does not subordinate one time or event to another: corporations erecting electric fences around public land, a deportation in Nice in 1943, Elizabeth's mother falling in love with a woman, the Profumo Scandal of

1963, an old man dying in a care home, the short life and astonishing work of Pauline Boty, the referendum. All are equally important and equally insignificant. Their narrative joining and ordering becomes the work of (often retrospective) interpretation which is itself a mutable history; a collage with several themes; white noise from which identifiable tunes emerge. To be alert to such semantic possibilities requires a Nietzschean untimeliness, a slight disjunction. The narrative voice thus pauses, several times, as do Elizabeth and her mother, to breathe and ponder the difficulty of identifying the theme and the tune. Here is a moment when Elizabeth reflects about a radio programme she heard that morning in which two spokespersons argued over immigration:

> It has become a time of people saying stuff to each other and none of it actually ever becoming dialogue.
>
> It is the end of dialogue.
>
> She tries to think when exactly it changed, how long it's been like this without her noticing.

(112)

The referendum, in *Autumn*, is a particularly egregious symptom of our peculiar 'now' and of *not* 'noticing' how fundamentally divided the country had become before the vote, let alone afterwards. This has been in the making for a long time, and given that dialogue and debate are at the heart of any functioning democracy, their absence does not bode well. The isolating 'bubble' effect of one's own echo chamber of shared opinions was immediately recognised by many students, who stressed the need for dialogue with Leave voters rather than branding them as racist working-class provincials. When later analyses identified age and education as decisive factors in voters' decision making, it came as no surprise either. All students (including those from the continent) saw themselves as benefactors of the free movement of services, goods and labour and fully intended to use their education to be part of that flow. But had they all exercised their right to vote, I wondered quietly. Had they realised that theirs was a future that needed defending against a larmoryant brand of nostalgia?

The pasts *Autumn* lets resurface resonate in the 'now' for good reasons, like a memory 'as it flashes up at a moment of danger' – a quasi-Benjaminian performance (1999: 247). The first few pages speak of the past as 'the junk shop of the self' (11). Junk shops return later on in Elizabeth's mother's participation in a daytime TV show called *The Golden Gavel*, a riff on popular programmes such as *Antiques Roadshow*, *Cash in the Attic* and *Bargain Hunt* in which participants hope junk turns out to be valuable antiques. It was a rather puzzling motif for the students, perhaps because they were not the regular demographic for such programmes. What kind of past does this country value, even fetishise to the point of musealising it in the domestic interior, in endless period dramas and antiques shops? Whose history is worth writing up and passing on, and whose story gets forgotten? Who decides about the value of the past? And suddenly Daniel Gluck's memory of his sister Hannah's rounding-up in Nancy in 1943 was not just part of that mnemonic driftwood washing ashore in the last days of life. She escaped once – more we can't know – through a single act of *sang froid*, and Daniel Gluck (perhaps once Daniel Glück?) came to a Britain that could bring itself to accept refugees. We noted the contrast in Smith's allusion to the war compared with the defiant 'splendid isolation' rhetoric of Farage and Johnson. I remember one student advising us that a new serialised adaptation of Len Deighton's counterfactual invasion fantasy *SS-GB* would be broadcast on BBC1 from February. Eyes rolled at such canny scheduling given the triggering of Article 50 at the end of March as if the audience had to be perennially reminded of the historic and contingent evils rushing towards them from the continent. The appeal of these nostalgic fantasies was not lost on the students. Just as the promise of Brexit had rekindled an imperialist fantasy of unlimited global trade in which everyone would scramble to strike swift deals with a self-sufficient small island graciously handing out three visas per year, so Trump had stirred dreams of returning to a manufacturing past of life-long, safe and lucrative jobs. Neither campaign had offered substance but succeeded in making the political establishment more unlikeable: voting for Brexit or Trump meant rejecting the social, economic and political complexities of a globalised 'now' in favour of an ostensibly simpler past.

'Why would you want to turn back the clock?' asked my older sister back in June 2016 in Germany. '*Downton Abbey* is a TV programme!' Of course our Central-European past was hardly liable to evoke nostalgia: our aged parents had fled the Red Army in 1945 and had worked hard to fit in hundreds of miles farther west. We had spent our childhood in the shadow of this monstrous Wall eight miles north of our small Franconian town where the Iron Curtain cut right through a village (Mödlareuth's death strip is now an open-air museum), all across Germany and all the way down to Trieste. It had very little to do with the retro chic of *Deutschland 83*. Controlling borders reminded us of whippersnappers in *Vopo* uniform strip-searching my frail father at the East German border; redacted telegrams from relatives no one could make sense of; hours of queuing at checkpoints; endless chicaneries with passports and visa applications. There is a wonderful Post Office scene in Smith's *Autumn* whose portrayal of a humourless clerk wielding mindless, obstructionist bureaucracy brought back memories of a Kafkaesque afternoon wasted at Prague central train station, being sent from pillar to post and failing the ostensibly simple task of buying a ticket to Munich. Anyone who has ever experienced the malign machinery of Soviet bloc officialdom will not bat an eyelid at the news of deportation letters being sent in error to EU nationals by the Home Office. If you want to deter foreigners you just create a hostile environment, but bear in mind that in the process you will make your own citizens feel equally unwelcome. Since June 2016 many a student has said to me in private, 'I feel ashamed at being British. I don't really want to live here anymore either'.

A mass culture of lies

The writer Olivia Laing, who interviewed Ali Smith for *The Observer*, raised with Smith what seems to have puzzled most other reviewers either side of the Atlantic, the extended references to the Profumo Affair and Pauline Boty's famous painting of Christine Keeler, *Scandal '63*. For Smith, 2016 and 1963 are linked through shameless political mendaciousness and its social consequences:

there has been a massive lie and the lie has come from parliament and dissolved itself right the way through the country
and things change. It's a pivotal moment. We were dealing with
a kind of mass culture of lies. And it's a question of what happens culturally when something is built on a lie.

(in Laing, 2016)

The Profumo scandal is often cited as having discredited the Tory
establishment, helping Labour win the 1964 general election and
changing the relationship between the government and the press. The
referendum in June 2016 was also a pivotal moment for its seismic
political outcome. The 'mass culture of lies' – from the Profumo affair
to the sleaze of the 1990s to the Iraq dossier to the expenses scandal
to the referendum – has steadily discredited politics and weakened
democracy itself. In our 'now' private citizens like Gina Miller have
to sue the government to involve Parliament. And paradoxically, the
'will of the British people' is cited as an authoritarian tool to shut
down debate over the extent and manner of exiting as if the blunt referendum's blunt outcome had given *carte blanche* to the government.
As Elizabeth Demand says, 'It's like democracy is a bottle someone
can threaten to smash and do a bit of damage with' (112). Perhaps
the most lasting legacy of the Profumo scandal and revelations about
public servants' mendacity is the MRDA meme that is often used
to dismiss predictable pronouncements based on obvious bias. It
refers to Keeler's friend Mandy Rice-Davies' streetwise giggle at an
aristocrat's denial of sleeping with her ('Well he would [deny that],
wouldn't he?'). In the subsequent decades the electorate has come to
fully inhabit Rice-Davies' cynicism.

Pauline Boty's painting *Scandal '63* only survives in photographs,
and it is of course itself a painting based on Lewis Morley's iconic
publicity shot of Keeler on a knock-off Arne Jacobsen chair (both are
now in the V & A). Boty's painting reverses the dynamic of the Profumo affair's narrative by making Keeler centre stage, literally margin-
alising the men who used her and then lied about it publicly. This was
the strand of the novel the students found most fascinating because
it made us realise how much its form resembled a Boty painting.

Reading *Autumn* did not feel like a strong wind in our faces despite the pace it described and its non-linear narration. Rather, it was like a long and slow contemplation of an enormous collage of scenes and images about our moment, and we had to work out what they all contributed to the 'structure of feeling' that is 'now'. What made Boty herself so 'untimely' in her own time was her ability to understand a consumerist age of images that constantly invite projection. Her collages and paintings re-circulate the icons of the era (Marilyn Monroe, Jean Paul Belmondo, J. F. Kennedy) while also tearing into its gender politics. In *Scandal '63*, *A Man's World I* and *II* and *The Only Blonde in the World* (on the rear end paper for *Autumn*), the meaning of the original photographs changes through their re-making as painted photographs because the audience is now aware of the photograph *as* photograph. They don't slip by as illustrations but are identified as simulacra peddling fictions and fantasies (another 'junk shop of the self'). As Smith notes in her interview with Olivia Laing,

> It reminds you to read the world as a construct. And if you can read the world as a construct, you can ask questions of the construct and you can suggest ways to change the construct. You understand that things aren't fixed.

Or, as Daniel Gluck says, 'whoever makes up the story makes up the world' (119). The referendum campaigns' stories about the UK, its past, its present and its future, utterly failed to resonate with the students and with many younger voters. Many do not recognize themselves in the Brexit fantasy and its rhetoric, which vacillates wildly between the vacuous and the antagonistic. Nor can I see any appetite among educated millennials for splendid isolation and a future constructed from a mythologised past. If they care enough about a global, European Britain to want to change the course of the ship Britannia, they had better start writing a story they can believe in – and vote for.

Bibliography

Adams, Tim. (2017). Interview with Claire Messud. *The Guardian*, Books, Monday 4 September 2017. Available at: www.theguardian.com/books/2017/sep/04/claire-messud-the-burning-girl-interview [Accessed 5 September 2017].

Anderson, Eric Karl. (2017). *Interview with Ali Smith*. Available at: www.penguin. co.uk/articles/in-conversation/interviews/2016/oct/ali-smith-on-autumn/ [Accessed 12 June 2017].

Barnes, Julian. (2017). Diary: Will People Hate Us Again? *London Review of Books*, 20 April 2017, pp. 41–3.

Benjamin, Walter. (1999). *Illuminations*, trans. Harry Zorn. London: Pimlico.

Gilbert, Sophie. (2017). Review of Autumn. *The Atlantic*, 15 February 2017. Available at: www.theatlantic.com/entertainment/archive/2017/02/ali-smiths-autumn-is-a-post-brexit-masterpiece/516660/ [Accessed 12 June 2017].

Laing, Olivia. (2016). Interview with Ali Smith. *The Observer*, 16 October 2016 Available at: www.theguardian.com/books/2016/oct/16/ali-smith-autumn-interview-how-can-we-live-ina-world-and-not-put-a-hand-across-a-divide-brexit-profu [Accessed 12 July 2017].

Smith, Ali. (2016). *Autumn*. London: Hamish Hamilton.

4

DO NOVELS TELL US HOW TO VOTE?

Sara Upstone

In 1991, the former Soviet Union was in the midst of political revolution. Reflecting on these events, the Russian scholar Maria Kamenkovich described how illegal copies of Tolkien's epic fantasy *The Lord of the Rings*, copied by *samizdat*, were distributed by pro-democracy political activists and passed from person to person. These were the only full copies of the text available because the first volume had been officially released only in censored form a decade earlier. Just before the siege of the White House, in which pro-democracy forces defended Gorbachev's government against a pro-Communist coup attempting to end his reform programme, the first official complete translation of the book was published. For Kamenkovich the popularity of the books amongst Gorbachev supporters signified anything but escapism. 'Many people remembered Tolkien when they made their barricades', she recalls:

> The war machine got as crazy as Oliphants [. . .] And Gandalf stood before the King of Angmar saying: "You shall not pass." Tolkien never meant to describe any real events either in the past or the future. But he certainly *added* something to earthly events. It just cannot be helped.
>
> (Curry, 1997: 44–5)

The dissolution of the USSR and the birth of Soviet democracy via a novel about furry-footed halflings. It's a funny example, bathetic perhaps. But Kamenkovich's reading of Tolkien is the literature academic's dream. It fuels our faith in the suggestion that texts can be socially transformative: that narrative might play a part – however small – in shaping the world in which we live. In such readings literature is neither simply a mirror of the socio-political circumstances in which it is produced nor a marginal interrogator of those circumstances but also a potentially active player in the shaping of popular consciousness and the actions stemming from it. The literary text is a fundamental part of a cultural imaginary – a way of thinking about the world informed and influenced by cultural texts such as literature, cinema, and art – that has the potential to contribute to political outcomes.

The theoretical discourse in support of this kind of cultural imagination is entrenched in the work of critics such as Homi Bhabha, Benedict Anderson, and Edward Said. What these critics all emphasise, with different focus and specific examples, is the ways in which not only do geographical borders shape identities and how we imagine them, but – conversely – how we imagine ourselves shapes borders, resulting in a cultural authority which is unstable and ambivalent because it is not merely documentary but also 'caught, uncertainly, in the act of "composing" its powerful image' (Bhabha, 'Introduction', 3). Said's *Orientalism* (1978) is ground breaking in this respect because it asks us to consider how entire identities might be constructed through cultural imaginaries – that, in essence, they exist not in reality but rather in the complex matrix of cultural representations that over time cement them into what appears a tangible presence. Developing Said's perspectives, both Bhabha in his edited collection *Nation and Narration* (1990) and Anderson in *Imagined Communities* (1983) have emphasised the imagined status of the nation in particular. Bhabha's recourse to the motif of 'narration' points not only to a metaphorical writing but also a literal one, where what exists is not the nation as geographical absolute but rather 'the cultural construction of nationness as a form of social and textual affiliation' (Bhabha, 'Dissemination', 292). Contemporary criticism has taken these ideas and shaped them into ever-more-dynamic and striking statements of literature's power: work such as Gabriele Schwab's *Imaginary Ethnographies*

(2012), for example, which presents literary texts as 'anthropologies of the future'. What makes examples such as Kamencovich's so attractive is that they take this theory out of the realm of abstraction and transform it into a much more concrete relation between the literary text and the political event.

In this chapter, I want to consider how our thinking around Brexit might change if we apply this understanding of the cultural imaginary and its political impact. In the wake of the Brexit vote, there has been intense media and academic speculation as to the driving factors behind the result. This attention has often been focused not on individuals but on communal responses and the circumstances surrounding particular voting constituencies. Special attention has rightly been paid to economic factors and questions pertaining to immigration levels. What has been neglected, however, in these accounts is discussion of how the cultural might form a contributory – if not determining – factor in voting patterns. This is despite the fact that there already exists an emerging literature on cultural imaginaries of Europe through works such as Anna Saunders and Laura Rotaro's *Essence and the Margin: National Identities and Collective Memories in Contemporary European Culture* (2009).

The absence of such discussions is to some extent understandable – it would be ludicrous, certainly, to suggest that a particular literary representation might in this case have provoked particular political responses to European identity. What is also clear, however, is that the role of the cultural text in the creation of British perceptions of both Britishness and the relationship between Britain and the global is something that is more generally acknowledged. In his seminal *The Break-Up of Britain* (1981) Tom Nairn explores the ways in which English nationalism is shored up by literary mythologizing: Enoch Powell advancing his 'conservative fetishism' (287) through writing poetry from the 1930s to the 1950s, creating both his own imaginary of Englishness and the myth he would then later promote to his supporters in the 1960s. Similarly, Stephen Haseler in *The English Tribe* (1996) explores the sedimentation of conservative and nostalgic Englishness through both powerful literary elites and television dramas of postcolonial melancholy such as *Brideshead Revisited* and *The Jewel in the Crown* (an updated version today might add *Downton*

Abbey to this list of high-profile productions): images sold to the global media marketplace for mass consumption but then reflected on to British identities through the very same media. More recently, Mark Perryman in his edited collection *Imagined Nation: England After Britain* (2008) invokes Anderson's theory in order to collect a range of voices including Paul Gilroy and Billy Bragg exploring the cultural imagining of England and asking whether the nation exists 'only in our imagination' (31).

It is in the context of these theories that we can speculate as to what role the literary text may have played in the Brexit vote. The idea that national and international identities are constructed presents a challenge perhaps to those who wish to uphold Europe's value in the current moment; a Europe that exists largely as discourse, constructed through cultural representations and historically entrenched only through these representations, with borders that exist not prior to these representations but in the wake of them, seems particularly vulnerable to naysayers. It presents a handy opening, perhaps, for those who wish to argue that there is, in fact, nothing special about the European Union at all, a susceptibility which is exposed by debates surrounding the possibility of a collective European identity given the diversity it must encompass (Delant and Rumford, 2005; Segers and Albrecht, 2016). Yet this is not the lesson of Anderson, Bhabha, and Said. These critical perspectives render the national identities that some pro-Brexit voices most strongly identify with equally intangible. Equally constructed, they are the subject of neither unified nor coherent geographies.

Such attention encourages a much longer view of Brexit beyond contemporary political events. Rather than focusing our attention on immediate socio-political contexts, cultural imaginaries ask us to consider how places and communities have been represented over time and to ask how attitudes to national and international identities and alliances exist as a result of a long process of representation. The individual cultural text (be it visual, cinematic, or written) exists as part of a complex cultural matrix of often reinforcing representations that produce a dominant cultural discourse surrounding issues of identity. It is not one text that tells us how to vote, for certain – but rather a plethora of texts that shape our sense of who and what we are in the contemporary moment. What is at stake, equally, is not necessarily a text explicitly speaking to particular events or people or being taken up by them but rather the potential for that text to have a wider political influence within the context of its existence amongst other cultural forms.

I want to suggest that such associations go far beyond the obvious. In particular, they are not simply about cultural texts which suggest a UK imagining itself as isolated from Europe or about a cosmopolitan cultural identity that is pro-EU against an older imaginary of political independence, xenophobia, and anti-immigration sentiment. One could imagine a selective reading of cultural texts that supports these assumptions, and such studies do already exist (see, for example, Dix, 2010; Blandford, 2007). What is more interesting, I think, however, is how readings of cultural imaginaries might allow us to consider deeper, more nuanced – perhaps more generous – readings of the Brexit vote. These readings ask us to consider the politics of the cultural imaginaries we create in ways beyond didactic intent. What is it in these cultural texts, we can ask, that has contributed to a community's way of thinking about itself that might have prompted a Brexit vote?

'On the outskirts of Luton, for heaven's sake'

In the spirit of this speculation, then, let us consider an example – the much maligned, much humorised, middle-England location that is Luton. Luton: where 56% of the vote was to leave the European Union. Luton: a place where the Brexit vote is easy to offer a rather obvious explanation of given that it is one of only three towns in the UK where people of white ethnicity are no longer a majority. Luton: where the leader of the English Defence League originates from, and where there have been notable clashes between Islamic and anti-Islamic groups.

Luton: a place, too, that exists within a particular cultural imaginary. When I was a child, Luton meant only one thing; it was the place defined by a 1979 Campari television advertisement series in which the model Lorraine Chase arrives in beautiful locations only to declare when questioned that she has arrived not from Paradise but from Luton airport. Chase's jarring cockney accent interrupts the advertisement's upmarket visuals, and by extension Luton emerges as the binary opposite of paradise, a dialectic to be resolved by the sipping of a cocktail. Chase's comic associations might have been my first encounter, but they were the continuation of a tradition begun by Monty Python in sketches such as 'Fly Me to Luton' and an image then resurrected in the 1980s by David Renwick, who frequently references the town in his sitcom *One Foot in the Grave*, most notably in an episode entitled 'In Luton Airport No One Can Hear You Scream'.

Whether an individual has encountered these representations directly is of less import here than the cumulative effect of these texts in contributing to an overall sense of Luton as a place – to, ultimately, creating Luton through the cultural imaginary. This is not the structural relation we see between Soviet protestors and *The Lord of the Rings* but rather a more amorphous influence. For this reason we can only speculate – but meaningfully speculate nevertheless – on the contribution such a cumulative representation makes to the identifications and attitudes which – again speculatively – may have led to the Brexit vote there.

It is into this pre-existing cultural space that Nicola Barker's *The Yips* (2012) enters, a novel that not only makes much of its physical location – 'the most flamboyant piece of comic fiction ever to be set in Luton', says the cover of the paperback – but that also contributes by these comic associations to Luton's pre-existing reputation. There is something intangibly comic about the idea of Luton which readers are here invited to partake in: a forerunning joke of which *The Yips* is only the latest instalment. Barker follows Campari's lead by presenting the town as a place of tastelessness where little of weight or significance takes place. The novel is populated by a series of cruder, larger-than-life characters, epitomised by the central figure of Stuart Ransom, a professional golfer who can be defined by his unsophisticated sexism and equally vile racism. Ransom is, however, hardly an exception; there is also Jen, whose peroxide hair, false eyelashes, and assessments of 'pure class' speak to the stereotypes of Essex girls and footballers' wives; and the other inhabitants of the Thistle Hotel in which Ransom stays, classless appropriations of wealth revealed by blond comb-overs, buttoned blazers, and lavender shirts. Wealth here is juxtaposed by accent in the same way as Campari's advert – the man in the blazer loudly shouts 'Oi' (168) in a manner which strips his outfit of any upper-class associations. Luton, readers are told, is a place that might attract wealth but never attracts class.

Barker's novel operates as satire. Yet the ironic gaze which she constructs does not lessen the cultural weight of her representation. The comic tone of Barker's novel rather serves to reinforce the sense of weightlessness presented by Campari, Renwick, and Monty Python, all of which present Luton via its airport as a place of transition: a necessary stopping point rather than a destination. The novel's claim to be 'the most flamboyant [. . .] ever' about its location reinforces the sense of Luton as a space on the peripheries. It would be much harder to make such an assertive claim about London or Manchester or Birmingham. Luton's position here as the setting for a novel, its back cover announces, is exceptional. Indeed, Barker's satirical style means that what might be substantial events in another novel are here swept aside in a swirling maelstrom of carnivalesque ludus. Glen has had cancer seven times, yet his internal consciousness and the trauma of the disease remains untouched; Valentine is agoraphobic and converts to Islam in the wake of her complex home life, but the narrative is more concerned with her career as a tattoo artist specialising in the artistic reinvention of female genitalia. Her mother has suffered irreparable brain damage, and the main focus of this is on her voracious sexual appetite. A man collects wallets made out of the skin of concentration camp victims and Jen is locked in the boot of a car, but these deeply disturbing facts come with only the most superficial psychological exploration. Barker here is no doubt commenting on the bizarre consequences of events through the creation of a stranger-than-fiction fiction – a world in which real life is presented as exceeding the normal realms of realism. Yet the consequences of this for Luton are that it becomes the epicentre of emptiness: a holding space for the intangible, unruly, and ultimately inconsequential. When it is revealed that Ransom's altercation at the hotel is to feature in a national tabloid newspaper, his immediate response is 'Right here in Luton of all places!' (260), the final three words postulating the incongruity of devoting a national headline to such a place.

This emptiness extends to the representation of Luton itself, which despite gracing the back cover of the novel exists as intangibly as the events which take place within it. Specific references within the novel to Luton are sparse – a nod to Havelock Park, Ransom's description of the local lake as a 'burst water main' (86). At one moment in the novel, Barker expands her narrative viewpoint, and we are given a glimpse of the wider town. A short paragraph of geographical references to the Windmill Trading Estate, St Mary's Road, and the X31 bus tell us that Barker has at least visited the town and walked the main road that joins the shopping district with the University of Bedfordshire. One wonders given this trail why the university itself does not feature – certainly this reinforces the absence of culture and intellectual life in Barker's representation of the town, but it also renders the uncomfortable possibility that Barker sees the life of the new university that Bedfordshire represents as offering little to complicate or enrich her representation. The Thistle Hotel in the novel is fictional, although ironically a Thistle Hotel Express did open in 2017, in largely the same location as Barker's creation. In this context, it is the Arndale Shopping Centre that is Barker's nod to Luton's real-world geography and a gesture towards materiality: the 'unforgiving slab' (1) against which the hotel sits. Barker's novel is set in 2006, the same year that the Arndale was developed and re-named The Mall. Yet there is no sign of this redevelopment in the description, and if Luton is on the brink of a development to change for the better there is little hint of this here. Rather, Luton exists as the counterpoint to London – the space 30 km southeast of the Bedfordshire town which, although equally undescribed, is assured by its capital status and broader cultural significance of an enduring presence. When Toby praises the hotel for its 24-hour concierge despite being 'on the outskirts of Luton, for heaven's sake' he is swiftly reminded by Gene that they are 'only forty-five minutes from London, after all' (228). London, though absent, has an enduring imaginary physicality, while Luton, in opposition, is always consigned to an imaginary immateriality.

In the wake of responses to Brexit documenting discontent with government polity on finance and immigration came another sense – of the vote as a protest against a broader feeling of exclusion and disenfranchisement, directed at metropolitan Westminster and its disregard for marginalised communities (Harris, 2016). What does it mean, we can ask, to live in a place that is always the other to a larger space and to one which is the seat of government? What does it mean to live in a place that is never taken seriously? What does this mean for one's sense of identity? For one's sense of entitlement? For one's sense of political enfranchisement? Barker is not from Luton; rather, *The Yips* exists in the context of a number of novels she sets in less documented places: *Darkmans* (2007), which is set in Ashford; *Wide Open* (1998), set on the Isle of Sheppey; and *Behindlings* (2002), set in Canvey Island. To be written of from outside in such a manner resonates with the notion of hermeneutical injustice: the ways in which those without social power are excluded from knowledge making about both themselves and others (Fricker, 2007). Perhaps, we might think, Barker's Luton speaks to a space in which a vote for Brexit is not only a vote against immigration but is also a vote to be taken seriously – to demand the political importance which comes with contributing to a dramatic change in Britain's global positioning. Perhaps it speaks to a desire to correct hermeneutical injustice through self-assertion. This, then, is not an argument solely about the demise of the white majority. It is an argument about political agency; it is an argument about political visibility and about political acknowledgment. If these are the terms by which Brexit becomes worthwhile, then to those who voted to leave it has already been a success. For here success is to be measured not by GDP, unemployment, or immigration figures but rather by the very acknowledgment that comes from the media and political reaction to the triumph of Brexit.

'The upholder of the sanctity of the great British pint'

Of course, acknowledging the possibility of a cultural imaginary surrounding Luton contributing to a Brexit protest vote does not detract from the fact that there was undoubtedly a response to immigration in the vote there. In this respect, Barker's novel does not straightforwardly encourage anti-immigration sentiment. What it does perhaps do, however, is contribute to an overall sense of ethnic division. Moreover, such division has explicit resonances with the town's relationship to the European Union.

The Yips predicts Luton's Brexit vote in its association of its anti-immigrant population with anti-European thinking. Near the beginning of the novel Ransom encounters a young man, Noel, whose mother once worked at the hotel. Noel arrives to meet Ransom with an appearance that is 'hollowed-out, withered, shop soiled' (47), smelling of cannabis and cigarettes and heavily tattooed, including the initials of Luton Town football club imprinted on his knuckles. Later in the novel, Noel's deceased father, Reggie, is revealed to be 'Luton's premier Nazi' (141). The narrative connects this racist thinking to Reggie's anti-European thinking. Readers learn that amidst his white supremacist activities, he also led a campaign against the local Trade and Standards Commission in the wake of the adoption of EU metric measures, winning him the label 'The Upholder of the Sanctity of the Great British Pint'.

Novelists such as Barker have the choice in this respect to challenge or uphold such associations: the choice, perhaps, between the stark pressures of realism and a more optimistic thinking that does not eschew these realities but nevertheless attempts to reshape them with an eye to the future. In the case of *The Yips*, the latter path is rejected as Reggie's anti-European, racist thinking comes in the wake of a more generalised acceptance within the narrative of ethnic division within the town. Despite Luton's ethnic diversity, there is only fleeting reference in *The Yips* to Luton's British Asian culture. Valentine's conversion to Islam is incorporated into the novel's satire – the satire from which nothing can be exempt in Barker's scathing, irreverent gaze – so that it is rendered here as part of the town's weirdness. The one notable moment of cross-cultural exchange within the town is a racist encounter in which Valentine and her Muslim friend Nessa, both in hijab, are kerb-crawled by a white man pulling down his trousers and simulating masturbation. While Valentine is angry, Nessa responds with the stereotyped resistance of the evangelical – claiming that such actions are 'our fuel' (425), a caricature which does little to explore the moment of feminist solidarity across cultural boundaries possible in such an experience.

So while the novel productively traces the beginnings of later racial tensions in the town, it does little to simultaneously foreground Luton's positive multi-ethnic community as it has been represented elsewhere, in the statements of community leaders but also in works such as Sarfraz Manzoor's memoir *Greetings From Bury Park* (2007) and his documentary *Luton Actually* (2005). In this respect, we might speculate that the Luton of this failed multiculture votes Brexit therefore as capitulation to the stereotype of its ethnic relations; it votes Brexit in the understanding that multiculturalism is impossible. It sees, perhaps, no possibility of a positive British identity that exists outside of homogeneity and reliance upon tropes of racial difference, within which the diversity symbolised by the European Union is both hostile and threatening. While in 1996 Stephen Haseler would write 'Twenty-first century Britons will see the British Isles as being a part of Europe [. . .] British sensibility will expand to encompass continental European history as part of its own' (185) the absence of positive cosmopolitanism for Barker's inhabitants renounces such possibility even as Brexit itself would speak similarly.

In this context, the vote to leave the EU is not a case in itself but rather a signifier of a much larger – and more urgent – problematic. It is this broader circumstance that is under-emphasised in online campaigns to hold a second vote or to declare the initial result invalid. For the vote to leave the EU is not the calamity itself but rather only the symptom of the calamity of internal division, disappointment, and despair that has befallen Britain. In this respect, Nairn's earlier assessment of the role of the EU in the breakup of Britain as an 'imaginary external solution: the magic escape-routes indulged in by one government after another' (53) continues to hold true only with crucial revision. For now it is no longer the government that holds this fantasy but rather the liberal and metropolitan centres of Britain, and the breakup that is threatened is not of Britain's constituent nations but of its very internal fabric: across towns and cities but also within them. As in Nairn's earlier formation, the enthusiasm for European identity has come too late and with illusory reasoning – for what is ultimately at stake is not membership of the EU itself but rather a broader set of values that many temptingly wish to believe continue to exist as long as membership prevails: the possibility, most notably, of communities of difference and political alliance founded not on cultural similarity but rather on the principles of tolerance and diversity enshrined in multiculturalism and cosmopolitanism and necessary for a European political identity which rests not on a fundamentally agreed definition of what it means to be European but rather the willingness to accept 'a community of strangers' in a world in which patriotism is neither expected nor secured by military conscription and where shared memories have yet to be imagined (Castiglione, 2009: 29). What the cultural imaginaries of places reveal in this context is the need for a reimagining of those places to contribute to the creation of a Britain in which there is not only economic but also cultural justice so that these values might become compatible with concepts of both national and regional belonging: a reimagining at once democratic and representative, but also radically speculative and creative. If the result of this is that membership of the EU is no longer either a cultural or economic threat or the cause on which to hang a wider disaffection and cultural alienation, then this could be an advantageous consequence. But to desire continued membership without this essential transformation would be to overlook the stark lesson in social and cultural division which the vote has painfully provided.

'Always give them a choice'

The cultural imaginary of Luton doesn't exist in a vacuum. It exists within a wider media discourse that negatively positions those who live in the town and denies them the hermeneutical justice to reshape that reality: a media discourse which declares Luton 'the worst place to live in Britain' (Boult, 2016) and 'the end of humanity' (Waugh, 2016), that declares its airport 'the worst airport in Britain' (Busby, 2017) and that defines it as the town tearing itself apart (Francis, 2012). It is tempting, in this context, to say that literature has little impact. Yet, conversely, it surely makes the contribution of literature even more vital.

Near the end of Ali Smith's novel *Autumn* (2016), a wonderful reflection on the hopefulness which is demanded of us all in the post-Brexit era, an elderly gentleman and a young girl debate the meaning of stories. They have written one of their own: a tale in which the young girl, Elisabeth, creates a man with a gun, and the old gentle-man, Daniel, imagines to her incredulity a person in a tree costume as the gunman's unlikely adversary. In the post-writing analysis, Elisabeth declares stories to be made up, while Daniel is at pains to tell her that they are 'no less true for that':

> And whoever makes up the story makes up the world, Daniel said. So always try to welcome people into the home of your story. That's my suggestion.
>
> (119)

When pressed, he continues:

> And always give them a choice – even those characters like a person with nothing but a tree costume between him or her and a man with a gun. By which I mean characters who seem to have no choice at all. Always give them a home.
>
> (120)

Elsewhere (Upstone, 2017), I have written of the contemporary novel's utopian potential and the possibility of that utopian poten-tial most particularly in relation to questions of race in twenty-first-century Britain. In keeping with my own sentiment, I continue to believe, like Daniel, that a story is a possible force for good that may shape ideas of diversity and tolerance in positive terms: that a story may, likewise, welcome you in and make you feel like you belong not only in that story, but in a place and in a community and in a nation. That it may do so even if, in reality, you don't feel that belonging. That it may, as Daniel suggests, offer you a choice you don't have in the moment before you read it but which you may have perhaps not on reading only that but in conjunction with other acts of transformation. At the same time, there is little tolerance in the kind of didacticism which would proscribe Barker's satire in favour of such utopianism. To casti-gate novels for their perpetuation of a cultural discourse is less helpful than to recognise the existence of such a discourse and its multi-fac-eted cultural presence – the subtle ways in which our imagining of place contributes to as much as reflects its real-world positioning. If Britain is to remain part of Europe, then we need a cultural imaginary which fosters not merely this identity but equally the broader social, political, and economic reality upon which it rests. The challenge to creative practitioners has never been greater or more urgent.

Bibliography

Anderson, Benedict. (1983). *Imagined Communities: Reflections on the Origin and Spread of Nationalism*. London: Verso.

Barker, Sarah. (2012). *The Yips*. London: Fourth Estate.

Bhabha, Homi. (ed.) (1990). *Nation and Narration*. London: Routledge.

———. Dissemination: Time, Narrative and the Margins of the Modern Nation. In: *Nation and Narration*, ed. Homi Bhabha. London: Routledge, pp. 291–322.

Blandford, Steve. (2007). *Film, Drama and the Break-Up of Britain*. Chicago: Chicago University Press.

Boult, Adam. (2016). Luton Named Worst Place in the UK – Do You Agree? *The Telegraph*, 20 January 2016. Available at: www.telegraph.co.uk/news/newstopics/howaboutthat/12110898/Luton-named-worst-place-in-the-UK-do-you-agree.html

Busby, Mattha. (2017). "The Ladies" Loos Are the Worst: Why Customers Hate Luton Airport. *The Guardian*, 31st August 2017. Available at: www.theguardian.com/world /2017/aug/31/the-ladies-loos-are-the-worst-why-customers-hate-luton-airport

Castiglione, Dario. (2009). Political Identity in a Community of Strangers. In: *European Identity*, eds. Jeffrey T. Checkel and Peter J. Katzenstein. Cambridge: Cambridge University Press, pp. 29–51.

Curry, Patrick. (1997). *Defending Middle-Earth: Tolkien, Myth and Modernity*. London: Houghton Mifflin.

Delant, Gerard and Chris Rumford. (2005). *Rethinking Europe: Social Theory and the Implications of* Europeanization. London: Taylor and Francis.

Dix, Hywel. (2010). *Postmodern Fiction and the Break-Up of Britain*. London: Continuum.

Francis, Nick. (2012). Hatred Tearing a Town Apart. *The Sun*, 27 February 2016. Available at: www.thesun.co.uk/archives/news/405096/hatred-tearing-a-town-apart/

Fricker, Miranda. (2007). *Epistemic Injustice: Power and the Ethics of Knowing*. Oxford: Oxford University Press.

Harris, Sarah Ann. (2016). Brexit 'Regretters' Say They 'Weren't Really Voting to Get Out of The EU. *Huffington Post*. UK Edition, 27 June 2016. Available at: www.huffingtonpost.co.uk/entry/brexit-eu-referendum-people-regretting-leave-vote_uk_5770e6b3e4b08d2c56397a46

Haseler, Stephen. (1996). *The English Tribe: Identity, Nation and Europe*. Basingstoke: Palgrave Macmillan.

Manzoor, Sarfraz. (2007). *Greetings From Bury Park: Race, Religion and Rock'n'Roll*. London: Bloomsbury.

Nairn, Tom. (1981). *The Break-Up of Britain* (1977). Second Expanded Edition. London: Verso.

Perryman, Mark. (2008). *Imagined Nation: England After Britain*. London: Lawrence and Wishart.

Said, Edward. (1978). *Orientalism*. New York: Pantheon.

Saunders, Anna and Rotero, Laura. (eds.) (2009). *Essence and the Margin: National Identities and Collective Memories in Contemporary European Culture*. Amsterdam: Rodopi.

Schwab, Gabriele. (2012). *Imaginary Ethnographies: Literature, Culture, and Subjectivity*. Columbia: Columbia University Press.

Segers, Mathieu and Yoeri Albrecht. (2016). *Rethinking Europe: Thoughts on Europe: Past, Present and Future*. Amsterdam: Amsterdam University Press.

Smith, Ali. (2016). *Autumn*. London: Hamish Hamilton.

Upstone, Sara. (2017). *Rethinking Race and Identity in Contemporary British Fiction*. London: Routledge.

Waugh, Rob. (2016). 'It's the End of Humanity': Luton Is Voted the Worst Town in the UK. *Metro*. UK, 19 January 2016. Available at: http://metro.co.uk/2016/01/19/its-the-end-of-humanity-luton-is-voted-the-worst-town-in-the-uk-5632960/#ixzz4sTbqqJTa

5

POETRY AND BREXIT

Anne Varty

Rarely have encounters between British poets and their audiences been as electric as those of Carol Ann Duffy's 'Shore to Shore' tour during June 2016. The unforeseen compression between political upheaval and the public performance of poetry amplified the tour's already heightened sensitivity to national identity, cultural borders, and the geopolitics of place. This chapter reflects on 'Shore to Shore' and the resonance of its poetry.

A year earlier Carol Ann Duffy planned a poetry road trip across the British mainland to celebrate the 10th anniversary of Independent Bookshops Week (18–25 June 2016), sponsored by her publisher Picador. Her fellow travellers were to be Gillian Clarke, outgoing National Poet of Wales, Jackie Kay, soon to be elected Scots Makar, and Imtiaz Dharker, pronounced 'world laureate' by Duffy. Their route from Falmouth to St Andrews charted a deliberately marginal course across the mainland, stopping in 15 small towns with thriving independent bookshops, aligning their map with the cultural politics of the parish. At each venue they were joined by a local poet, further promoting the significance of community. This apparent celebration of decentred independence might seem at odds with the ardent Remain convictions of the entire touring company. No-one could have foreseen that the referendum would take place 5 days into the tour, nor that its end date, 2 July 2016, would be the day on which Jackie Kay as Makar would address the opening of the new session of the Scottish Parliament with her poem 'Threshold'. The journey itself gave the travelling poets a unique opportunity, as Kay asserted, 'to take the political temperature of the country' (Kay, 2016). This included observation of their own experiences, which were recorded in a diary of the tour, published by the *Guardian* online.

I went to the reading in Oxford on 21 June where, after the bright fanfare by accompanying musician John Sampson, Clarke opened the performance with 'Daughter', written in October 2012 for the murdered 6-year-old April Jones. She dedicated it anew, by suggestion rather than by name, to the memory of Jo Cox, Labour MP for Batley and Spen, murdered for her 'Remain' politics on 16 June 2016 outside her surgery office in Leeds: Clarke's refrain, 'everyone's daughter', the plea, 'Let her change us forever'. Guest poet Bernard O'Donoghue followed. His work also struck a tone of elegy mixed with apprehension in 'The Year's Midnight' and 'The Day I Outlived my Father': 'So I am in new territory from here on . . . at liberty at last . . . to swim against the tide'. Kay's selection included 'Extinction'; its working title had been 'Planet Farage', 'We closed the borders, folks, we nailed it. / No trees, no plants, no immigrants. . . .'. Dharker read poems linked by the theme of the language of public discourse including 'The Right Word', a unsettling poem which domesticates our relationship with terrorist threat.

Carol Ann Duffy was the last to read. She opened with 'Prayer' (the closing poem of *Mean Time*, 1993). The poem, in the context of 'Shore to Shore', articulates how the island nation, and indeed the individual represented by extended metaphor, is threatened from both within and beyond its boundaries:

> Darkness outside. Inside, the radio's prayer –
> Rockall. Malin. Dogger. Finisterre.

With its submerged invocation of 'Britain' through its play with the BBC Radio 4 shipping forecast, the tone is foreboding. It pictures the island nation held captive by the elements and guarded by place names that are both familiar and threatening, from 'Rockall' to 'Finisterre'. Exposing their etymology and conjuring with the fragments of the words, all rock, mal, dog, dogged, and the end of the earth, this 'Prayer' warns that Britain contains and is contained by its own uncanny alter ego. The shore, like a hard border, protects by excluding others and contains by isolating the inhabitants.

On the eve of the referendum they were in Monmouth, in the borderlands between England and Wales. This was a felicitous alignment of place and event: the referendum itself was experienced with the force of a physical border, as articulated by a text received by the tour organiser, Helen Taylor. In the 'Shore to Shore' diary, published in the *Guardian*, one of her daughters on the way to vote on 23 June texted, 'See you on the other side'. The results of the vote coming in overnight, Duffy concluded her diary entry, 'As I write, it's approaching 6am and JK Rowling has tweeted that Cameron's legacy will be the breaking of two unions. His unleashed genie has indeed given us our country back – torn in two like a bad poem'. The first reading after the result was known took place in the Shropshire town of Bridgnorth on Friday 24 June. Their guest poet was Liz Lefroy. 'The audience give their local poet . . . enthusiastic applause when she says she comes from a family of Huguenot asylum-seekers and chooses to be European. She reads her poem Michelangelo's David: "Love can be translated into time in any language"'. Imtiaz Dharker, writing this entry for the tour diary, continued, '[a]ll of us shift our readings slightly. Gillian reads "Lament", Jackie "In my country", Carol Ann "Weasel Words": all poems written years ago, but relevant today. There are no overt political statements but the choices are fierce. The people who come to speak to us at the signing tell us that the poetry has helped' she wrote in the *Guardian* Diary. On Saturday they travelled to 'the borders of another language, landscape, culture, a cliff-edge in the heart,' Gillian Clarke records, the Welsh town of Oswestry. 'Suddenly,' Clarke continues, 'all exclaim at a sight that Liz Lefroy warned us of last night, a monstrous construction in a field: fly-tipped junk, a garish "sculpture", a tipped boat with a sly insinuation of refugees. Immigrants on a sinking ship, the loveless word LEAVE in weeping paint. A word to wound, not heal; to sink us, not save us'. Again Clarke began her reading with 'Lament'. Written originally about the Gulf War of 1991, the title of the poem is an imperative verb, the poem an inventory of mourning: 'For the ocean's lap with its mortal stain. / For Ahmed at the closed border. / For the soldier in his uniform of fire'. As Clarke read the poem aloud, she was 'wondering what our listeners see. In my head is a sinking ship, wreckage, the work of a fly-tipper in a green field'. The following morning Clarke notes that '[m]y daughter considers applying for Irish citizenship, as her grandmother was Irish. Sackings and resignations in the Labour party. Yeats speaks in my heart. "Things fall apart, the centre cannot hold," and the premonition: "And what rough beast, its hour come round at last, / Slouches toward Bethlehem to be born?"' New allegiances, changed identities, an abandoned and abandoning homeland, all adjuncts of border crossings to which the 'Shore to Shore' poets had become so finely attuned, were announced as internalised and familial.

Jackie Kay, in the *Guardian* diary, commented on how both the meaning and reception of her poem 'Extinction' changed with the referendum result:

> It was written as satire and every night before the referendum it had audiences killing themselves laughing. Now that satire has become a reality, it suddenly isn't funny anymore. When I finish reading the poem, there's now a drop in temperature, moments of extended silence, then people kick into life and clap and cheer, as if they want to identify themselves straight away, adding their vigorous voice. As if they want to be on the side of poetry.

'Extinction' was one of the 20 poems Carol Ann Duffy commissioned in May 2015 for the *Guardian* newspaper's 'Keep it in the Ground' campaign to engage with Climate Change. Launching that collection of poems, Duffy wrote, '[i]nformation . . . is not enough. . . . As Rusbridger says, journalism is a "rear view mirror": good at telling you what has happened but not so good at explaining what's round the next bend'. 'Extinction' matches the destruction of natural diversity (which happens faster when borders are closed or islands are isolated) with the homogenising grip of racist, sexist political extremes.

The poem's shift from 'satire' to 'reality', as Kay saw it, came faster than most anticipated: 'We took control of our affairs. No fresh air/No birds, no bees, no HIV, no Poles, no pollen'. ('Take back control' was a favourite slogan by Vote Leave, repeated by Boris Johnson and Nigel Farage on the eve of the referendum.) Kay's version of the poem 'Extinction', printed in the *Guardian* on 2 July 2016 and performed at all her readings during 'Shore to Shore', differs from the first publication as printed in the *Guardian* on 15 May 2015 on precisely the topic of borders. The tour version opens with three new lines: 'We closed the borders, folks, we nailed it. / No trees, no plants, no immigrants/No foreign nurses, no Doctors; we smashed it'. These lines are additions to the 16-line poem of 2015, which opens 'We took control of our affairs'. Expanding to 19 lines, the poem itself has no closed boundaries, as though its aesthetic form embodies the politics for which it stands, assuring its own survival in an era of extinction.

On 28 June the poets were performing in Carlisle Cathedral, approaching the next border for negotiation, between England and Scotland. Dharker noted the hybrid aspects of their location, the city 'feels like it has one foot in Scotland', the cathedral was 'a site of worship for almost 900 years, which still has the Norman nave from the 12th century', and it had emblematically astonishing acoustics. Dharker notes that 'It also suits the music of guest poet Jacob Polley's voice, and the perfect pitch of his poems'. He read 'The News':

> The moon's not sad; the sun won't worry.
> Despite your suffering, England's still
> And only some of us are sorry.

This poem was published in *The Havocs*, a collection composed between 2006 and 2012. It was not written in response to a specific event, but it is one utterance in the mounting, and with hindsight prophetic, expression of civic unease which sounds throughout Polley's volume. 'The News' chimes too with the 1916 poem by Thomas Hardy which Gillian Clarke invoked in her diary entry for the following day, 'In Time "of the Breaking of Nations"', 'Yet this will go onward the same / Though Dynasties pass.' The articulation between poets, poems and audience became profound and shifting under the pressure of political tumult. It encompassed not just the immediate shared experience of performance. Social media, text, tweet, Facebook also enabled those absent to overcome geographical distance and join in. But for all its inclusive aspiration, the more articulate and mutually affirming this Remain community became, the starker the division between it and those who voted Leave.

That division was particularly inscribed by the border between England and Scotland, separating the land of the Leavers from the land of the Remainers. Their crossing was described by Jackie Kay on 30 June: '[t]hen there's a huge sign: Welcome to Scotland. We all cheer. I have never felt more pleased to cross the border. "Je suis haggis," Carol Ann shouts. We're all Scottish now'. The wit of Duffy's border greeting is far-reaching. 'Je suis haggis' adapts the French slogan 'Je suis Charlie' designed by Joachim Roncin and posted on Twitter hours after the terror attack on the office of the satirical journal *Charlie Hebdo* in Paris on 7 January 2015, spreading rapidly across the world as a statement of defiance. Duffy's use of a foreign language to assert a home identity places Duffy firmly on the 'other' side, where the self is hybrid and the outlook transnational. It doubles Scotland with Europe (both are home), and her use of French in particular recalls not simply *Charlie Hebdo* but also the Auld Alliance between Scotland and France, agreed in 1295 to contain English expansionism, its legacy stretching beyond the 1707 Act of Union into the present day. Finally, 'je suis haggis' acts on the imperative of the political majority in England, 'Leave'. That is just what these poets, in this moment, chose to do: 'We're all Scottish now'. Interviewed in the *Sunday Herald* on 10 July 2016, Kay recalled the powerful emotions which accompanied the choice: 'When we crossed the border in that minibus, we all cheered, we all broke out into applause, and we were all visibly moved. Some of us were in tears. We just felt very, very, very grateful"'. The geopolitical boundary represents an ideological line whereby Scotland, the stateless nation and threatened minority partner of England, comes to represent a refuge. It is a paradox that what qualifies Scotland as a home place is the fact that it voted for open borders and free movement, yet it can only be accessed by crossing a line which here functions to exclude and protect. It is a further paradox that Kay's urgency to reach 'home' is a conceptualising of the border which contradicts her satire on the aggression of the exclusive border which was articulated by 'Extinction'.

The 'Shore to Shore' Tour was billed by the sponsor, Duffy's publisher, Picador, as a 'Celebration of Poetry and Community'. It was unforeseeable how successfully poetry and community would come together through these readings. Nor could it be anticipated how the independent bookshops in association with which the tour was arranged would find themselves at the heart of national turbulence rather than local stability. 'Subtly, subversively, words speak to the heart, the hurt, the anxiety of a nation in crisis. We see it, and hear it, in every audience, every town, every stopping-place on this journey', wrote Gillian Clarke. The national poets were important for the success of the tour because of their repertoire, experience, and fame, yet it was clearly poetry itself which came to the fore, 'words speak[ing] to the heart'. The sheer number of poets taking part, not only as performers but also, like Hardy, Yeats or Adrian Mitchell, as off-stage presences, their work quoted or honoured during the two-week period, meeting sell-out audiences in encounters of evident intensity, demonstrates the vital place of poetry in the public life of the nation and its role in this time of Brexit.

Bibliography

Unless specified, all the prose comes from the *Guardian* 'Shore to Shore' diary. This begins in the Guardian, 21 May 2016, and carries on as a column until July.
Kay, Jackie. (2016). Interview. *Sunday Herald*, 10 July 2016.
The poems performed are as follows:
Gillian Clarke: 'Daughter'; 'Lament'
Imtiaz Dharker: 'The Right Word'
Carol Ann Duffy: 'Prayer'
Jackie Kay: 'Extinction'; 'In my country'
Bernard O'Donoghue: 'The Year's Midnight', 'The Day I Outlived my Father'
Jacob Polley: 'The News'
I am grateful to Camilla Elworthy at Picador for information about planning the tour.

6

ENGLISH LITERATURE SAVED MY LIFE

Bryan Cheyette

I launched my last book with a talk called "English Literature Saved My Life". This was an odd thing to do as the book *Diasporas of the Mind* (2014) was about different kinds of literary diasporas and contained very little canonical "English literature". But the reason why I called the talk "English Literature Saved My Life" was that, as an 11-plus failure in Leicester, my secondary modern school did not offer English Literature "O" Level (in the days before GCSEs), and I had to consume the forbidden fruit after school. I might as well have been given crack cocaine, as I was hooked. Thanks to a wonderful teacher, Stephen Charlton, myself and three other students memorized Francis Turner Palgrave's *Golden Treasury of English Songs and Lyrics* (1861) and managed to achieve the English literature grades necessary to move on and study "A" Levels (the other 296 students in our year remained 11-plus failures). My life was saved.

One way of telling this life story is to make it a story of assimilation into Englishness. After all, Palgrave's *Golden Treasury* represents a certain kind of Victorian English sensibility not least because of Palgrave's close friendship with Sir Alfred Lord Tennyson and his work as a Private Secretary for William Ewart Gladstone. Tennyson encouraged Palgrave to edit the *Golden Treasury*, which became a bestseller and led to Palgrave's election as Professor of Poetry at Oxford University. Palgrave's Jewish heritage, which he was unaware of until his adult life, has once again become relevant to the story. It turns out that his father Francis Cohen was only permitted to marry his mother Elizabeth Turner if he converted to Christianity and took his wife's mother's maiden name, Palgrave, as his own. Such was the extent to which Francis Turner Palgrave was assimilated completely into Englishness, notwithstanding the poet Algernon Charles Swinburne sniping at Palgrave's "Cohenisms" in his letters.

So how does this story of assimilation – my potential assimilation and Palgrave's actual assimilation – relate to Brexit? Many of those who voted Brexit objected not only to new immigrants on these shores but to the fact that these new immigrants are now more assertive about their differences (religious and otherwise) than previous generations. As someone whose grandparents came from Ireland, Latvia, Russia and Poland and very quickly gave up their Yiddish language and culture, I am only too aware of the pressures to assimilate and hide your ethnicity. This version of assimilation has a long history, going back to the Victorian period, and it only began to wane in the 1970s when I was reading the *Golden Treasury*. Many postwar literary critics, whom I found interesting, such as Q. D. Leavis, Al Alvarez or John Gross, were in the same assimilationist mould as Francis Palgrave, although I was not aware of this on first reading. The polymathic George Steiner, writing from a strident central European perspective, was the exception to the rule and, for this reason, I found him particularly attractive. But very soon after the publication of Steiner's *Language and Silence: Essays 1958–1966* (1967) he was refused the right to examine by the English literature department at the University of Cambridge. This was not a coincidence, as Steiner's insistence on the need to look beyond national borders, to move from provincialism to cosmopolitanism, was rightly seen as a slight on the English literature department at Cambridge.

Looking back on these heady days before university, when I was devouring T. S. Eliot, James Joyce, Franz Kafka, Sylvia Plath and Anne Sexton, I thought I was assimilating not only into English literature (although none of these favourites were English) but also into the English language (I was obsessed with the etymology of words; one of my favourite books was the *Little Oxford English Dictionary*). My undergraduate degree at the University of Sheffield was a conventional Beowulf-to-Virginia Woolf course, which I loved. Coming from a comparatively bookless home (dominated by *Reader's Digest*), everything I read at university was new and exciting. Not only was I the first in my family to go to university, I was the first on my father's side who was relatively literate (my father's mother couldn't write a word of English; my father's education was interrupted by the Second World War and did not continue much into his teenage years). Not unlike many working-class scholarship students, such as Richard Hoggart, I was cut adrift and torn from my local culture. Hoggart wrote memorably about these class fissures in his *The Uses of Literacy* (1956). Literature saved my life because it acted as an anchor, giving me a language to understand the gulf between generations in my family which were gulfs in both class and ethnic assimilation.

So why didn't I write conventional English literary criticism after my time at university and assimilate in my writing as I did in my life? I still don't understand why I chose to write on British-Jewish literature and on representations of Jews in English literature for my doctorate. Perhaps it wasn't exactly my choice, as there was a very particular context in the early 1980s for this work. Assimilationism was being challenged by compelling voices such as Salman Rushdie (most especially) and his generation of writers – Martin Amis, Ian McEwan, Angela Carter – who were all looking elsewhere for their inspiration. The rise of post-colonial studies at the time reflected a growing sense of multiculturalism and a critique of Empire and challenged the various ways in which imperialism was still part of the British imaginary. I learned a good deal from the so-called holy trinity of post-colonial theorists – Homi Bhabha, Edward Said and Gayatri Spivak – all of whom articulated racial and colonial discourse in ways which spoke either explicitly or implicitly to the history of Jewish assimilation into Englishness.

This was a time, in other words, when the history and place of migrants in Britain was being understood from a positive perspective and other options, rather than mere assimilation or disappearance, were being voiced. It was also a time, rather like today, when a young graduate, faced by a radical right government, had very little hope for the future. I was rightly advised by Neil Corcoran to "write from the heart" (we were later to bond over a mutual love of Bob Dylan) and so chose to work on new areas of research which spoke to my sense of self (and my parents' and grandparents' identity) that explained the processes of assimilation. My literary criticism, underpinned by youthful idealism, was the discovery of new fields which were ignored wilfully by the English literature mainstream. While this made it difficult to get an academic job in departments run by mainstream literary critics, it did energize my work and gave it an ethical purpose (to speak about dehumanizing racial discourses or unheard-of minority canons when others were silent) in a poor imitation of George Steiner. The 1980s was a time when literary criticism (Angela Carter, F. R. and Q. D. Leavis, Raymond Williams) had a prominent place in bookshops and there was an expectation that such criticism mattered and was on the side of social change. This was also the expectation of my youthful self, not least that the ethical dimension of literary criticism could bring about change which was progressive and humanizing. But, of course, one's youthful self is always deluded by idealism, and all that was changed by my research, alas, was the academy.

Which brings me back to Brexit. My main objection to Brexit is that it creates the illusion, which currently is our reality, that there are no other futures than the nation-state for the United Kingdom or Great Britain (both misnomers, as Scotland and Northern Ireland voted Remain and, if there was a vote today, so would Wales). I have always thought that a focus on the nation-state closes off many more possibilities than it opens up. That is why my work has attempted to expand the canon of English literature into minority and diasporic literatures so as to show the straightjacket on the imagination of national ways of thinking. I admire those contemporary writers such as Elaine Feinstein, Gabriel Josipovici (in this volume), Clive Sinclair and Muriel Spark, whose imagination begins in a minor key but is not confined by any one nation and soon opens up new vistas. Brexit means that our national straightjacket – Englishness, not even Britishness – becomes much tighter and the value of a migrant's perspective becomes increasingly discounted and devalued.

And so, after all, this is a migrant's story. It is the story of someone who found a home in English literature and in so doing changed its conventions and expanded its subject matter like many migrants do. Migrants start with nothing; after all they are considered to be mere observers of a national history that began long before they arrived on these shores. If you have to discover this culture for yourself, so that it becomes who you are, then you are prone to take the culture exceedingly seriously. What is the point of writing a book if it doesn't say something new or, at least, try to say something new? In other words, if you come from a relatively bookless world, and reading books becomes something that you do outside of school for pleasure (so that you can end up in a school and university that *does* teach English literature rather less pleasurably), then the bar is raised pretty high for the kind of book that you will end up writing. This has been called an insider/outsider perspective, and it is this perspective which I value, although, needless to say, it is not mine alone.

A migrant's perspective is at the heart of English literature – Joseph Conrad, Jean Rhys and Zadie Smith – of English cinema – Sarah Gavron, Mike Leigh, Karel Reisz – of English theatre – Julia Pascal, Harold Pinter, Arnold Wesker – of English art – Frank Auerbach, Lucian Freud, Josef Herman – and I could go on. This is not only a migrant's "contribution to civilization", as it used to be called, as all of these figures, and many, many more, have remade and rethought English "civilization" (as we like to think of it) in their own diverse ways. But these stories are little known as our national story still dominates (as I write this the film, the history and the myth of "Dunkirk" is everywhere). The culture of Brexit wants to put our national story ahead of everything else as if withdrawing from the European Union were another "Dunkirk" with Britain standing alone in need of last-minute help from a reluctant United States.

But we cannot turn the clock back to Britain's "finest hour" or to the height of the Empire in Victorian Britain when migrants were meant to disappear from public view ("assimilate" as soon as they arrived and, at best, practice their odd religions in their homes). This is a Brexit fantasy, as we head for an uncertain future by hanging on to the spurious certainties of the past. But what can I, now a member of the metropolitan elite and detached from my fellow 11-plus failures, do? Leicester voted Remain not least because it is the first British city where the so-called ethnic minority is actually the ethnic majority.

I often think about those students who I lost touch with, many of whom came from families who supported the National Front (a nastier version of UKIP). They may well look at me now, ensconced in my ivory tower, and argue with some justification that I do not know how hard their lives are without their jobs being undercut by new migrants who are willing to work long hours at a cheaper rate than they can afford. But now that they live in a city of migrants I would like to think that they have some appreciation of the qualities which their fellow citizens can bring. After all, the city of Leicester has been united by the body of King Richard III, whose ancestry is open to dispute and who lived at a time when Britain was riven by civil strife (the War of the Roses). What a perfect symbol for our present civil strife, and the perfect conversation starter to bridge the gulf between myself and those whose nation-thinking would want the migrant to disappear.

Bibliography

Al Alvarez. (1966). *The New Poetry: An Anthology*. London and New York: Penguin Books.

Cheyette, Bryan. (1995). *Constructions of "The Jew" in English Literature and Society: Racial Representations 1875–1945*. Cambridge: Cambridge University Press.

———. (ed.) (1998). *Contemporary Jewish Writing in Britain and Ireland: An Anthology*. Lincoln: Nebraska University Press; London: Peter Halban.

———. (2014). *Diasporas of the Mind: Jewish and Postcolonial Writing and the Nightmare of History*. London and New Haven: Yale University Press.

Corcoran, Neil. (ed.) (2017). *"Do You Mr Jones?" Bob Dylan with the Poets and Professors*. London and New York: Penguin.

Eliot, T. S. (1963). *Collected Poems: 1909–1962*. London: Faber & Faber.

Gross, John. (2002). *A Double Thread: A Childhood in Mile End and Beyond*. London and New York: Vintage.

Joyce, James. (1917). *A Portrait of the Artist as a Young Man*. London: The Egoist Press.

Kafka, Franz. (1937). *The Trial*. London: Martin Secker.

Leavis, F.R. (1948). *The Great Tradition*. London: Chatto & Windus.

Leavis, Q.D. (1932). *Fiction and the Reading Public*. London: Chatto & Windus.

Otton, Megan Nelson. Francis Turner Palgrave (1824–1897). *Dictionary of National Biography*. Available at: http://dx.doi.org/10.1093/ref:odnb/21158 [Accessed 12 September 2017].

Palgrave, Francis Turner. (1861). *Golden Treasury of English Songs and Lyrics*. London: J. M. Dent and Sons.

Plath, Sylvia. (1965). *Ariel*. London: Faber & Faber.

Sexton, Anne. (1966). *Live or Die*. Boston: Houghton Mifflin.

Steiner, George. (1967). *Language and Silence: Essays 1958–1966*. London: Faber & Faber.

7

MIGRANT BRITAIN

Ankhi Mukherjee

This is the time of the greatest refugee crisis the EU has known, in fact, the greatest refugee crisis since World War II. There is no more appropriate juncture to revise critical thinking on dispersed populations, and no more apt novel, I'd argue, than the Beirut-born Rawi Hage's *Cockroach* (2008) for inaugurating this revision, at this historical moment, with thousands fleeing the crises of Africa and the Middle East, Syria and Libya in particular.

Cockroach is about a migrant who has escaped the decade-long Lebanese civil war (and a personal trauma) to arrive in "frozen" Canada and who imagines himself half-cockroach: wretched, driven underground, hungry and scrounging. In one of his hallucinations, a cockroach doppelganger says: "We are ugly. But we always know where we are going. We have a project. A project to change this world" (102). I was reminded of Hage's ugly and wily cockroach when, in summer 2015, during a tour of South East Asia, prime minister David Cameron described migrants trying to reach Britain as a 'swarm' ("Calais Crisis"). "He should remember he is talking about people and not insects. I think it's a very worrying turn that he appears to be wanting to be divisive and set people against, whip people up against, the migrants in Calais," Labour's Harriet Harman had said in the chorus of condemnation that followed. This was in the context of Calais, where hundreds of migrants had tried to enter the Channel Tunnel overnight, and thousands had been trying to reach the UK from Calais. Nine people had died attempting to cross the Channel in June. Cameron's exact words, uttered in Vietnam, were "a swarm of people coming across the Mediterranean, seeking a better life, wanting to come to Britain." The leader of this imperial nation told the BBC that "everything that can be done will be done to make sure our borders are secure and make sure that British holidaymakers are able to go on their holidays." I offer my thoughts on Brexit and migrant Britain in the immediate context of not just 23 June, 2016, but with reference to the scenes that unfolded soon after Cameron's comments: hundreds of migrants piled up in the nineteenth-century rail station, Keleti, in the Hungarian capital, while European leaders bickered over who should take responsibility for these unwanted arrivals; hundreds taking off from Budapest on foot; the image of three-year-old Aylan Kurdi face down on a beach in Turkey.

Hage's novel is set in Montreal. His insect-like protagonist, scuttling around for food and love, is the swarming unconscious of the icy city. The city becomes an "urban text," to quote Michel de Certeau, a system produced by the very act of walking, just as a language is produced by speech-acts (93). The narrator is not an enunciating subject. His peregrinations and disconnected conversations, in which he is more analysand than analyst, stand in for (the absent) plots to reconstruct memory palimpsests of topological spaces that have started to become foreign to themselves. *Cockroach*. When we meet the walker-writer at the outset, we learn that he had tried to commit suicide, was sectioned, briefly, and is now ordered by the state to visit a therapist, Genevieve, every week. The narrative comically alternates between the hallucinatory reality of the protagonist's waking and dream lives – his memories and traumas, his thieving and larceny, his sexual fantasies and sexual shenanigans, his ragtag socioeconomic milieu, comprised of émigré hustlers and con artists (Iranians, Albanians, Algerians, Lebanese) – and the deadpan exchanges with the uncomprehending therapist in the public health clinic. The narrator, unnamed, has fled his Middle Eastern home (identifiable as Beirut) for a modern city (identifiable as Montreal, which Hage once described as "a large military industrial complex"). The protagonist's troubles can be traced to the death of his sister, beautiful, reckless, and fatally attracted to a violent man: we gather that it is his unwitting complicity in the sister's tragic death that has brought him to Montreal. Here, he falls madly in love with Shohreh, a beautiful, wilful Iranian woman who uses him for sex but doesn't love him back. His suicidal thoughts are quickly forgotten, and he becomes embroiled in Shohreh's perilous reinvention of herself from victim to perpetrator of violence after she meets an Iranian politico – one who raped and tortured her in Iran – in the restaurant where the narrator works as a busboy.

Unlike a lot of writing we have come to identify as diaspora literature, with the "ex-centric communicative circuitry" (Paul Gilroy's phrase in *Against Race* 129) of its patterns of power, communication, and conflict, Hage's novel takes little interest in dismantling the colonialist centre-periphery binary that continues to polarise postcolonial geography. Its prime focus is not on transforming metropolitan space for dispersed populations to, and I quote Gilroy again, "converse, interact, and . . . synchronize significant elements of their social and cultural lives," but to find a room without light where the narrator can break down in peace. He is scathing on the question of assimilation or embourgeoisment, as seen in his attitude towards Reza or the Professor, experts at playing "the fuckable, exotic" foreigner. He abhors the affluent French Canadian women who fall for his 'noble savage' act and whom he subsequently robs. He can live in filth and hunger if Shohreh will sleep with him, he insists:

> I can tolerate filth, cockroaches, and mountains of dishes that would tower above our heads like monumental statues, like trophies, testifying that we value lovemaking and a hedonistic experience, and that all else can wait!
>
> (52)

This is not to say that the narrator does not register or is not enraged by the growing inequalities of the city or the growing rift between the global north and south. His narrative testifies repeatedly to the quandary, pain, and mortality of raced subjects: "I was split between two planes and aware of two existences, and they were both mine" (119).

However, though he jokes about enjoying a spot of "anti-imperial looting" (251), helping the janitor's Russian wife steal from an old lady in her care, whose British officer husband, according to the janitor's covetous wife anyway, "stole everything from the Indians, or the Chinese" (41), *Cockroach* is about a deterritorialisation without the constraint of reterritorialisation: it is about coming undone, but without a transformative vector, and it is about a protagonist who rejects alike the seductions of archaism and futurism (Deleuzian terms). The narrator seems to suggest that his psychotic episodes are, in fact, involuntary acts of non-conformity with power, which is inherently predatory.

> How can I tell her [Genevieve] that I do not want to be part of anything because I am afraid I will become an invader who would make little boys hunger, who would watch them die with an empty stomach.
>
> (210)

What Rawi Hage's *Cockroach* represents, by way of urban text, is the mental underground, laying claim to a psychiatric culture that had hitherto denied the colonised, the by-products of coloniality, and the wretched of the earth, the civilizational benefit of possessing an unconscious. Echoing Freud's there is no 'no' in the unconscious, Hage writes, "The drain swallowed everything, nothing was filtered, recycled, tossed away." However paranoid and restrictive the immigration policy of the world above ground, "All was good, all was natural, all was accepted by the underworld" (156). Back in the stratified urban space of Montreal, the narrator realises that liberal universalism is predicated on the creation of racial and cultural others and their systematic exclusion or violent expulsion. The unnamed narrator in *Cockroach* likens his therapist to the Sultan in the *Arabian Nights*. Here's a snippet of that conversation:

> Who is Abou-Roro?
> My mentor. A thief in the neighbourhood.
> Genevieve nodded. She looked intrigued but held her composure Her pen made its way inside her lips, and I could see her breathe in a steady, regular motion, in time to her heartbeat.
> The doctor, like sultans, is fond of stories.
>
> (102)

He will need to baffle the epistemic greed of the police state through silence, half truths, and innuendo in every exchange. Hage's *Cockroach* makes its leading character, an active, not passive subject, a migrant who refuses to be read, neutralised, or immobilised.

I have discussed *Cockroach* in some detail here, as it helps us imagine the future anterior of Brexit literature, the deferred re-articulation of the shocks and aftershocks of this epochal event. The future anterior "never will be, but always will have been," as Gayatri Chakravorty Spivak states (25). The phobic 'swarm' of migrants of David Cameron's articulation give over, in the future perfect of Rawi Hage's *Cockroach*, to the fantasy of a gigantic insect, an avenging machine. This is the migrant as a character dreamt up by Kafka (Gregor Samsa) and Burroughs (*Naked Lunch*). He is a visionary, like Dostoyevsky's Underground Man; and he represents the "anonymous collectivity" (Albert Memmi's term) of Ellison's Invisible Man. A thief, anarchist, and a social satirist made ill by his own bilious observations, he jogs memories of Céline, Rimbaud (Drunken Boat) Camus, Genet, Cronenberg.

Needless to say, the imaginative literature of Brexit remains to be written. Until such time as it is fully elaborated, the text of the EU referendum will be indissociable from the acrimonious "pamphlet wars," primarily instigated by the publication of the net migration figures (333,000 in 2015 according to the Office of National Statistics, showing a dramatic rise of 20,000 from the previous year) in the first week of the referendum. "The economy was the most covered campaign issue, with 7,028 articles compared with 4,383 about immigration, though the latter were more prominent" says Jane Martinson in *The Guardian* (May 10, 2017). Media interest in immigration tripled in the 10 weeks of the campaign, a report into UK news media revealed: 99 front pages were about immigration during this period, compared to the 82 devoted to the economy. Most of these had been published by pro-Leave newspapers. The *Mail*, the *Sun*, the *Express* became countervailing forces in the forms of hypermediated storytelling Brexiters used. The *Mail* front page, "Let us in: we're from Europe," needed a correction after it was discovered that the refugees depicted were from the Middle East. Nigel Farage's infamous "BREAKING POINT: The EU has failed us all" poster, purportedly showing migrants and refugees arriving in hordes to a Britain made borderless by the EU, used a photograph of migrants cross-ing the Croatia-Slovenia border in 2015. The sole white person in the photograph had been hidden by a box of text. When challenged on the paranoia-stoking, hate-inciting nature of the message, Farage maintained that it was an accurate and undoctored photograph of the genuine refugee crisis that followed Merkel's call in summer 2015, adding that we could never be sure if any of these people were actu-ally refugees, as defined by the Geneva Convention. Similarly, the big red bus promising £350 million more a week for NHS was a mobi-lised lie [treasury figures for UK contributions to the EU budget revealed that it was just £156m a week for 2016/17]. The mass hys-teria around Turkey – population 75 million – joining the EU was also deception in dire breach of electoral law. In an implausible (in other contexts) but utterly believable turn in Brexit sophistry, the phrase "Project Fear" was attached to the Remain campaign, not the paranoid style of Gove, Johnson, and Farage. Referring to predictions from the Remain campaign of a profound shock to the economy in the event of Brexit, it was cited 739 times in the 20 national, daily, and Sunday newspapers in Britain.

A leaked document from the Home Office, dated August 2017, proves that a key objective of Brexit was indeed to put an end to the free movement of labour, reduce lower-skilled EU migration, and develop a UK-focused – 'Britain First' – immigration policy. As Alan Travis, the Home Affairs editor of the *Guardian*, observes, it "fills the hole in the middle of Brexit." While the document does not promise a cut in immigration, the rhetoric is one of "taking back control" and achieving "sustainable levels" of net migration. It is a no-brainer that the hysteria around migration from the EU masks another. A net 164,000 non-EU immigrants came to the UK in the year ending September 2016: this is almost equal to the 165,000 that came from the EU. "If border checks have left non-EU immigration at this level, why would imposing post-Brexit controls on EU citizens bring their numbers down?" asks Michael Skapinker in the FT. It is almost as if the government is using the Leave voters' demand for significant reduction in EU immigration to crack down on immigration from non-EU countries. Theresa May, whose own brand of "Project Fear" has, in the past, manifested in draconian measures meted out to international students, was recently cautioned by Conservative and Opposition MPs about overestimating the risk of students remaining in Britain illegally. New data published by the Office of National Statistics estimates that the number of students overstaying their visa is 4,600 (and not 100,000, the number the Home Office had been using as evidence). According to Sir Vince Cable, the former Business Secretary (to May's Home Secretary during the 2010–2015 Coalition), May's crackdown on international students since 2010 has resulted in 48,000 being sent home illegally and wrongfully. Even when Cable's Department for Business stopped stringent controls, large numbers of foreign students were deterred from coming to the UK, says the new leader of the Liberal Democrats.

PM May's strong and stable animus towards international students has drawn severe criticism from the public, the Parliament, and the Government, especially since there is no public pressure to maintain this stance. International students bring substantial income (to the tune of £25.8bn) for universities and support approximately 206,000 jobs: they are vital to making universities excellence-led, internationally competitive, and global partners in shared pursuits. Citing a Migration Observatory poll of 2011, which found that while 69 per cent of people wanted immigration to be controlled, only 29 per cent considered students to be immigrants, Skapinker states,

> Indeed, there is no obligation on the government to have an immigration target, let alone one of reducing net immigration to the tens of thousands. And if it insists on one, Oxford university's Migration Observatory has pointed out that the easiest way to get close to it would be to stop counting international students – there were 134,000 of them last year – as immigrants.

In 2013, the Migration Observatory at the University of Oxford, quoted here, published a report which revealed that, between 2010 and 2012, the word most used in conjunction with "immigrant" in broadsheet, mid-market, and tabloid newspapers was "illegal." Chitra Nagarajan lamented in the *New Statesman* that having lived with signs of racism in the Oldham of the 90s, she "never would have thought it would be the government, not far right racist groups, who would be telling people to 'go home' twenty years later." Nagarajan's article came out in 2013. At least, the immigration-centred campaign culminating in June 2016 has made the distinction between far-right racist groups and the government easier to dismantle. Nigel Farage is said to have cheered when Michael Gove and Boris Johnson adopted UKIP's policy of promising an Australian-style points system. The language of occupation, infestation, and encroachment is no longer the prerogative of right-wing rants, as was the case in the good old days. By 2015, it was occasionally difficult to distinguish PM Cameron's anti-immigration rhetoric from that of Nigel Farage's. On ITV's *Good Morning Britain*, Farage had described the experience of being stuck in a motorway as being surrounded by "swarms of potential migrants to Britain and once, even, they tried the back door of the car to see whether they could get in" (cited in "Calais Crisis"). Earlier this week, I heard Roger Scruton in conversation with Patrick Wright on Radio 4. The conservative philosopher, who fondly refers to his Wiltshire home as "Scrutopia," spoke in elegiac cadences of an idea of England that, according to him, was threatened with extinction. The particular focus of his musings was the "higgledy piggledy humanism of the English common law," which, thanks to Brexit, will now be able to overthrow the yoke of the "overwritten" European Convention on Human Rights. In a conversation whose gentle undulations would be soporific had it not been for the incantatory use of the noun "encroachment" (and its menacing verb forms), the soft-spoken Scruton asked why the "illegal immigrant convicted of rape" should have the right to private life, as dictated by the Human Rights Act. The EU had encroached on English fundamentals, its wolf-free pastoral, its local distinctiveness, its ability to proceed from contingent particulars to the abstract principle (not the other way around, as was the case with what Scruton termed as the "Roman law" countries). Speaking of wolf-free pastures, Scruton's reference here is to Robert Winder's *The Last Wolf: The Hidden Springs of Englishness* (2017), which pivots on a definitive event in 1209 – the killing of the last surviving wolf in the Western shires by a Shropshire knight commissioned by the crown. This allowed Britain to become a giant sheep farm, according to Winder, and the wellsprings of English identity could hitherto be found in the weather, in the countryside and countryside pursuits, in Britain's splendid insularity, and its agrarian resilience to industrial modernity. Now that is a timely post-Brexit yarn, Winder's *The Last Wolf*, though it does not pull the wool over the eyes of this migrant from a brutalised British colony.

Bibliography

de Certeau, Michel. (1988). *The Writing of History*. New York: Columbia University Press.

Elgot, Jessica and Taylor, Matthew. Calais Crisis. *The Guardian*, 30 July 2015. Available at: www.theguardian.com/uk-news/2015/jul/30/david-cameron-migrant-swarm-language-condemned

Gilroy, Paul. (2008). *Against Race*. Cambridge, MA: Harvard University Press.

Hage, Rawi. (2008). *Cockroach*. London: Penguin.

Nagarajan, Chitra. We Need to Change the Very Language We Use to Talk About Immigrants. *New Statesman*, 15 August 2013. Available at: www.newstatesman.com/politics/2013/08/we-need-change-very-language-we-use-talk-about-immigrants

Scruton, Sir Roger. The English Fix. *BBC Radio 4*, 14 September 2017.

Skapinker, Michael. Theresa May's Clampdown on International Students Is a Mystery. Financial *Times*. Available at: www.ft.com/content/a1b695da-07e7-11e7-97d1-5e720a26771b

Spivak, Gayatri Chakravorty. (2012). *Outside in the Teaching Machine*. New York: Routledge.

Travis, Alan. Home Office Document Exposes Heart of Theresa May's Brexit. *The Guardian*, 5 September 2017. Available at: www.theguardian.com/politics/2017/sep/05/home-office-document-exposes-heart-of-theresa-mays-brexit

8

SCRATCHING THE POST-IMPERIAL ITCH

Anshuman A. Mondal

On 24 June, Nigel Farage declared with typical overstatement that 23 June 2016 would henceforth be remembered as Britain's "independence day". Those of us who have concerned ourselves with the fates of nations and societies that achieved their independence from European colonial and imperial rule in the latter half of the twentieth century know that "independence" means no such thing, that it is perhaps the most dazzling and distracting term in the lexicon of the political snake-oil salesman. By that very token, however, it must be acknowledged that it still wields incredible and immeasurable rhetorical force, especially in an era marked by an intensification of globalisation that has enmeshed all nations, states, cultures and identities in an intricate web of reciprocal – albeit highly unequal and uneven – interdependencies.

As a rhetorical device, "independence" clearly evokes and draws sustenance from the emotional resonance of the United States' Fourth of July celebrations, and in so doing it also evokes ideas of colonial dependency, of a struggle for freedom from an autocratic, unaccountable and distant centre of power. But it also enacts a reversal: Britain, for so long held to account by the forces of "political correctness" (i.e. anti-racist activists, multiculturalists and guilty liberals) for its imperial and colonial overlordship and the historical crimes perpetrated in its service, could now be positioned as itself a victim of a kind of colonial dependency and, at a (rhetorical) stroke, its colonial history could be at once evoked and obscured. The moment captures, I think, the extent to which Brexit was energized and motivated by still-resonant imperial-era imaginaries and ideologies, which circulated with wild abandon during the lead-up to the referendum and have become almost entirely rehabilitated since.

In the immediate aftermath of the referendum result, a dominant narrative was quickly established that Brexit was some kind of working-class revolt against cosmopolitan elites – those wealthy, footloose "citizens of nowhere" as Theresa May described them in her first party conference speech as Prime Minister whilst hitching herself as tightly as possible to the hardest of hard Brexit bandwagons (May, 2016). Brexit, so this argument runs, was the revenge of those "left behind" by globalization: by the vagrant capitalism that has benefitted only the few that are literate enough in the lexicons of neoliberalism and turbo-charged finance, or those with the skill sets to establish themselves as online entrepreneurs riding the wave of a revolution in information technologies, or those who have been in the right place at the right time (and with the right connections) to have exploited the opportunities afforded by wholesale privatisations of state assets as wave after wave of nation-states succumbed to the imperatives of the IMF and the World Bank; according to this narrative, Brexit (and later, the election of a populist right-wing president in the US) was a splenetic expulsion of rage by these "left-behind" working classes at a world beyond their control that has betrayed all the promises of the post-war settlement.

In this narrative, much of the responsibility for Brexit was placed on the shoulders of the Labour Party, which was apparently deserted by millions of its working-class voters because it was perceived by them to be aligned with precisely the kind of cosmopolitanism against which they took aim. But amid the swirling currents of claim and counter-claim, the facts tell a different story that opens a different perspective on the referendum result and much that has followed in its wake. According to analysis of the referendum voting patterns by YouGov, 65% of Labour voters from the 2015 general election voted to remain. By contrast, only 39% of Conservative voters followed their leader and Prime Minister in voting to remain in the EU. The Liberal Democrats – who positioned themselves before the referendum as the most committed pro-Remain party – still only managed to "deliver" 68% of their voters, and it is worth bearing in mind that, given their disastrous performance in 2015, that means that 32% of *their most committed voters* still voted to leave the EU. As for the SNP, for all the talk of Scotland being the most pro-Remain region of the UK, its governing party – one that had swept to a landslide victory in the 2015 election and is firmly committed to the EU – still could not persuade 29% of its voters to back its position and oppose Brexit (Moore, 2016).

When measured against the baseline of votes accrued by each party at the 2015 general election, therefore, more Labour voters voted to remain in the EU than those of any other party: 6,075, 748 out of the 9,347,304 that voted for them in 2015; by contrast, David Cameron managed to secure the votes of only 4,420,485 of the 11,334,576 who voted Conservative in 2015, and only 1,642,786 out of 2,415,862 Liberal Democrats put an "X" in favour of the EU. And even though all 38 of the Scottish referendum constituencies voted to remain in the EU, the 68–32 margin nationwide translated into only 1,661,191 votes for remain, of which 1,032,650 were SNP voters.

Clearly there is a bigger story here than simply disaffected working-class Labour voters deserting the party because of its alignment with neoliberal globalisation during its term in office, and the apparent cosmopolitanism of its political leadership and middle-class metropolitan voters. Obviously, *some* Labour voters who voted for Brexit would fall into this category, and many of the "left behind" had already deserted the party prior to the 2015 General Election, embracing either the Conservatives or UKIP. But the scale of the Leave vote across the political spectrum cannot be wholly accounted for by this group. It is, rather, that the Leave vote coagulated a number of different and disparate constituencies that must have encompassed large swathes of well-off – indeed, very well-off – voters in the rural and suburban "Tory shires" as well as disgruntled working-class voters in Labour's urban heartlands.

The question is what, if anything, bound these groups together, and it is here that the referendum itself perhaps offers an opening. For it may be objected that it is meaningless to compare each party's votes in the 2015 general election with the breakdown of voters at the referendum: the latter was not just a different vote but also a different *kind* of vote. But herein lies the rub: the referendum distilled all the complex factors that go into voting intention into a simple binary choice that would not usually obtain in a general election on the one hand, and, on the other hand, it also offered a clear and direct target for some voters toward which to direct their concerns about immigration. Immigration would be an important issue at a general election but not so unambiguously the *most* important one – as it clearly was in the referendum.

And it is here that we might pick up on certain continuities in discourse and rhetoric between arguments against EU immigration *now* and post-war immigration from formerly colonised countries in order to suggest that people did not vote Leave principally because of right or left-wing socio-economic programmes; and they didn't vote for or against economic neo-liberalism. Rather, the Leave appeal was entirely emotive and based on striking several chords that resonated with people from working-class and middle-class backgrounds who have not quite gotten used to Britain's post-imperial decline from top-dog to also-ran.

The effects of neoliberalism contributed to this, certainly, both in an objective and subjective sense, but the "left behind" voters have responded not to the economic arguments of the internationalist left but the hymns of nostalgia peddled by the nationalist right. Symbolically, the EU represents this decline from imperial autonomy and "absolute" sovereignty (another myth) better than anything else. Just being in it is a stark acknowledgment of that fact.

This imperially nostalgic nationalism is the only thing that working class leavers in the post-industrial wastelands of 21st-century Britain and the well-to-do leavers in the leafy Tory shires have in common, and it is rooted in what Raymond Williams calls the "structure of feeling" produced by ideology, in this case the structure of feeling produced by imperial ideologies and imaginaries that have still not fully wound their way through the digestive tracts of the United Kingdom's body politic (Williams, 1977).

The principal ingredient in this structure of feeling is race. This is not to suggest that everyone who voted to leave the EU is either an open or closet racist; but I would suggest that the way in which any suggestion that racialised imaginaries might be at work (and play) in arguments for Brexit have been batted away as yet more evidence of the sneering condescension of the metro/cosmopolitan elites – ironically, a particularly heavy-handed and egregious example of political correctness (or populist correctness, as the journalist Arwa Mahdawi [Mahdawi, 2017] pugnaciously calls it) – has obscured the extent to which race does indeed animate the Brexit imaginary and the imperially nostalgic structure of feeling it articulates.

One should not be distracted by the fact that anti-EU immigration sentiment appears to be principally directed at obtrusively *white* migrants from eastern Europe because, to a certain extent, this is a displaced proxy for still embedded antipathies towards non-white migration from outside the EU – as evidenced by the ways in which fear and loathing of African, Middle Eastern and Asian refugees and migrants crossing the Mediterranean into the EU was sutured to arguments against migration of EU citizens. This was most notoriously apparent in the UKIP referendum poster showing a queue of refugees snaking its way to the distant horizon, which was widely condemned for its reprisal of Nazi imagery (Stewart, 2016). In any case, the idea that the whiteness of EU migrants somehow provides a cast-iron alibi against the pressures of racialisation can be refuted by pointing to the long pedigree within British racial and racist discourses which has pointed to various "white" peoples as surrogates for black, Asian and other "coloured" others: the Irish as the "niggers" of Europe; the Latin southern Europeans – the Spanish, the Portuguese, the Italians – with their long lexicon of associated racial epithets (Losurdo, 2011); the belief in the environmentally engineered racial degeneration of the white Creoles of the Caribbean as so memorably captured in Jean Rhys's classic novel *Wide Sargasso Sea* (Rhys, 2000). And, of course, there are religious inflections too, since the Latinate southern Europeans are Catholic and "Papist" whilst other "white" (racially speaking) peoples at the margins of Europe, most notably the Turks, immediately invoke a repository of anti-Muslim antipathies that resonate particularly strongly in the current conjuncture when

Islam is once again seen as a major civilizational threat (Daniel, 1993; Matar, 1998; Matar, 1999): another key rhetorical tactic by the Leave campaigns (principally by the UKIP-led unofficial one, Leave.EU, but also – *sotto voce* – by the official Vote Leave) was to insinuate that the EU would soon be "swamped" by nearly 80 million Muslims when (not if) Turkey joined, thereby bringing into play a cluster of associations surrounding "terrorism", violence, fanaticism, barbarism and so on that all play their part in the kind of othering on which racialized imaginaries feed and thrive (Erlanger, 2016).

But the most important way in which race operates in the Brexit imaginary is to put the structure into the structure of feeling. Racism goes beyond mere prejudice and is not merely a way of classifying human populations according to physical characteristics that ground psychological attributes and cultural predilections; above all it is a way of distributing these groups along a *hierarchy*. In terms of the British empire, colonial racism's first task was to establish slavery in the Caribbean and American plantation colonies as part of the natural order of things, and thence, as the British empire expanded, to establish a geo-political order across the globe by correlating Britain's position at the centre of a global imperial system with whiteness as the apex of the racial hierarchy. Crucially, this would index not just global political relations but also the distribution of capital and the dynamics of structural (under)development to the racial hierarchy: the "White Commonwealth" of settler colonies – Canada, Australia, New Zealand, South Africa – were offered early Dominion status so that they could begin establishing autonomous economic pathways to development, whilst the "black" commonwealth was deemed by both liberal and conservative political opinion to be "not yet" ready for self-government on the basis of racially determined prejudices and stereotypes about the capabilities and capacities of entire peoples – a sensibility that affected liberal critics of empire as much as their opponents, as the crucial final passages of E.M. Forster's *A Passage to India* suggest, where even the "sky" and the "trees" recognize the solid imperturbability of the colonial hierarchy and its associated racial cleavages (Forster and Stallybrass, 1979).

Of course, this structure of feeling determined to a very large extent British attitudes to non-white immigrants in the decades

following the Second World War, which coincided with decolonisa-
tion, on the one hand, and the establishment of the phase of "postcolonial" capitalist globalisation on the other – along with the creation
and expansion of the European collaborative project that would cul-
minate in the EU. The rise of the EU, then, coincided with Britain's
post-imperial decline even though the globalisation to which it (the
EU) is a response has largely kept global hierarchies established during the centuries of European imperial rule intact; the latest phase of
globalisation has displaced this only somewhat, with countries like
China, India and Brazil and some parts of sub-Saharan Africa emerging as stronger – although still under-developed – economies in their
own right. Meanwhile, other Asian countries such as Taiwan, South
Korea, Indonesia, Malaysia and, of course, Japan now constitute an
economic centre of gravity to which white commonwealth countries
like Australia and New Zealand look instead of the Mother Country. But while it would be foolish to pretend that global economic
and political relations have not changed at all, they have perhaps not
changed quite as dramatically as many people might imagine; crucially, however, Britain's global "imaginary" – its picture of itself and
its place in the world at large – appears to have changed very little: it
still dreams of its place at the head of the diplomatic table.

The extent of this psychological inertia was revealed when it was
reported that Whitehall officials had christened ministerial aspirations
towards re-establishing the Commonwealth as a post-Brexit free trade
zone "Empire 2.0" (Coates, 2017). Even allowing for the fact that this
was quite possibly an ironic jest by Whitehall mandarins about the
delusions of their ministerial masters, it nevertheless does speak to the
purchase of imperial fantasy within the Brexit sensibility. Indeed, in
the pro-Brexit press there was even talk of welcoming that prodigal
son of Britannia, the United States, back into the imperial family as
an "associate member" of the Commonwealth, which is a desperate
but nevertheless revealing piece of wishful thinking (Rogers, 2017).

Ironically, Britain's decline relative to its former colonial depend-
encies would be amplified by Brexit because the EU, as a bloc, has
retained many of the structural advantages accrued by European
economies during the imperial period. Outside the EU, on its own,
Britain would not possess quite the economic leverage that Brexiteers

imagine. As the *Financial Times* (Blitz, 2017) has noted, in 2015 44% of Britain's exports went to the 27 countries of the EU as opposed to a mere 9.5% that went to the entire 52-nation bloc passing under the title of the "Commonwealth" (which is about as abject a misnomer for an entity so deeply scarred by Britain's former colonial rapacity as can be imagined). Only 1.4% of Australia's trade is with the UK, whilst three times as much goes to the EU. None of this seems to bother the Brexiteers, however, for whom the disengagement from the EU offers the opportunity to establish new economic relations with the "Commonwealth" that would see Britannia, in their view, once again "ruling the waves" as it did during its imperial heyday. This is a salutary reminder that "free trade" has always been inextricably and intimately woven together with empire, something that Amitav Ghosh's magisterial *Ibis Trilogy*, and in particular its second volume, *Flood of Fire*, rehearses at great length and with keen historical insight (Ghosh, 2015). Many of the ardent free-trade advocates for Brexit, such as Douglas Carswell and Daniel Hannan, are genuinely appalled by the toxic racism that circulates within much Brexit discourse, but they are (wilfully?) forgetting that "free trade", as Ghosh suggests, really is no such thing: it is shaped by power relations that are structurally embedded and enforced by a battery of juridical, bureaucratic and economic instruments that are underwritten, in the final analysis, by the calculus of military force. That the former colonies cannot so easily be threatened with gunboat diplomacy or subdued by military conquest is welcome, but the reflex persists – especially in the guise of humanitarian interventionism, and even more so when that interventionism barely conceals the naked commercial and economic interests of those wishing to subjugate others in order to set them free.

We should remember that imperialism has long been the safety valve through which the political establishment of the United Kingdom has channelled working-class disaffection so as to disperse its energies elsewhere on distant shores (Judd, 2001). The British labour movement, much as it sometimes likes to imagine itself as part of an international vanguard of working peoples, is deeply scarred by its investment in and complicity with colonial racism both in these islands and across the world. During both the boom of the 1960s and the economic crises of the seventies and eighties, black and Asian working people in the United Kingdom could not depend on their trade unions to set aside their racial antipathies and work on their behalf (Sivanandan, 1981); nor were the working-class communities that solidly supported the then highly left-wing (and indeed anti-EEC) Labour Party immune from scratching Britain's post-imperial itch when Margaret Thatcher's Conservative party called upon them to defend the tiny last vestiges of Britain's imperial territories in the distant south Atlantic in 1982 – and then, riding the crest of the imperial exuberance that followed victory over Argentina, aiding and abetting the landslide election victory that duly followed, one that unleashed the economic forces that now, some three decades later, has delivered the political recoil of Brexit. The salutary lesson to be learned here is that dreams of imperial glory can easily dazzle people into voting against their own interests. Throughout this period, the leafy shires of Tory England have quietly dreamed their dreams of "taking their country back" from the hordes of unwelcome foreigners "swamping" their communities even as the metropolitan centres of England have hesitantly embraced the fragile multi-cultural, multi-racial *modus vivendi* that emerged from the racial paroxysms of the eighties and early nineties. Now, those dreams have emerged into the political spotlight, and they have been rehabilitated, made respectable. Racism is no longer quite so unacceptable as, for a brief time, it once was. And it is not for nothing that throughout the long, drawn-out setting of Britain's imperial sun Kipling's "If" has remained Britain's favourite poem. For all the easy eloquence with which it exhorts its readers toward apparently simple and straightforward virtues, it is nevertheless a call to arms, a hymn to Britain's imperial destiny, and one can't help feeling that the overtones of territorial possessiveness in its final line – "yours is the earth and everything in it" – remains key to its enduring appeal.

Bibliography

Blitz, J. (2017). Post-Brexit Delusions About Empire 2.0. *Financial Times*. Available at: https://www.ft.com/content/bc29987e-034e-11e7-ace0-1ce02ef0def9

Coates, S. (2017). Ministers Aim to Build 'Empire 2.0' with African Commonwealth. *The Times*.

Daniel, N. (1993). *Islam and the West: The Making of an Image*. Oxford: Oneworld.

Erlanger, S. (2016). Britain's 'Brexit' Debate Inflamed by Worries That Turkey Will Join E.U. *New York Times*.

Forster, E.M. and Stallybrass, O. (1979). *A Passage to India*. Harmondsworth, Penguin, 1985.

Ghosh, A. (2015). *Flood of Fire: A Novel*. New York: Farrar, Straus and Giroux.

Judd, D. (2001). *Empire: The British Imperial Experience, from 1765 to the Present*. London: Phoenix.

Losurdo, D. (2011). *Liberalism: A Counter-History*. London: Verso.

Mahdawi, A. (2017). Populist Correctness: The New PC of Trump's America and Brexit Britain. *The Guardian*.

Matar, N.I. (1998). *Islam in Britain*. Cambridge: Cambridge University Press.

Matar, N.I. (1999). *Turks, Moors, and Englishmen in the Age of Discovery*. New York and Chichester: Columbia University Press.

May, T. (2016). Keynote Speech to Conservative Party Conference.

Moore, P. (2016). *How Britain Voted* [Online]. Available at: https://yougov.co.uk/news/2016/06/27/how-britain-voted/ [Accessed 15 September 2017].

Rhys, J. (2000). *Wide Sargasso Sea*. London: Penguin Books.

Rogers, J. (2017). USA Could Be 'Associate Member' of Commonwealth to Reap Rewards from Forgotten 'Treasure'. *The Daily Express*.

Sivanandan, A. (1981). From Resistance to Rebellion: Asian and Afro-Caribbean Struggles in Britain. *Race & Class*, 23, pp. 111–52.

Stewart, H. (2016). Nigel Farage's Anti-Migrant Poster Reported to Police. *The Guardian*.

Williams, R. (1977). *Marxism and Literature*. Oxford: Oxford University Press.

9

CRUEL NOSTALGIA AND THE MEMORY OF THE SECOND WORLD WAR

Robert Eaglestone

In this chapter I mention the War. I argue that while statistical, social science accounts of Brexit are useful, we can make that narrative deeper by exploring what literary theorists call 'affect', or – an older phrase – 'structures of feeling'. 'Structures of feeling' are always 'feelings about' something: in this case, about the memory of the Second World War. This turn to the past means that Brexit is *not quite* an example of what the leading affect theorist Laurent Berlant calls 'cruel optimism': instead Brexit is a 'cruel nostalgia'. I explain what this means and give some notable examples from both 'Leave' and 'Remain' and then look at the some of the limitations and the damaging consequences of cruel nostalgia.

Calculation, community, cues

A "braiding" of "cost-benefit *calculations*, feelings of attachment to the wider *community* and *cues* from political leaders" (147) (my emphasis) shaped the outcome of the referendum, argue the political scientists and statisticians Harold Chalk, Matthew Goodwin and Paul Whitely in their substantial *Brexit:Why Britain voted to leave the European Union*. This braiding follows closely Aristotle's famous account in his book dedicated to explaining public and political arguments, the *Rhetoric*: he says that arguments appeal to *logos* (reason, calculations), *pathos* (feeling) and *ethos* (to the sorts of people and community we take ourselves to be, or wish to be). While the traditional statistical accounts tell us a lot about how opinions change, about calculation (*logos*), their accounts of *pathos* and *ethos* are underdeveloped. The Brexit questions used by pollsters, for example, ask for a one-word response to the question 'describe your feelings about EU membership' (uneasy, confident, proud and so on). More, these sorts of statistical accounts don't take into account the sense that emotions, *pathos* and *ethos*, are intrinsically and inextricably part of the wider and longer narratives we tell ourselves about ourselves, nor do they address or explain the content of these feelings. (Compare: it's not enough to tick a box asking if you are in love: we want to know who with and how badly.) None of this is to say these surveys are wrong: they are often useful indicators of voting. It is only to say that these positivistic approaches are limited. When the triage nurse asks you to rate your pain from one to ten, this is helpful: but a number fails to describe the quality of the pain, what it means to you or in your life. To get a fuller picture of something like Brexit, you need a sense of depth too.

Fortunately, there is a discipline which specialises in the profounder understanding, contextualisation and thought about *ethos* and *pathos*, about the meaning of emotions (among other things). It does not proceed in the strictly social-scientific way of statistics but through detailed description, deliberation, conversation and argument, the methodologies of the humanities. That discipline is the study of literature. Literary study since its emergence in the late nineteenth century has been involved with ideas about 'how we live', with politics. And in recent years, research in literary studies has come to explore these issues of the politics of *pathos* and *ethos* ("feelings of attachment to the wider *community* and *cues* from political leaders") through what is called 'affect theory'.

Affect theory analyses one of those things that we all acknowledge but is very hard to pin down (in surveys, for example). Affect is not simply 'emotion': rather, it is something like the cultural atmosphere in which our emotions form. The great Welsh critic Raymond Williams wrote, a generation ago, of "structures of feeling" beyond the simple material of everyday life and culture: this gets some of the sense.

Affect theorists talk a lot about 'in-betweenness': affect is both inside us and in between us and others, us and the world and so on. In an illuminating essay in the magazine *N+1*, the historian Gabriel Winant explains that affects are "the way social life makes itself felt, leaving deposits in individual people, which we then process into our own emotions" (Winant 112). "I feel terrible" is an emotion, he says, but "this makes me feel terrible" is affect, "making explicit and external something otherwise tacit and internal" (Winant 113). Affect is simple to understand, because we all experience it, but complex to explain because it goes against the grain of our thought (which is based on a division between individuals, and between individuals and society): however, this idea of affect slips in everywhere. For example, our political science statisticians make an illuminating remark: they say that voters' "attitudes towards immigration and their feelings of national identity" were "'baked in'" long before the referendum campaign (Chalk et al. 2017: 176). This is a perfect image of this 'in between' aspect of affect. An attitude is both 'ours' and 'baked into us' (by someone? The baker presumably . . .). We both own the attitude (it's ours, inside us) yet it's also done to us. What hardens the bread? The interaction between the oven and the bread.

Affect is crucial for the political world (as Aristotle realised) because while we are rational and calculative (we use *logos*), we are not *only* rational and calculative. As Laurent Berlant, one of the most influential affect theorists, writes, "a public's binding to the political is best achieved neither by policy nor ideology but the affect of feeling political together" (Berlant 224). Moods and affects are not fixed but relentlessly moving: events or political leaders can (through 'cues') shape or change them. Berlant again: our public spheres are "affect worlds" and are "constantly negotiated" by our interactions with each other, with the media, with the world (Berlant 226).

As the distinctions *pathos* (feelings), *ethos* (community) and *logos* (or rational calculation) suggests affects are not arguments or propositions *per se*: they are shared moods. This is why they are hard to pin down. Describing an affect might be 'it makes me feel' or 'we feel . . .' rather than 'I think . . .' or 'I argue'. Affects do not lead directly to policies: politicians leading parties which are dominated by affect do not have clear, complex policies but rather seek to embody moods, as a journalist writes of 'the public mood'. But moods are moods about *something*. They have a hard-to-pin-down history, form and shape and can cannot be easily analysed (in a survey) but they are still there and potent. Indeed, they carry meanings or consequences of their own.

Berlant's most celebrated book about the consequence of affect is called *Cruel Optimism*. Optimism becomes cruel when hoping or striving for what you desire is actually harming you. The object of your desire can be political (a 'change's gonna come', 'making America great again') or personal ('when I'm thin') or both, as in the case of Berlant's real target, the American Dream in an era of post–credit crunch financial depression ('when I get rich'). But the object of desire remains a fantasy, and your commitment to that fantasy damages you: 'get rich or die trying' isn't healthy. As Berlant writes, "an optimistic attachment is cruel when the object/scene of desire is itself an obstacle to fulfilling the very wants that people bring to it: but its life organising status can trump interfering with the damage it provokes" (Berlant 227). If you shape your life around your dream, and pursuing that dream is, in fact, damaging you, it's hard to re-organise your life in your own, less dreamy, best interests when you can live among the ruins. Focusing on how much you love tomorrow or on the land over the rainbow or how to stay positive means that how you are today goes unheeded.

Brexit is – nearly – a very good example of 'cruel optimism'. The 'cues' given by the Leave campaigns and by the Brexiteers in Teresa May's government suggest broad sunlit uplands after the UK leaves the EU (£350 million for the NHS; world trade; 'taking back control'): the reality already looks materially grim. (But the benefits of Brexit are often not seen as material: a YouGov poll, 1 August 2017, found that "Six in ten Leave voters and a third of Remain voters say significant damage to the economy would be a price worth paying to get their way on Brexit".) However, Brexit offers one crucial difference from the more American 'structure of feeling' Berlant analyses. Most affect theory deals with the present or (as in the case of cruel optimism) a focus on the future which ignores the detrimental effects in the present: but Brexit focusses on the past. Not cruel optimism but *cruel nostalgia*.

Don't you know there's a war on?

To understand cruel nostalgia and the pull of Brexit, we need to put together the more normal ideas of our affective interactions, which are usually rooted in the present or aimed at the future, and the much more established scholarly discussions of collective memory: cruel nostalgia is a form of affect-memory.

Collective memory is one of the most – if not the most – powerful affective social forces. Shared cultural memory is inchoate, created through the whole gamut of culture both private (family stories, shared reminiscence) and mass (films, television, novels, computer games). Indeed, the relationship between community and memory is deep and reciprocal: part of the point of shared memory is to create that sense of community through shared narratives, frames of reference and 'forms of life'; part of the point of community is to preserve memory (war memorials, for example, remember the dead for the present community). Collective memory becomes affect memory when it becomes powerful and visceral. A deeply felt affect-memory is evoked through a cue ('we happy few', from a politician, for example), a piece of material culture (a Spitfire fly-past) or something more ephemeral, a tune, say. Most people don't actually remember the impact of 'We'll meet again' or the moan of an air-raid siren because they weren't alive during the Second World War but may still be profoundly moved by the 'memory of the memory' (some experts in memory studies call this phenomena 'post-memory').

Affect-memory does not check evidence, has no rules, no form of argument, no need to be consistent or to be engineered into a full, explanatory account. This is why there are 'memory wars' and why people on both the left and right try to construct or debunk views of the past through whatever means they can. This is also why, despite the sometimes-stated desire to be 'doctors of memory', historians are rarely able to 'cure' or end these memory debates: simply put, arguments over memory do not follow the historians 'rules of engagement' and argument and are less about facts and evidence (or even how facts and evidence are constructed) than about affects, emotions and ideas about community. There are two dominant forms of affect memory in the UK at the moment: one is the memory of Empire and the other, and I think more powerful, is the memory of the Second World War.

What makes up the affect memory of the War is hard to pin down in precise terms. (Imagine the limitations of a survey: how does the memory of the Second World War make you feel?) It is possible to draw some broad outlines, however. The War in memory stands for a time of *national anxiety*: a sense of fear, a moment in which the whole polity itself is in danger, 'all-out war'. It does not stand for the hope and magnanimity of victory: who could confuse the visceral fear evoked by the air-raid siren for a jaunty victory march? (This is why Nigel Farage, constantly keen to invoke the War, could not refer to victory in the referendum as, say, a kind of VE day. Instead he called it 'our independence day', recalling the US, of course, and many other formerly colonised nations who had become independent from Britain, as Anshuman Mondal discusses in his chapter in this volume.) As importantly, the War also stands for a *shared common purpose*: a sense of a national unity, deep comradeship across classes and, within the UK, national identities, when 'none was for a party' and 'all were for the state' (Macaulay). The War also stands for *defiance* against the enemy, against the odds, alone, and with that, a kind of *certainty* and *pride*: that 'we' know who 'we' are. This means it has a kind of 'meta' meaning too: if you don't share this feeling, you are not 'one of us', not rooted in the same past. The War is a kind of signifier for a rooted Britishness or even Englishness: interwoven with Empire and race, certainly, and different perhaps in the four nations of the UK, but also a marker of nationality. It stands also for *bearing up* to hard times, *keeping calm* and *carrying on* and as a way of overcoming ('Britain can take it!'). There is much more to be said about these, too, but my concern here is less with those affects and more with their meaning.

This affective-memory of the War, then, is a geological layer running under British cultural life: mostly unseen, it emerges in outcrops and shapes the surface of the land above it. And – to extend this metaphor – this geological layer is 'weaponised' as combatants dig up and catapult rocky chunks of this affect-matter at their enemies.

This happens, for example, when the *Daily Mail* demands 'who will speak for England?' (3 February 2017). It echoes the famous attack on Chamberlin in 1939 and claims for itself the voice of common purpose. It happens again in a tweet on the election of Macron by Leave. eu:"The French rolled over in 1940. This time they've saved Germany the fuel and bullets. #Presidentielle2017" (Twitter 12:51 p.m. – 7 May 2017). The Leave campaign and its associates used images which refer to the war (Spitfires, White Cliffs) and made constant appeal to Churchill and Churchillian language. The War appeared, too, in the post-referendum assertions that the civil service could 'handle' Brexit because they had 'handled' the War. It appears as a clear echo in the title of Tim Shipman's widely-acclaimed account of the referendum campaign: *All-out war.*

Another, more deeply illustrative example is Andrew Mather's short book *Brexit: Why We Won: Explaining a Historic Vote to Your Friends* (2016). It's also subtitled 'What remain will never understand about the leave victory'. Mather writes that

> in order to counter the threats and claims of Remainers, it has been apposite to remind them of our history vis a vis the French and the Germans. Freeing Europeans against political dictators has been a fairly constant occupation for this nation.
>
> (11) (sic)

And again: "we twice defeated a 'unified Europe' under Napoleon, twice under Germany" (80). Mather suggests that there is "peace in Europe not because of the EU but because we devastated Germany and gave them such a bloody nose, they have no desire to see that repeated in living memory. They have no qualms however about a more insidious 'peaceful' version" (80). Despite his hatred of liberals ("we hate liberals" 48) he is happy to fight for 'remainer' London because "that land is ours by blood right: we died for it, and we died protecting Europe" (87). During the campaign, he writes,

> it actually seemed we might win, so much so that at a wedding complete with bells, I imagine the same bells ringing out over

England on VE day, Victory over Europe, on pretty much the seventieth anniversary of an earlier VE day.

(69)

And again, the campaign "was fought and won for the same reasons we fought and won in two world wars: we don't like other people telling us what to do or threatening our freedom" (12). He concludes by echoing Shakespeare's Henry V, and Churchill, by declaring that "We 'happy few' of seventeen million have every right to feel proud of what we achieved" (89).

Arron Bank's *The Bad Boys of Brexit* (2017) is another example. The book fails to express any deep thought on Europe or the UK or the reasons behind Brexit: in part, this is because it is a day-to-day chronicle of the events of the campaign; in part, because it is ghost-written (the 'editor', Isabel Oakeshott, writes that she drafted in "several researchers who helped trawl through thousands of emails and text messages sent and received by Arron . . . as well as twitter accounts, media reports and Leav.EU press releases" (vii)). Indeed, apart from a lot about Bank's constant international travel and holidays, about Bpop (his Brexit pop festival which never happened), Bank's hero-worship of Nigel Farage and how much he hates Tories, there is very little in this thoughtless book – not even much 'bad boy' behaviour. There is one very emblematic moment, however. Banks is watching Nicholas Soames argue, on television, that his grandfather Winston Churchill would have voted 'remain': after some insulting crudities at Soames' expense (including calling him 'Two Belts'), Banks says he was handed a letter and donation for £30 by a World War Two veteran: "I am an old soldier from the last war. I remember the French and Belgians in 1940, what we called the surrender monkeys . . . who we saved. My father was an old contemptible in France in 1914. He says you can't trust them and they proved him right. We were never thanked". He uses this to refute Soames: "Take that, Two Belts". One wonders about the authenticity of this ('Surrender monkeys' as a description for the French is generally thought to have been coined in 1995 on an episode of *The Simpsons* and isn't a usual phrase from the Second World War.) But it also shows something else. Notice he doesn't say this refutes Soames's assertion about Churchill or something like that. 'Take that, Two Belts' is not arguing through reason but through emotion: evoking the small against the great, the old against the powerful, claiming (despite 'surrender monkeys') an authentic link to the heroic past and sounding full of rude, boisterous energy, fearless of offence against the television: 'take that'. This is not dialectic but affect, deploying a mood, not making an argument.

However, because the affect memory of the War, this deep cultural geology, is not an argument, that means others can use it too. Politicians of the left also turn to Churchill's language and yearn, too, for the apparent certainties of the 1945 Labour Government. Gordon Brown's short film intervention during the campaign made a case of the EU as 'winning the peace'. After the referendum, Michael Heseltine made an odd but revealing comment: while "Germany lost the war . . . We've just handed them the opportunity to win the peace".

A significant example of the use of the memory of the War by the Remain side is the publication, in summer 2017, of *Guilty Men* by 'Cato the Younger'. Its title, form and structure as polemic directly draws on a very famous book of 1940, again *Guilty Men*, by 'Cato' (a pseudonym for Michael Foot, Frank Owen and Peter Howard), which attacked those guilty of appeasement. This 'Brexit edition', with a quotation from Churchill on its wartime faux-aged beige cover, begins with the famous David Low 'Very well, alone!' cartoon from 18 June 1940. It contrasts the Beach at Dunkirk with the Beach at Kos, a war crisis with a refugee crisis. As Cato the Younger writes, the 'very well, alone!' sentiment of defiance was and is consistently evoked by Brexiteers (in his essay below, Thomas Docherty draws attention to Johnson's version of this, for example). But standing alone was both a last resort and – bearing in mind the Empire – not entirely true. Taking the idea that Britain "was greatest in its history when it stood alone" (9) is simply upside-down: Britain is greatest when engaged with other nations. The *Guilty Men* of 2017 – as the 1940 book does – goes on to excoriate fifteen men and women, from across the political spectrum, responsible for Brexit. This imitation says: Brexit is as much a failure and as deep a shame as appeasement. Cato the Younger implies that our decade is as deceitful, as avaricious, as lacking in leadership and as brim-full of hubris and meanness as the thirties was dirty, low and dishonest.

But it's not actually a war . . .

The strong, visceral affect memory of the War does not make us think about things rationally: it makes us feel things. These feelings can be deployed as part of the *ethos* and *pathos* of winning people over to your side in a political argument ('take that!'). This means that the affect memory of the war is not a kind of 'false consciousness', as Angus Calder's famous *The Myth of the Blitz* argued. Calder showed that in the War years, the country was disunited and fractious (more strikes, fear of robbery, looting, and so on) but that even from then, the dominant and developing cultural memory was of a 'business as usual' unity. Similarly and more recently, Paul Gilroy argued that the continual reference to the War in British culture, high and low, was because the memory of heroic resistance plastered over moral questions over the post-war settlement, race and Empire, over migration and, of course, Europe. The affect memory can be used this way, of course, but because it sums up feelings, not arguments, it need not be. Indeed, as soon as the War is evoked and these feelings emerge into a rational argument – from beyond 'take that', from *pathos* and *ethos* to *logos* – their limitations and serious consequences are illuminated.

When the War as a time of *national anxiety* is invoked as part of a rational argument, the question is begged: who has put the country in danger? Where are the invaders? What threat? The answers to that are as different as the factions involved. Mather and others on the right would claim that 'liberals', 'immigrants' and sinister Europeans intent on refighting the War are the culprits ('Saboteurs', 'Enemies of the People') – one wonders if the UK in was in such dire peril. After Article 50, perhaps, as Cato the Younger suggests, it is.

When the *shared common purpose* comes to the fore (as in the accusations that 'remoaners' are 'talking down the country') there is the sense implied that 'normal' politics, the negotiations of different interests, represented by parties within a state, needs to be put on hold. More, those who protest this are somehow failing their national duty or not behaving appropriately. Whenever politicians speak, as Nigel Farage did on the night of the referendum, for 'real people . . . ordinary people . . . decent people' or some such and invoke the especially strong form of nostalgia, the memory of the War, they evoke this step beyond faction and party to a 'whole' which works by excluding those it defines as, in this case 'unreal', 'extra-ordinary', 'indecent': not-British, unreal citizens of nowhere. There is an implicit threat here. Once a person is made 'unreal' or outside the frameworks of rights and legal identities, they become vulnerable to forms of extra-judicial action. The most extreme case of this exclusion is, as Hannah Arendt describes, in totalitarian governments: the totalitarian move-ments claim to bypass the political and to speak for the whole (the 'volk' for the Nazis, the 'workers' for the Soviets) and so exclude and then eliminate those who do not share that voice. This is why not to do 'politics as usual' is not to do politics at all. This exclusion is also why the affect memory of the War is often seen as racist and can be used for racist arguments and 'dog whistle' politics. That said, the affect – memory is also the source of counter-racist arguments (by stressing, one example from many, the many hundreds of thousands of Imperial and Commonwealth troops who fought in the UK and all over the world). It is by global involvement, for example, rather than by standing alone, that Britain is greatest.

The affects of *defiance* and *certainty* also become contorted in a similar way when they are moved from feelings to thinking. Against whom is one defiant? Similarly, Mather identifies those 17 million who voted to leave as 'we happy few' (those at Agincourt transposed to the RAF in the Battle of Britain transposed to the 'leavers') and so positions 'remainers' not as his fellow citizens but as his and the state's enemies. The liberals suddenly become the medieval French or the Luftwaffe. More, the memory of the War summons up what Gilroy rightly calls a sense of "unimpeachable moral authority", the sense of certainty (Gilroy 127). But certainty and moral authority about what? A free-floating sense of certainty and moral authority is dan-gerous (as well as illogical: but that's exactly the point). The enemies in Brexit discourse are *within* the polity, and as 'we wax hot in faction' those with different political positions become more 'hateful than a foe' (Macaulay again). *Pride* is the most complex affect evoked by the memory of the War. Pride in the real achievement of one's forbears is significant and real: but when this tips into an illusion that you your-self have some part in their heroic actions, something is amiss. When Banks says he is "back in Blighty" (Banks 93) he is not returning from combat in Normandy but from yet another holiday in the Caribbean.

Finally, as the War signifies *bearing up* and *carrying on* it begs the question of how these hard times began: they are in no small measure self-inflicted. The poster bearing the slogan 'Keep calm and carry on' was not, in fact used during the War (it was a draft) but now sums up this generally admirable sentiment and is used, reused, altered, reshaped in many different contexts, although each evocation retains a trace of the War. But 'Keep calm and carry on' as we destroy ourselves is cruel nostalgia in a nutshell.

When will the war be over?

The promise of a shared common purpose in a time of national anxiety, with its attendant defiance, certainty and pride and the sense that we can bear up and carry on, all help form the cruel nostalgia of Brexit, before, during and after the referendum campaign. On the one hand, these affects represent something to which damaged and worried communities and people can turn. On the other, they are a set of easily accessible affective cues which politicians and others can manipulate. This swirling mixture of *pathos* and *ethos* make it hard to focus on other kinds of arguments about Europe: arguments about the future (you can't look forward if you're always looking back); arguments which seek to move beyond the memory of the 1945 settlement.

For those on the Remain side, their use is equivocal. The rhetorical strategy of the 2017 *Guilty Men* cuts two ways: it certainly uses the affect-memory of the War against the Brexiteers and tries to offer a new context for the memory of the War. It concludes with a description of how the young of the countries of the UK, betrayed by Brexit, head to the beaches of Southern Europe to aid the Syrian refugees, as their forebears headed in little boats to Dunkirk. But in so doing, perhaps it gives too much to cruel nostalgia, to the sense of British identity rooted in the 'keep calm and carry on' of the Second World War, and does not begin to find or establish a new form of European identity (Cato the Younger accuses Tony Blair of a similar fault while he was leader: 'ducking the advocacy' and failing to transform the UK's view of the EU). But serious Brexiteers, who revel in the War, also ought to be wary of this affect memory: the affects evoked in cruel nostalgia – anxiety, community, pride – run deep. If, 'when the war is over', there are no blue skies over white cliffs, there may be much to answer for. In Churchill's bathetic phrase, 'the sky will be dark with pigeons coming home to roost'.

Finally, almost as a footnote, cruel nostalgia reveals that the War itself has moved from living memory – with its fluidity, confusing currents, difficulty and perhaps trauma – into myth and into history. What once was the living sea has now become sediment, petrified as sentiment, a thick, significant layer in the geology of British memory. Now it is a seam to mine for explosives to throw at one's political enemies; it is a site of careful archaeological excavation and thoughtful historical preservation. But, with a peculiar and exquisite irony, perhaps Brexit shows that the real War is over and the mythic Second World War has begun.

Bibliography

Arendt, Hannah. (1973). *The Origins of Totalitarianism*. New York: Harcourt Brace.

Banks, Arron. (2017). *Bad Boys of Brexit*, ed. Isabel Oakshott. London: Biteback Publishing.

Berlant, Laurent. (2011). *Cruel Optimism*. Durham: Duke University Press.

Calder, Angus. (1991). *The Myth of the Blitz*. London: Pimlico.

Cato the Younger. (2017). *Guilty Men*. London: Biteback Publishing.

Chalk, Harold, Goodwin, Matthew and Whitely, Paul. (2017). *Brexit: Why Britain Voted to Leave the European Union*. Cambridge: Cambridge University Press.

Gilroy, Paul. (2004). *After Empire: Multiculture or Postcolonial Melancholia*. London: Routledge.

Mather, Andrew. (2016). *Brexit: Why We Won: Explaining a Historic Vote to Your Friends*. Self-published.

Shipman, Tim. (2016). *All Out War: The Full Story of Brexit*. London: William Collins.

Winant, Gabriel. (2015). We Found Love in a Hopeless Place. *N+1*, 22, pp. 110–28.

YouGov. Available at: https://yougov.co.uk/news/2017/08/01/britain-nation-brexit-extremists/ [Accessed 1 August 2017].

10

BREXIT AND THE AESTHETICS OF ANACHRONISM

Michael Gardiner

In the early 2010s, I argued that the unwritten British constitution had a surrogate in the organization of writing that would develop into the university discipline of English Literature. I also argued, though, that over recent decades there had been a movement away from this universalism and a rise of a politics of place. One such revolt of place, the activism that surrounded the 2014 Scottish Independence Referendum, has a string of historical precedents to help us read it. Less so the EU Referendum Leave vote, which seems to have, on the surface at least, a completely unrelated politics. But I will suggest that, as tricky as this may seem at first, the Leave vote was in some ways a comparable revolt of place, and was levied, consciously or not, against the same British universalism. And this should be see against the fact that this rejection of Britain's ethical universalism was revealed by breakdowns of the vote to be quite class specific, as those with the lowest incomes overwhelmingly voted Leave (Joseph Rowntree Trust, 2016).

It is now over 40 years since, Tom Nairn suggested that Britain might be understood more as a social class than a nation. For Nairn, a middle class emerging unusually early was able to merge with an existing agrarian establishment to form a 'natural governing elite' and so withstand the later popular pressures of European revolutions, particularly using a deeply embedded 'civil service intelligentsia' to absorb any such Jacobin hankerings (Nairn, 1981: 24–37). Nairn's thesis is widely known of, but its implications are not always grasped. For what cements Nairn's ever-expanding, anti-revolutionary and utterly stable middle class is its strictly 'apolitical' understanding of government as an arbiter of financial exchanges. The tendency to define all relationships in economic terms is familiar from today's neoliberalism, but, as neoliberalism's '70s architects were readier to explain than have been recent critiques of this movement, this tendency *extends* an existing 'hardwired' Hanoverian stress on the primacy of the economy in defining the social. In Hanoverian thinking, the perpetual dissolution of 'despotic' power to individual property owners proceeded according to natural and universal rules of movement, somewhat equivalent to movements in Newtonian space. For John Locke in particular, an enlightened government merely protected these universal laws of the movement of money towards individuals (cf. Locke n.d., 1689). In the Lockean tradition of natural law that would become 'eternal' in the modern British state, the only possible conception of progress is financial, and progress itself is always measured in terms of individual property. Property is time's arrow. And threats to this natural progressive, conversely, will seem like 'backward' and uncivilised actions undertaken by those proven incapable of property ownership. Which, of course, is how the Leave vote has typically been described, as backward, resentful, uncivilized, unprogressive.

Progressive, then, we assume on a British level to mean forward in a self-evidently civilised, fair way. But more fundamentally, in a state form stuck 'eternally' with Lockean natural law, it means forward through expanding the ground from which individual property can be created. And refusals of this vision of the progressive, since these are also refusals of universal or natural rules, tend to be written off as 'nationalist', a familiar accusation to anyone who follows Scottish independence issues. The 2014 Scottish independence debates showed how powerful this term was in poisoning attempts to circumvent the basis of sovereignty in the economy – as 'nationalism', Scottish attempts to *hold on to* public service provision could paradoxically be described as anti-social, un-public-minded, even as hatred. The power of this term allowed for some astonishing acts of disavowal by Nairn's 'civil service intelligentsia': immediately before the 2014 referendum a *Guardian* editorial admitted that Scottish independence would bring exactly the public measures the paper claimed to want, then explained that its readers had to argue against it, because '[n]ationalism is not the answer' (*Guardian*, 2014). This understanding of 'nationalism' stands in an invisible contrast to everyday naturalist effusions of British 'patriotism', in a formula going back to George Orwell's 'Notes on Nationalism' (1945), which contrasted a benign and productive British patriotism with 'fascistic' Scottish and Irish nationalism (Orwell, 2007). Nationalism is dangerous because an unnatural violence and a disruption to the organic unfolding of time. Or, as I've argued elsewhere, nationalism typically just means *politics*.

There probably was a degree of 'English nationalism' in Brexit, and cultural responses grasped this. It's not that Scottish Leave votes were negligible or that there were no English Remain pockets – but in England Leave was an at-hand nationally specific form. Henderson et al. describe an attitudinal link between Leave voting and self-identifying as English-rather-than-British not true of any other British nationality and argue for Brexit to be grasped in terms of its English dimension (Henderson et al. 2016). However, the almost total invisibility of English agency until very recently also makes 'English nationalism' a very diffuse phenomenon, stretching from a simple misunderstanding of the term as state citizenship at one end to a powerful localism at the other, a diffuseness that makes it peculiarly resistant to organisational taxonomies and management. This helps explain why English nationalism is so loathed on a British level, even amongst those who grudgingly see Scottish nationalism as a familiar part of the landscape. The St. George's Cross has long been an article of embarrassment and disdain for the British liberal ruling class, and Emily Thornberry's 2014 'white van tweet' (BBC News, 2014) only scratched the surface of this. Moreover, a relative lack of attention to First Minister Nicola Sturgeon's attempts before the Referendum to explain how the result could lead to another Scottish independence vote suggested that, for a large number of Leave voters in England, and despite the Union Jack waving that accompanied the official campaign, the threat to the British union was not that great a disincentive (Henderson et al. 2016: 188).

However, as problematic as it may seem at first, I would like to suggest that 'nationalism' in this broad sense, which is to say the political, or what stands outwith an economic conception of authority, can yield shared forms of action that we had thought were lost – especially if these forms seem 'out of time'. If the British economic underpinnings of progress point to a single temporality, a time that simply naturally unfolds, then 'nationalism' could mean local points of temporal unevenness, or anachronism. The potential for questioning from the absolute sovereignty of the economy can be glimpsed in such glitches of apparently natural developmental time.

Literary examples of this kind of glitchscape became especially visible in the decade before the Leave vote, in England as well as Scotland, and not merely from the realms we would expect of Leave voters. Laura Oldfield Ford's *Savage Messiah* (collected 2011), for example, introduced by Mark Fisher as a text that uses 'anachronism as a weapon' (Oldfield Ford, 2011: n.p.; Fisher, 2011: x; cf. Fisher, 2014). Documenting a series of walks around London, its half-forgotten and abandoned reaches, *Savage Messiah* undertakes an archaeology of the collectivities thought to be lost under the era of temporal flattening we now call neoliberalism, and turns up raw bits of past that have not yet been processed. The characters remembered on these walks, anarchists, ravers, drifters, punk musicians, musicians, protesters and nomads, seem to have nothing to do with 2016 Leave voters, but they share a lived environment and a sense of the devastating consequences a universalist conception of development can have. These walks are marked by a political commitment that is also felt as a tendency to anachronism, a sense of being drawn to events or objects that disturb the development that seems natural and organic but is revealed to be driven by the inexorable spread of individual property. Brexit might be read, to some extent against the grain, as channelling comparable desires for collective action that have been frustrated by the naturalness of property as a general good, demands now made not only in terms of physical property but also on a psychological or cognitive level in terms of the way we should view one another as individuals made of market choices. Or put otherwise, to assume that the Brexit vote means masses of people have been conned into xenophobia by pragmatic leaders creating a fearful fantasy world (cf. Curtis, 2016) might also risk showing too much readiness to give up the agency contained in the vote's collective act of defiance against the ethics that led to the current 'communal' alienation. But to hear such an agency under the deafening demands for individuation that characterise cognitive capitalism may mean a tricky openness to the 'counter-intuitively' and untimely.

Originally a series of hand-produced zines, Oldfield Ford's loosely connected stories use typewritten and corrupted text, grainy photos, cut-ups and bits of flyer to document the wandering explorations she calls *drifts*. These drifts look much like Situationist *dérives*, 'through / Demolition Sites / Conjuring up semiotic ghosts', traversing what is now 'an anodyne vision of London designed by the "creative industries"'. The borders of the individual at times seem permeable, or to be in a place means actual contact between self and environment – '[t]his decaying fabric, this unknowable terrain has become my biography, the euphoria then the anguish, layers of memories colliding, splintering and reconfiguring'. The city is remapped through mixed and imperfect forms, spoken in terms less of appeals to individual consumers than flows of desire, it 'pulsates with libidinal excess', and the walker struggles to retain social memory under the layers of gentrification, individuation, 'yuppiedromes'. Although these archaeological walks look like psychogeography – and cite common roots in European thought (Vaneigem, Deleuze and Guattari, Bataille, Laing) – for Fisher this commitment to social memory from the developmental time that seems to have buried it entirely means that it might be better described in terms of *hauntology* (Fisher, 2011: xiv). This term, borrowed from Derrida's *Specters of Marx* and suggesting an ontological centring on absence, has been used since the mid-2000s or so to suggest the traces of a past that, precisely because it is lost, cannot be recuperated into the empty time of heritage, or 'retro', and so retains its political potential (Derrida, 2006: 10–11; Fisher, 2014: 2–29). Only in their pastness, in their having been experienced in a mutable human time, do these past political desires avoid being drawn into retro's 'quick fix', its adjustment of shared memory to the terms of individual market rationality (Fisher, 2014: 15). Where the past is increasingly reduced to a source of financial value ('heritage'), shreds of sociability have to be actively unearthed, and when they are they look dirty and battered. 'Abandoned dreams reside here, unharnessed and unchannelled. Step over them in carefully avoided cracks in the pavement'. Brexit, for all else it might be, can be seen as a vast repository of such untimely traces.

Despite the obvious similarities to French Situationism, this form of archaeological search for intact pasts is specific to the localities – and, in a trickier sense, to the nations – of the UK. For if retro and the heritage economy seem oddly 'at home' in the UK, it is because here the recuperation of the past is just property creation as usual, simply moved on, in a post-industrial economy, to a psychological or cognitive level. As in Locke, this property creation happens in the name of an abstract 'social' good that at base is really an economic good – as in the business of 'nation branding' that rehearses the story of British progress for cultural export. In which sense Fisher's description of hauntology is close to Nairn's (2002) polemic *Pariah*, which describes the (Blairite) economy's 'music-hall' performance of itself, its obsessive creations of a branded version of a 'past' (Nairn, 2002). The anachronistic aesthetic of *Savage Messiah* is a fly in this retro ointment: the fragments of pastness it finds are unreconstructed and unreconstructable, it agitates against privatisation, it looks for the fragments of collectivity that look out of time in a world of individual development. The ghostly search for lost futures in the ruins of development Fisher calls *hauntological melancholia* – a term he carefully distinguishes from *postcolonial melancholia*, or the longing for lost imperial privilege (Fisher, 2014: 24–5; cf. Gilroy, 2004). This is a crucial distinction, since to brush off the hauntological need for historical memory as a wish for a return of British imperial privilege is to do neoliberalism's work for it – it is to reject the local desire for class consciousness that are caught within the Leave vote, and so most of the desire for collectivity in the post-war history of these islands.

In *Savage Messiah*, the developmental destruction of public housing is moreover associated with the timeframe of the modern British state. For one thing the traces it finds are often medievalist and pre-Hanoverian, that is, they come from outwith the rationalism of the Protestant work ethic and its demands on nature – magical places, stone circles, ley lines, 'ancient paths and hidden footbridges', tropes which recall '70s localism and are common to hauntology in music, where the term has mostly been used. (The Ghost Box record label, to use one well-worn example, with its 'untimely' presentation of the lost worlds of collective cultural production, library music, comprehensive school textbooks, local government pamphlets, Public Information Films, Pelican paperbacks and all the innovative but mass-appeal cultures that Fisher calls *popular modernism*.) Oldfield Ford explicitly recalls *Concrete Island* (1974), J.G. Ballard's ironic echo of that Hanoverian narrative of property, *Robinson Crusoe*, which had replaced *Crusoe*'s 'nature' with the wastelands lying amongst motorways, trade routes, defined by compulsory speed. The insistence on walking in the drift/*dérive*/car crash then becomes a temporal intransigence that demands the occupation of place, something it shares with other psychogeographic treks (e.g. Sinclair, 2013) and with an older England-specific history of walking politics (cf. Gardiner, 2012: 23–30). Unlike most Anglo-psychogeography, though, Oldfield Ford's characters have lived precariously in these wastelands and have been moved on by the 'economic good' of property prices. And like Leave voters, their collective and class politics have been dismissed in describing them as backwards and incapable of development.

Or to put this conversely, we might read Brexit as a rejection not only of the voting instructions of that other 'remote authority', the British leadership (now peculiarly aligning themselves with European government, in an odd reversal of Nairn's anti-revolutionary middle class), but also of the British liberal conception of development itself. The potential of this is perhaps clearer if we go back to the double sense of this term nailed down by Lockean natural law: the vote's apparent threat to cosmopolitanism ('social development') is also a threat to cheap flows of labour ('economic development') – and there are strong vested interests in transposing the two. Otherwise, why has the era during which equal opportunities has come to be rigorously institutionally policed also seen a dramatic *increase* of inequality? (And this inequality itself, inevitably, splits along race lines: British liberalism's fundamental problem with race thinking is simultaneously that it is unethical and that it blocks individuation – the terms of race must be perpetually *repeated* but also perpetually modified and put to work.) Why is the London that was during Brexit debates claimed as a beacon of cosmopolitanism also, on some metrics, the most unequal city in the Western hemisphere (e.g. Dorling, 2011)? The extent to which critiques of the use of absolutely free markets in labour to depress wages had been made by 2016 to seem xenophobic might be seen as one of neoliberalism's most extraordinary victories of neoliberalism. Similar arguments on wage depression were made by Bennite 'Out' campaigners during the 1975 EEC referendum, including Jeremy Corbyn, but on this by 2016 the Labour left had meekly conceded defeat.

The Estate Agents' pamphlets that litter *Savage Messiah* are much less reticent about what the neo-Lockean extension of individualist development has meant: *development* is both a change to be naturally desired and a synonym for *privatisation*. Public housing broken down into individual properties is development's overarching mode, and often draws from collective heritage by making it non-collective. Especially in that most patriotic space of the Olympics to come, 'overshadowed by the looming megalith of "London 2012"' (and soon, of course, to be seized on by the Opening Ceremony's repurposing of the welfare state for nation branding), development makes 'systematic social cleansing' appear as a public good. Against such an architecture, even brutalist tower blocks hold a hauntological potential in their sociality, their popular modernism recalcitrant and stubbornly anachronistic. The traces of the lost collectivities long since denounced, whether as ugly brutalism or as ugly brutal 'nationalism', can linger on only in hauntological terms. And such traces, marked by their failure to 'keep up to speed', will always seem somehow wrong or imperfect or ill conceived or backward. There will always be something jarring about them, just as any real social value that can be taken from Brexit will be entangled with the jarring, the unethical, and the unacceptable.

Anachronism, of course, is not the same as 'backward' at all. As a disturbance of the present that has been emptied out by the abstraction of development, anachronism can be 'forward' or 'backward' – and these qualifiers might rather be seen as genres of anachronism. Something like 'forward anachronism' characterised much of the Scottish fiction of the early neoliberal era (the 'Third Scottish Renaissance'), at the head of which stood Alasdair Gray's *Lanark* (1981), now widely celebrated for its metafictional impulse to depict a Glasgow assumed (by characters) to have no presence on wider public stages (Gray,

2011). Gray's 'forward anachronism', itself drawing from a Glasgow science fiction interest going back through the '60s (Edwin Morgan's 'popular modernism' most obviously), would become a motif for independence campaigns' speculative commitment to the temporally unfamiliar, the desire (in a quotation he adapted) to 'act as if you are living in the early days of a better nation'. If the out-of-timeness of 'backward anachronism' suggests traces of collective thinking in neoliberalism's buried pasts, the out-of-timeness of 'forward anachronism' imagines that neoliberalism's ban on collective thinking has gone. If 2014 was partially defined by Scottish 'forward anachronism', 2016 was partly defined by English 'backward anachronism', and I suggest that the 'direction' matters less than the hope that other possible histories exist. These genres of anachronism moreover have certain odd symmetries – many Ghost Box artists could be set against the slightly earlier output of the Scottish duo Boards of Canada, with their own anachronistic registration of future shock. Indeed, these forms of anachronism might be seen as working in concert – certainly not consciously, but not entirely by accident either, and perhaps able to face the might of British liberal realism together.

Nor is anachronism the same as nostalgia. In fact it's unclear where a British *nostos*, the long return home of Homer's hero, would go – the modern British state is at heart a financial displacement, its 'localities' exactly what home is not (cf. Baucom, 1999). Unlike nostalgia, anachronism is fundamentally – and perhaps despite itself, in the case of Brexit – a politics of change, since it refuses the fixed progressive that keeps emptying out the present and making change impossible. And nor can anachronistic desires be reduced to a question of whether (some) traditions are 'invented', as in the title of the celebrated collection by Hobsbawm and Ranger – a book firmly in the tradition of Orwell, since it exempts the UK from any such accusations of inventedness (Hobsbawm and Ranger, 1983).

But how wishful is it to see this 'nationalist' voice as holding potential for a social response to neoliberalism? It would help if we grasped that the ability to produce and manage a terminology of equal opportunities is itself a form of property, and one that confers crucial advantages on those who have access. Access to this language is strictly economically guarded, indeed is increasingly the condition of entry into Nairn's civil service intelligentsia. It relies on a specific form of eloquence that takes an increasingly large up-front investment (university tuition fees), increasingly presented in starkly cost-benefit terms. Under late neoliberalism, or 'authoritarian liberalism', when a language of absolutely equal opportunities – of what 70s neo-liberal theorists called individuals' 'market equivalence' – is enforced with potentially draconian penalties, the 'ownership' of the language of equal opportunities has become *a primary mode of the diffusion of inequality*. An increasingly pressured middle class needs these cognitive skills to maintain a slender edge, and for that matter to keep them from ending up in the same economic position as the poorer immigrants whose 'inclusion' is now the source of their material advantage. To most people on these islands, this advantage is obvious. But if it is obvious, there is no obvious language in which to say it, because the language open to them is always receding. If Brexit shows such a language losing its power to command, does it show catastrophic racism on the part of the bulk of this country's poor, or does it show an exhaustion with a market realism for which access to a managerial language of equal opportunities is a source of inequality? Or both? And how sure are we about this?

I'd suggest that this question of a collective voice freed from performing neoliberal market equivalence should not merely be seen as a failure of sympathy, but can also be approached through hauntological desires and through anachronism. Indeed, rejections of neoliberal individualism are *necessarily* anachronistic, since in everyday life they have become almost impossible to think. Anachronism feels wrong, embarrassing, troublesome, unrepresentative, raw and sometimes inappropriate or ill considered – and yet it is a release from those processes of mediation that are ultimately the market management of the present, a release from the need to keep adjusting the self to this story of development, or what Oldfield Ford calls 'the pressure to be yourself, the slow unravelling of biopolitical identity'. A serious engagement with the collective desires hidden within Brexit's apparent rejection of civilized values would recognise that such an anachronism has a human value. But problematically, it would also have to be able to actually hear those people whose lack of access to linguistic currency, since it produces cognitive 'property', has been defined as a perverse kind of social good. To stay middle class during tough times for the 'immaterial economy', you have to keep denouncing the language of those beneath you.

Of course, Brexit England is really a *mix* of hauntological melancholia – the desire for past collective political potential – and postcolonial melancholia – the desire for lost imperial privilege. But Fisher's distinction between these two forms is crucial – where the former can be easily neutralised by invoking the latter, where Brexit is reduced to old-fashioned racism, the crucial traces of collective action the vote contained, traces that are becoming harder and harder to find, are easily crushed in the name of values that turn out to be devastatingly alienating.

Perhaps what is most worth noting after all is the lengths to which the poor have gone to try to speak. Huge numbers of Leave voters have made personal sacrifices. For none of this is to claim that Brexit will make things better. Brexit will not make things better. Brexit will make things worse. Those regions most likely to vote Leave were also those that most needed EU support (Hobolt, 2016). The 21st-century Tory conception of an Anglosphere is a grimly monolingual and anti-intellectual echo of the mid-Victorian empire (cf. Kenny and Pearce, 2016). An old anti-Jacobin resentment of Europe is at work in Brexit, as well as the market-scepticism I have perhaps fancifully suggested can be drawn out with anachronism. Many Brits wouldn't want to take part in an international union they can't lead (or which Germany seems to lead). Half the country is now often casually viewed as racist. Meanwhile, post-Referendum attacks on Poles and other nationalities, particularly in some of the country's poorest areas, have been real and horrifying. A UK without the flow of continental European peoples is a nightmarish prospect. Environmental policy and employment policy will offer less protection. And a stylish European bureaucracy will be replaced by a soul-destroying British bureaucracy run by the kind of people who introduce their mistakes with the word 'unfortunately'. This all seems more ripe for dystopia than hauntology. And yet, any interruption of neoliberal realism necessarily comes as a shock. In its shock, its unpalatability, its inappropriateness is the nature of its interruption. It will always seem like the wrong way to go about things, like a muddled and irrelevant answer, probably be vaguely offensive, and above all like a kind of anachronism. But in anachronism, there are the traces of political potential lost to the empty present.

Of course, suspending neoliberal realism long enough to glimpse political potential was supposed to have been the job of the left. Once upon a time, even the British Labour Party sometimes made Marxisant noises about being guided by the actual experience of the masses, noises that seemed distant in 2016. Serious responses to the vote might rather go with the grain of its collective and localist thinking than react against it. These responses would be concerned with social class in a way that now often seems archaic. They would attempt to hear the unmediated and unadjusted voices of those whose exclusion had been a necessary tenet of an economy of 'inclusion'. The splashes of proletarian colour sometimes found in an Ian McEwan or a Martin Amis won't do it – their Dickensian rascals locked up in inverted commas have nothing to tell us about this. And for that matter, it's hard to see what we would get from the psychological creations of literary realism: if the developing individual self of Locke's *Essay Concerning Human Understanding* was a cornerstone of the *Bildungroman*, then *Lanark* and similar 'decomposition' Scottish novels of the '80s and '90s worked as *anti-Bildungsroman*, and in this was part of their challenge. This may involve fragmentation, repetition, lacunae as story. And it will be unlikely to come from a well-connected ambitious novelist looking for a likely moment of zeitgeist – though inevitably some of these will appear. The language in which it speaks will probably seem largely unacceptable. And even hearing it within the institutions currently remoulding themselves in terms of authoritarian liberalism will take tremendous levels of will and patience.

Bibliography

Ballard, J.G. (2008). *Concrete Island*. London: Fourth Estate.

Baucom, I. (1999). *Out of Place: Englishness, Empire, and the Locations of Identity*. Princeton, NJ: Princeton University Press.

BBC News. (2014). Labour's Emily Thornberry Quits Over "Snobby" Tweet. 21 November. Available at: www.bbc.co.uk/news/uk-politics-30139832

Curtis, A. (2016). *HyperNormalisation. BBC TV*.

Derrida, J. (2006). *Specters of Marx*, trans. Peggy Kamuf. London: Routledge.

Dorling, D. (2011). *Injustice:Why Social Inequality Persists*. Bristol: Policy Press.

Fisher, M. (2011). Introduction: Always Searching for the Time That Just Eluded Us, in Oldfield Ford. *Savage Messiah*, pp. v–xvi.

Fisher, M. (2014). *Ghosts of My Life: Writings on Depression, Hauntology, and Lost Futures*. Winchester: Zer0.

Gardiner, M. (2012). *The Return of England in English Literature*. Basingstoke: Palgrave Macmillan.

Gardiner, M. (2017). Thatcherism as an Extension of Consensus. In: *The Politics of Legality in a Neoliberal Age*, eds. Ben Golder and Daniel McLoughlin. Abingdon: Routledge, pp. 44–63.

Gilroy, P. (2004). *After Empire: Melancholia or Convivial Culture*. London: Routledge.

Gray, A. (2011). *Lanark*. Edinburgh: Canongate.

The Guardian. (2014). The *Guardian* View on the Scottish referendum: Britain Deserves Another Chance. 12 September 2014. Available at: www.theguardian.com/commentisfree/2014/sep/12/guardian-view-scottish-independence

Henderson, A., Jeffery, C., Lineira, R., Scully, R., Wincott, D., and Wyn Jones, R. (2016). England, Englishness and Brexit. *Political Quarterly*, 87 (2), pp. 187–99.

Hobolt, S.B. (2016). The Brexit Vote: A Divided Nation, a Divided Continent. *Journal of European Public Policy*, 23 (9), pp. 1259–77.

Hobsbawm, E. and Ranger, T. (1983). *The Invention of Tradition*. Cambridge: Cambridge University Press.

Joseph Rowntree Trust. (2016). *Brexit Vote Explained: Poverty, Low Skills and Lack of Opportunities*. Available at: www.jrf.org.uk/report/brexit-vote-explained-poverty-low-skills-and-lack-opportunities

Kenny, M., and Pearce, N. (2016). After Brexit: The Eurosceptic Dream. *Juncture*, 22 (4), pp. 304–7.

Locke, J. (n.d.). *Two Treatises on Government*, Part 2 Ch 9. Available at: www.gutenberg.org/files/7370/7370-h/7370-h.htm#CHAPTER_XI, 1689.

Nairn, T. (1981). *The Break-Up of Britain: Crisis and Neo-Nationalism*. London: Verso.

Nairn, T. (2002). *Pariah: Misfortunes of the British State*. London:Verso.

Oldfield Ford, L. (2011). *Savage Messiah*. London:Verso, 2009.

Orwell, G. (2007). *Notes on Nationalism, Essays*. London: Penguin, pp. 300–17.

Sinclair, I. (2013). *London Orbital*. London: Penguin.

11

FAKE NEWS LITERARY CRITICISM

J. A. Smith

In July 2017, the pro-Remain *Financial Times* disinterred the old argument of C.P. Snow, that Britain is intellectually riven by its 'two cultures' – science and the humanities – with the 'natural luddites' of the latter holding too much sway over the establishment: a case made in Snow's Cambridge 'Rede' lecture of 1959 (Collini, 1998; Ortolano, 2011). Taking its tone from Boris Johnson's pompous classical analogies, Michael Gove's literary pretensions, and the campaign director Dominic Cummings's hinterland of historical reference, 'Leave', it turns out, was the creature of a humanities fancifully separate from the tough-minded realities of industry and science (Gapper, 2017). The application of Snow's idea doesn't hold up long (David Davis studied molecular science, and Remain was led by undistinguished humanities and social sciences graduates as well). But it may be disconcerting all the same for the many academics in English studies who automatically see Brexit as a defeat for their side; for cultured, enquiring internationalism, as against a brutal inward-looking nativism and an illiterate press. This conflict, I suggest, is rooted in an unresolved tension within English studies itself, which Brexit supplies the unexpected provocation to examine. This requires us to return to the reply Snow's Rede Lecture received from one of the most significant architects of English studies in Britain, F.R. Leavis, in his Richmond lecture, also at Cambridge, in 1962.

This is worth doing because it suggests how two different but structural aspects of Leavis's thought, and, I suggest, of English studies as such, have ended up falling either side of a fault line that Brexit has exposed: and in turn it reveals something complex about the nature of Brexit. While Leavis himself has for some time been well out of fashion in the academy, his view of English studies as including among its tasks the training of a rigorous eye for falsehood, wooliness, and propaganda remains an important part of the discipline's self-representation. It is also part of 'Remain's' self-representation as a beleaguered corner of good sense, in the face of an increasingly depthless 'post-truth' environment of 'fake news' and populism. On the other hand, there is the side of Leavis's thought that is unoptimistic about cosmopolitanism as defined by effete elites, insists on the desirableness of homogeneous 'organic' community, and – because 'a language has its life in use' (Leavis, 1972: 183) – is suspicious of literature in translation. Needless to say, these smack of 'Leave', and it is not incidental that *Nor Shall My Sword* (1972), Leavis's collection of his mainly 1960s writings building on the Richmond lecture, begins and ends with unenthusiastic (though not un-nuanced) comment on the manner of Britain's original accession to the European Communities. This side of Leavis – when it is remembered – is yet more unfashionable, but I aim to show that it is not so easily separated from the 'rigorous eye for falsehood' part of his thought that the discipline is still happy to retain. Thus, I start by considering the meaning of the Snow–Leavis controversy to our current predicament in a quite different way to the *FT*, before taking pause over the origins of English studies' claim to speak for clear-headed scrutiny, at last making what is the superficially perverse assertion that it is actually through the 'other' 'communal' part of Leavis's thought as presented in *Nor Shall My Sword* that we can find a productive response to the alleged populism of our present moment.

It should be said that the chapters of *Nor Shall My Sword* yield diminishing returns after the Richmond lecture and its follow-up, 'Luddites? *or* There is Only One Culture'; tellingly, while the earliest essays were placed in *The Spectator* and *Times Literary Supplement*, the later ones ended up in *The Human World*, a small journal run by one of Leavis's more conservative students and named after a passage in the Richmond lecture (MacKillop, 1995: 386–7). These last are marred by some of the more objectionable versions of the habits of 'late style' (Said, 2006): repetitiveness, a narrowing of sources of information, and a 'stating' of quite banal opinions – on immigration and international aid especially – in a manner only haphazardly integrated into the systematic thought that provided Leavis's credentials for public utterance. There is an expectation that a public intellectual uses their platform to say things that they uniquely are in a position to say, on the basis of their particular 'discourse' established elsewhere: and – whatever one thinks of the views in question – *Nor Shall My Sword* contains moments that are not that. At the same time, the challenge Leavis lays down in the book, over where cultural value is to be placed if not, as he represents Snow and his ilk as believing, solely in economic growth, is a substantially unanswered one. That it seems an even more uncomfortable question now than it did at Leavis's time of writing is itself part of a constellation of cultural facts that includes the divisions that produced – and have been exacerbated by – the 2016 referendum result.

I

Snow, a former research scientist, civil servant, and successful novelist, praised in his Rede lecture what he considered to be the undervalued heroes of science and industry, who were on the cusp of bringing peace and prosperity to all, thus seizing an optimistic zeitgeist between the 'never had it so good' Macmillan '50s and the 'white heat of technology' Wilson '60s. For Snow, this progress could only be held back by the hauteur of what he called the 'traditional culture', a rather dubious conflation of some pre-war modernist authors, the political establishment, and, it sometimes seemed, literature as such (Trilling, 1965: 156; Edgerton, 2005). Leavis's famously fearsome reply insisted on literature's capacity for responding to technological advance in far more subtle ways than Snow understood and includes in its genealogy the claim that the government consensus Snow himself belonged to was indebted to some of the very nineteenth-century authors he dismissed as 'luddites': 'it was Ruskin who put into currency the distinction between wealth and well-being, which runs down through Morris and the British Socialist movement to the Welfare State' (Leavis, 1972: 57–8).

By contrast, Leavis characterises the priorities of Snow and his culture as follows:

> 'standard of living' is an ultimate criterion, its raising an ultimate aim, a matter of wages and salaries and what you can buy with them, reduced hours of work, and the technological resources that make your increasing leisure worth having, so that productivity – the supremely important thing – must be kept on the rise [. . .] Such a concern is not enough – disastrously not enough.
>
> (59)

I address the subtlety of what Leavis *does* feel risks being lost in this optimistic economic map of the future in a moment. For now, it is enough to stress that, while Leavis's habitual tone is that of the unheard and unattended outsider, this question of where – at a time when living standards are rapidly rising and exponential economic growth is anticipated for the future – cultural value is to be placed was evidently in the air. The three years prior to Snow's Rede lecture saw the publication of the following: 1956: Anthony Crosland's *The Future of Socialism*; an attempt to reconcile the Labour Party to the new consumer culture, making an elaborate socialist case for its vast acceleration; 1957: Richard Hoggart's *The Uses of Literacy*; an avowedly Leavisian critique of the coarsening effects of consumer culture but adding an analysis of the forms of resistance already built into working class culture; 1958: J.K. Galbraith's *The Affluent Society*; which contended that the very tools of economics themselves had become inadequate to interpret the new situation of growth, and that growth was currently being pursued for its own sake, to the cost of many other areas of economy and life. These texts are very different from each other and from the Leavis of the '60s, but collectively they reflect what a more sustained analysis could call a 'literature of growth', a culture of moral and intellectual response to the question of what becomes valuable when exponential economic growth means that material needs can be taken care of: a state of affairs that didn't seem far away.

It now seems difficult to deny that the succeeding decades *have* suffered by a lack of vocabulary for talking about cultural value outside the economic. This lack would be one thing if the belief in the inevitable advance of material living standards cultivated in the '50s and '60s had continued. But we return to the 'literature of growth' in a situation in which the whole terms of debate have been turned inside out. Economic growth has had its relationship to wages and material living standards – axiomatic for Crosland and Snow – severed (Institute for Public Policy Research, 2017); consumer goods are entangled in a destabilising culture of personal debt, not to mention a violent system of globally exploitative manufacture (Pettifor, 2017: 17–18); and automation and digital technology now come with the imposition of the unaccountable power of tech companies over our daily lives in the present and the prospect of mass unemployment in the future (Srnicek, 2017).

In this changed context, a lack of cognizance for anything beyond the economic was nonetheless, by design, the underpinning of the campaign to remain in the EU. The campaign leader, Craig Oliver's (2016) memoir reveals the guidance taken from two distinguished pollsters: Andrew Cooper: 'These people are vociferous in their dislike of the EU, but what will sway them is if their pocket is likely to be hit' (42); and Jim Messina: 'They aren't going to be won over by telling them how wonderful the EU is – they want to know the cold, hard economic facts. Will it hit them in the pocket or not?' (84). 'We know', Oliver adds, 'that there has been no election in the last hundred years where people have voted against their direct financial interest' (114). Economic stability was sure, then, to trump xenophobia and other wild but ultimately secondary emotional sallies. But that rule only applied for as long as the economic success of the country was something people personally identified with: for as long as the destiny of that signifier, 'the economy', and one's own seemed authentically at one. Both in the country at large as well as more specifically in crucial areas of the north of England (Hazeldine, 2017: 66–8), the uneven recovery after the economic crash and the complete non-relationship between what the Treasury called growth and people's standard of living had been surreptitiously working to undermine that attachment. With those ties of identification loosened, it became increasingly possible to think, *why not . . .?*

II

After the victories of Leave and Donald Trump, one sometimes heard among those working in the humanities a slightly wounded opinion about their own significance. The 'fake news' that dogged those elections and the uncritical publics that voted in them were said to be related to the decline in esteem for the humanities that has accompanied the growing marketization of the university. The humanities, after all, are there to teach us to differentiate fact from fiction, a revealing metaphor from a rhetorical distraction, humane and creditable argument from exploitative jingoism. (George Osborne overstated – and was seen as overstating – the immediate consequences of a Leave vote [Shipman, 2016: 372], but even the most high-minded Leavers must concede their campaign tended to the second of each of these pairs.) Helen Small calls this idea, that the qualities the humanities train somehow contribute to the quality of the politics of a culture, the 'democracy needs us' defence but notes that while its adherents often date it back to the nineteenth century, the most commonly cited progenitors have usually been misremembered in the details. Mill, Ruskin, and Newman did indeed speak about the training that would be required to create a critical civic public, 'but none of these writers thought that the arts and humanities had a privileged, let alone primary role to play' (Small, 2013: 134; on the complicated case of Arnold, 69–88).

The connection had to wait until university English started to take the role for itself in the milieu of Cambridge after the First World War. I.A. Richards recast Matthew Arnold's position that poetry was to emerge to 'maintain the psychological coherence of existence' (Mulhern, 1979: 26) into newly sophisticated psycho-linguistic terms in *Principles of Literary Criticism* (1924); but it was in some of the detail of the more classroom-focussed sequel, *Practical Criticism* (1929), that Richards's mix of ethics and aesthetics began to show its application to politics. A signal virtue of Richards's approach to poetry was the training it offered in overcoming and avoiding 'stock responses' (revising Arnold's 'stock notions') 'in all forms of human activity – in business, in personal relationships, in public affairs, in Courts of Justice' (Richards, 1964: 240). Those who had undergone rigorous training in the reading of complex poems were less likely to let the clichés that stultify all aspects of public life pass and more likely to look for 'ways in which they may be overcome'.

Richards's casual remark that a stock response was 'like a stock line in shoes or hats' proved perspicuous, as its logic was transported into the remarkably complex apparatus of the *Scrutiny* project from the start of the 1930s: an apparatus encompassing the literary journal of that name, mutually reinforcing monographs by its contributors, school textbooks, and sympathetic teachers who, taught by Leavis, sent their pupils to undertake the same (Hilliard, 2012). Common to each ingredient was the conviction that transformations of 'sensibility' in poetry and the disastrous effects of the mass press, state propaganda, commercialised leisure, and advertising were sociologically connected phenomena and could be analysed – and in the latter case inoculated against – using the same tools (Smith, 2014: 321–3).

The 'valuation' of creative writing and the scrutiny of broadly 'political' discourse met in *Culture and Environment* (1933), which Leavis wrote with Denys Thompson, but it was Thompson (who acquired a reputation for making the *Scrutiny* case in broader brushstrokes than Leavis) who made the connection most clearly in another book of model 'practical criticism' exercises, *Reading and Discrimination*:

> (Samuel) Johnson could in favour of a book cite the approval of the Common Reader. Today the commonest readers are those of the *News of the World*. What one reads matters more today than ever before, but discrimination is harder than ever to acquire.
>
> (Thompson, 1934: 4)

While Leavis identified culture's problems too far inside the structures of the establishment for him to endorse the phrase, 'democracy needs us' could not be articulated more barely than in a book training distaste for Milton ('soporific', 'monotonous' [22]) and Lamb ('a vehicle for charming whimsies' [39]) in exactly the same terms as for contemporary political speeches and advertising copy.

Nearly three decades later, and in what we have seen are the changed circumstances of 'the affluent society', the Richmond lecture remains a model of the same case. Leavis argues that under conditions of rapid scientific development, productivity, and standards of living, we are going to need 'something with the livingness of the deepest vital instinct; as intelligence, a power – rooted, strong in experience, and supremely human – of creative response to the new challenges of time' (Leavis, 1972: 60–1). The qualities being trained have become more abstract, but the horizon is still 'to create an educated public that politicians will fear and respect' (183) and is still envisaged as being undertaken in a 'vital English school' (63). Actually, the abstractness of what is being trained – its disappearance into different ways of articulating the often-criticised metaphysical Leavisian notion of 'life' – is reinforced by the actual use of literary texts throughout *Nor Shall My Sword*. This takes the form less of sustained analyses than of representative 'lightning-strike' moments from Conrad, Eliot, Dickens, Blake, and most of all Lawrence, authors Leavis had been crystallizing his view of for decades.

Where 'practical criticism' of the kind *Scrutiny* had advanced *is* present is in the treatment of Snow himself. Leavis's remark that Snow's text, misguidedly set in schools, would only be valuable there 'as a document in the study of cliché' (Leavis, 1972: 50) is – like many of the allegedly excessive insults that have troubled the lecture's reputation – actually of defining importance to the argument. There are a number of reasons to dismiss Leavis's belief that we can infer quality of thought, of 'mind', from prose style; but the example of Snow does not help one to such a dismissal. Leavis's dismantling of Snow's first pretending to a fashionably tragic view of existence ('we die alone') before moving brightly to the 'social hope', the 'jam' (Leavis fixes on the toe-curling metonym), of life's pleasures and prosperities, is devastating. Literature itself is doing some other, higher work in Leavis's discourse here: it is on Snow himself that Leavis sets the power of critical reading. In this sense, Leavis's claim that Snow is a 'portent' – not so much saying as personally enacting everything that is wrong with the culture – is mirrored by the way Leavis's text does not so much describe as enact the cultural cure.

III

Raymond Williams said of the Bloomsbury group that while its members held admirable views against ignorance, poverty, imperialism and so on, the alternative they presented came not in the form of an appeal to 'any alternative idea of a whole society' but to 'the supreme value of the civilised *individual*, whose pluralisation, as more and more civilised individuals, was itself the only acceptable social direction' (Williams, 1980: 165). The observation should make adherents of the 'democracy needs us' view of the humanities suddenly self-conscious: for it strikes at its fundamental ambiguity. If the basic unit of a 'political humanities' is the right-thinking individuals it has produced, then there are political philosophers who would deny that it represents a politics – as opposed to a 'mere' individualised ethics – at all (Mouffe, 2013: 16–17).

Leavis would have been perturbed to have the charge made to him. In *Education and the University*, he refers sardonically to those who view literary studies' function as 'adding to the few people who can talk intelligently about Stendhal' (Leavis, 1948: 107). But in the first instance, it applies. Leavis shared with many intellectuals of his generation the view that modernity had shattered us all into mutually uncomprehending individuals. At the same time, the very method of his writing and teaching – the quotation, the judgement, and the famous communal gesture: 'this is so – isn't it?' – trusted that at least one perfectly comprehending community was in fact close to hand (Anderson, 1992: 102). Yet as some who were taught under this regime have testified, the effect of it was sometimes less a productive intersubjectivity than a near-Calvinist focus on oneself and what it said about you if you got the answer wrong (Ellis, 2013: 25).

It is – perhaps surprisingly – from the more metaphysical side of Leavis's thought in the Richmond lecture that a more valuable 'political' response to our current predicament might be inferred. In the demolishing of Snow's idea of a 'social hope' in progress that transcends or compensates individual tragedy or finitude, Leavis asks 'what *is* the "social condition" that has nothing to do with the "individual condition"? [. . .] Where, if not in individuals, is what is hoped for – a *non*-tragic condition one supposes – to be located?' (Leavis, 1972: 53). Later, he connects this to the experience of poetry itself:

> the poem comes to be established as something "out there", of common access in what is in some sense a public world [. . . but] can have its life only in the living present, in the creative response of individuals.
>
> (62)

The habitual vitalism of this language aside, what is significant here is the retort that the important divide is not between tragic individuality and a hopeful broader politics but in the – as it were – constitutive divide, the generative gap, that produces both individual and 'public world' out of itself. (In the Lacanian tradition, this 'gap' would be precisely the definition of the tragic in itself [Smith, 2016: 158–60]).

To see this in play, let us take a closing concrete example. Leavis's passing slight to Marshall McLuhan elsewhere in *Nor Shall My Sword* – that to announce 'that mass-media have turned the world into a village' is to 'demonstrate that he doesn't know what a village was' (184) – seems quaint on the face of it in today's context of an increasingly digital capitalism. But Leavis's mistrust of McLuhan's interrelated technophilia and under-developed valorisation of community may be unexpectedly instructive in that context. The claim made by today's political populists that they bypass elites, phony experts, and unaccountable institutions in order to speak – without mediation – *for the people*, is a point of view that we have already had some training for in our digital lives in the 'global village' online. As I argue more fully in my book *Other People's Politics*, the crucial relationship between digital media and populism is not the one of liberal paranoia about fake news, online trolls, and 'bots' from Russia. Rather, it appears in the way that in the past decade, every area of life has been made the – at least potential – object of digitised data interpreted by algorithms: from advertising to finance to university rankings to the granting of loans to employment policies to electioneering to 'lifestyle' fitness apps to personalised music and video recommendations online, and so on (O'Neil, 2016).

In a time of straitened finances, policy makers have been especially amenable to the promises of Silicon Valley, that their algorithms can bypass traditional experts, editors, and other 'elite' decision makers to make more accurate decisions based on anticipated human choices, just as long as they are permitted to hold data on enough of our *past* choices in aggregate (Morozov, 2013). This has for some time been the real 'voice of the people': the way in which the digital traces of so much of what we do can be disinterred and conjured to speak as one. It is also the point on which the ambiguity in Leavis I have been discussing becomes unexpectedly useful. Leavis's response to the question of the individual within the communal is reiterated twice in *Nor Shall My Sword*, once attributed to Lawrence and once to Blake. Leavis refers to 'the Laurentian maxim "nothing matters but life"', remarking that Lawrence 'insists on the truth that only in living individuals is life there, and individual lives cannot be aggregated or equated or dealt with quantitatively in any way' (53–4). Later, we are told that 'to emphasise creativity as Blake did is to be committed to bringing home [. . .] that you can't generalise life, that individual lives can't be aggregated or averaged, and that only in individual lives is life 'there' (127–8).

This, I think, is one way in which Leavis's contribution to the 'literature of growth' can become instructive again under muchchanged conditions. Both the populism that brought us to Brexit and the use to which digital technology is being put at the present time make precisely this claim to treat lives in 'aggregate'. For that reason, they can only speak, or claim to speak, for human behaviour as – on average – it *has* been. What they are cut off from is the capacity to speak of what it *may* be; which can be seen to emerge, as Leavis describes, out of the contingency of this strange generative gap between 'public world' and individual lives. For this reason, my assertion is that the most important thing English studies has to offer in the face of malign forms of populism is *not* the kind of reactive inoculation against fake news that we have for a long time reassured ourselves is one of the more robust by-products of trained 'close reading'. Instead, Brexit should be recognised as a wake-up call about what happens when we allow the terms of 'the communal' to go unexamined or forget about the unpredictable forms of agency people are liable to suddenly show if decision makers allow them to be treated 'in aggregate' for too long.

Bibliography

Anderson, P. (1992). *English Questions*. London: Verso.

Collini, S. (1998). The Critic as Journalist: Leavis After *Scrutiny*. In: Grub *Street and the Ivory Tower: Literary Journalism and Literary Scholarship from Fielding to the Internet*, eds. J. Treglown and B. Bennett. 1st ed. Oxford: Oxford University Press, pp. 151–76.

Edgerton, D. (2005). C.P. Snow as Anti-Historian of British Science: Revisiting the Technocratic Moment, 1959–1964. *History of Science*, 43 (2), pp. 187–208.

Ellis, D. (2013). *Memoirs of a Leavisite: The Decline and Fall of Cambridge English*. Liverpool: Liverpool University Press.

Gapper, J. (2017). The Fatal Divide for Business in Brexit Britain. *Financial Times* [online]. Available at: www.ft.com/content/f8658320-661d-11e7-9a66-93fb352ba1fe [Accessed 20 September 2017].

Hazeldine, T. (2017). Revolt of the Rustbelt. *New Left Review*, 106, pp. 51–79.

Hilliard, C. (2012). *English as Vocation: The Scrutiny Movement*. Oxford: Oxford University Press.

Institute for Public Policy Research. (2017). *Time for Change: A New Vision for the British Economy: The Interim Report of the IPPR Commission on Economic Justice* [online]. Available at: https://ippr.org/files/2017-09/cej-interim-report.pdf [Accessed 20 September 2017].

Leavis, F. (1948). *English & the University: A Sketch for an 'English School'*. 2nd ed. London: Chatto & Windus.

Leavis, F. (1972). *Nor Shall My Sword: Discourses on Pluralism, Compassion and Social Hope*. London: Chatto & Windus.

Leavis, F. and Thompson, D. (1933). *Culture and Environment: The Training of Critical Awareness*. London: Chatto & Windus.

MacKillop, I. (1995). *F.R. Leavis: A Life in Criticism*. London: Penguin.

Morozov, E. (2013). *To Save Everything, Click Here: Technology, Solutionism and the Urge to Fix Problems That Don't Exist*. London: Penguin.

Mouffe, C. (2013). *Agonistics: Thinking the World Politically*. London: Verso.

Mulhern, F. (1979). *The Moment of 'Scrutiny'*. London: New Left Books.

Oliver, C. (2016). *Unleashing Demons: The Inside Story of Brexit*. London: Hodder & Stoughton.

O'Neil, C. (2016). *Weapons of Math Destruction: How Big Data Increases Inequality and Threatens Democracy*. London: Penguin.

Ortolano, G. (2011). *The Two Cultures Controversy: Science, Literature and Cultural Politics in Postwar Britain*. Cambridge: Cambridge University Press.

Pettifor, A. (2017). *The Production of Money: How to Break the Powers of Bankers*. London: Verso.

Richards, I. A. (1924). *Principles of Literary Criticism*. London: Kegan Paul.

Richards, I. (1964). *Practical Criticism: A Study of Literary Judgement*. 11th ed. London: Routledge.

Said, E. (2006). *On Late Style: Music and Literature Against the Grain*. London: Bloomsbury.

Shipman, T. (2016). *All Out War: The Full Story of How Brexit Sank Britain's Political Class*. London: Harper Collins.

Small, H. (2013). *The Value of the Humanities*. Oxford: Oxford University Press.

Smith, J. (2014). *Scrutiny*'s Eighteenth Century. *Essays in Criticism*, 64 (3), pp. 318–40.

Smith, J. (2016). *Samuel Richardson and the Theory of Tragedy: Clarissa's Caesuras*. Manchester: Manchester University Press.

Srnicek, N. (2017). *Platform Capitalism*. Cambridge: Polity Press.

Thompson, D. (1934). *Reading and Discrimination*. London: Chatto & Windus.

Trilling, L. (1965). *Beyond Culture: Essays on Literature and Learning*. New York: Viking.

Williams, R. (1980). *Culture and Materialism: Selected Essays*. London: Verso.

12

THE PSYCHOPOLITICS OF BREXIT

Martin Murray

Conflict

To say that the West is beset by political division right now is not to say anything unusual or controversial. For example, the US electorate is obviously and fiercely divided between those who support Donald Trump and those who abhor him. Similarly, in Europe, there are deep divisions over comparable political issues, including immigration. Conflict has 'broken out' between (and within) many different demographic and socio-political groupings throughout the Western World. It has been exacerbated by new media, especially social media. Key among the conflicts that are fuelling (and being fuelled by) the dissension that presently troubles the West is Brexit.

Socio-economic, racial and gender divisions clearly underpin all the conflicts troubling the West, yet they don't straightforwardly scan onto traditional political differences. In general, political parties, or positions, are divided *in themselves*. All of this Western political conflict is easy enough to see, especially 'in the media'. It's acted out dramatically – even melodramatically – in both 'mainstream' and social media by the hour. It captivates us.

What's *not* so easy is to get beyond the conflict. Being 'political' seems to demand adopting a position defined as *against* something:

the enemy, injustice, unfreedom, barbarism, the invader, the establishment, the élite. The position will concomitantly be thought and felt to be 'good' and its opponents presumed to be bad. It is exactly at this point that one is *caught* in a political conflict, when one thinks and feels one knows one is right, but one *is* so by having created an 'other' that is one's nadir and that is 'wrong'. Political oppositions (e.g. left/ right; Remain/Leave) seem clear, but they are not. They are treacherous and conceal depths of dissension and deception that are hidden behind headlines and nullified by news narratives.

Here is an example. Before, during and after Trump's election, some US Democrats, liberals and leftists couldn't help but see his supporters how they saw him: vulgar, unintelligent, racist, sexist and lacking in human empathy for the oppressed (Hymovitz, 2017). Yet in doing so they were often maligning, misrepresenting and misunderstanding the American working class, themselves the oppressed, and the constituency that much liberalism and leftism was historically designed to defend (Williams, 2016). Identifying an enemy is not the solution to a political conflict, it is the start of it, and escaping such conflict requires more than the enemy's elimination. It requires understanding and crediting the enemy and imagining what it feels like to be on the opposite side to one's own. None of this necessarily means abandoning one's own political argument, but it at least means opening it to question, although this is much easier said than done, including and especially around Brexit.

Psychoanalysis is one of the primary 'conflict-facing' approaches that the humanities and social sciences have used in their sincere efforts to grapple with conflict, and I draw on this here in my analysis of Brexit, or, more specifically the British political attitudes and positions that have been adopted in response to it.

Some argue that critical approaches which do not demand loyalty or commitment to a unilateral 'position' or 'identity' are out of date. For many, right across the political spectrum, it now seems better that one should stick to one's principles consistently (or dogmatically) rather than 'deconstruct' them. Strongly identifying with and holding oneself and others to sets of principles is what sometimes gets described as 'identity politics'. Such politics can be seen to be – and sometimes *are* – *anti*-theoretical, in the sense of being indifferent or hostile to argumentative complications of their basic premises. One of the practical real-world correspondents of such theoretical pre-emption is 'no-platforming', the practice of excluding speakers from events on the presumption that they will say something that contradicts or offends certain views that one holds *in principle*, thus precluding any possibility of testing those principles via disagreement with them.

Yet this sort of 'post-theoretical' adoption of political positioning heightens the very conflict that it is intended to eliminate. The Republican Democratic prejudices against Trump supporters are one example of this (they make conservative push-back worse); the way liberal hegemony and 'political correctness' provoke alt-right rage is another (Nagle, 2017: 68–85). Political disagreement in such cases may seem principled, but it reduces, in effect, to a play of power: holding to a firm and exclusive political line is an attempt at gaining or retaining or recovering such power. If we accept Nietzsche's premise that force often prevails (for example, over 'truth'), but that it also necessitates counterforce, then principled political arguments will always not only censor other arguments but also invite counteraction against themselves (Nietzsche, 1989: 77). Political principles – especially identarian ones – create as much conflict as they resolve.

It's on the basis of this sort of argument that I'm choosing to consider political conflicts – specifically over Brexit – here. From both a metaphysical and a psychological point of view, the left and the right both depend on and feed off each other, as do Remainers and Leavers. The resources of psychoanalysis offer the possibility, however momentarily, of not taking any of these sides and of understanding them all the better as a consequence.

Decisions

I am not arguing that having political views, especially strong ones, is disingenuous or a waste of time nor that political choice or action is useless or is voided by conflict. Indeed, there are ways in which action, including political action, can be seen as *having* to come out of conflict. The best way to show this, in my view, is via a philosophical argument that has a psychological dimension.

The case that political action can come out of conflict can be made as follows. It's only because one *can't* ultimately know what the perfect resolution to a dilemma is that one *must* choose between the options that it offers. If there wasn't any question of how a given issue might be resolved, one would already know what to do to resolve it, or one would already *be* resolving it, or one wouldn't feel any need to resolve it. Thus one takes action – and responsibility for that action – *because* one is aware of the conflict that requires it. To take a prescient example, one chooses to stay with or leave one's partner because one feels conflict about being secure but unhappy with her (or him) or being alone and afraid but free (in case it isn't obvious, I'm employing an analogy that compares sexual relationships and Britain's partnership with the EU). The decision to stay with or leave one's partner and *acting* on that decision doesn't necessarily make one happy, but it can at least reduce the conflict that prompted it. According to this sort of view, conflict, including political conflict, is the precursor and instigator of action (Sartre, 1996: 433–556).

Yet when decisions are made or actions are taken in doubt, there are *other considerations* one is setting aside, or eschewing, in order to make them. From a psychoanalytic point of view these other considerations – which might be other thoughts or facts or even desires – could well be denied and/or unconscious. This may even be *necessary* for a decision to be made. When I make a difficult decision to do A rather than B, I sometimes have to put B 'out of my mind'. For example, if I have the choice, I may choose to become a lawyer rather than a musician. I find the former boring and the latter stimulating, but the former will pay the rent and support my family, whereas the latter will probably not. I then have to 'forget' about my dream of becoming a musician. If I am successful and the dream doesn't return, it may have been 'repressed' into my unconscious. It lives on there, but I cease to remember or be aware of it. The psychoanalytic approach to the question of conflict and decision thus takes account of unconscious considerations (one even might say 'motives') and the various repressions they involve. It thus throws a different light on conflict and decision both.

Academia

Before showing this, I'm going to note how psychoanalytic analyses of politics are often 'done'. I'll be doing this because I want to conduct them slightly differently here.

In so far as it has contributed to analyses of culture and politics, psychoanalysis has mostly been deployed from a liberal or left position. This is particularly, although not exclusively, true of academic deployments of psychoanalysis. Examples of influential academic writers who have employed a sort of political psychoanalysis that has liberal or left inclinations are Herbert Marcuse, Slavoj Žižek and Judith Butler. The objects of their analyses have usually been explicitly or implicitly conservative or right wing: authoritarian institutions or social structures, conservative or reactionary attitudes, conventional social formations or prescribed identities (including sexual and 'racial' identities), bigoted or prejudicial ideologies, and cultural products. This adoption of a critical left-wing attitude towards purportedly right-wing objects has been maintained in a number of recent psychoanalytic studies of Brexit (see, for example, Morgan).

Yet a left-wing or liberal political inclination is not so marked in psychoanalytic practice, that is psychoanalysis practiced by psychoanalysts rather than academics. Some psychoanalysts *are* left wing or liberal, but this is by no means true of all of them. Freud was not unambiguously left wing or liberal either. Although there are undoubtedly radical and liberal aspects of his theory, both Freud and his work can be seen to have distinctively conservative elements. The institutions and analysts that have developed Freud's legacy and tradition have often also displayed conservatism too. The International Psychoanalytic Association (IPA), the umbrella association for Freudian (and Kleinian) psychoanalytic societies worldwide, has been and is accused of various sorts of conservatism. This criticism has included a long-standing charge of heterosexism among IPA societies and affiliates (the IPA did not formally state that homosexual men and women were admissible for training until 1998), charges from within and without Freudian culture that Freud's theories are sexist (see, for example, Grigg and Greer) and a charge, often made by Lacanians, that IPA-sanctioned therapeutic practices are inflexible and authoritarian (see Murray, 2016: 127–30).

Put simply, academics have tended to situate themselves on the left and analyse the right. Further, academics tend to use psychoanalysis as a sort of tool to analyse objects (literary, filmic, cultural or whatever) but unlike psychoanalysts, they don't also apply this tool to their own analyses of such objects or to themselves. In psychoanalytic terms, they and their arguments have tended not to take account of the 'counter-transference'.

However, here I'd like to do what academics often don't do: (psycho)analyse liberal/left as well as right-wing attitudes, specifically to Brexit. Although I acknowledge that it is a generalisation, liberal/left attitudes have tended to inform Remain voter opinions, while more conservative and right-wing attitudes have tended to shape Leave ones (although of course there are Lexiteer leavers and Conservative Remainers). What follows will analyse Remainer views as well as Leaver ones and will involve some analysis of my own views in the process.

Brexit

In the UK, Brexit is about as conflicted as a political issue can be. For the sake of full disclosure, I should say that I voted to remain in the EU. I am still of the view that remaining would have been the best choice for Britain and even think that a grave mistake was made in the referendum. I feel that I have strong political and economic reasons for thinking as I do. Yet I do not think that denying the reality of the vote or finding some way to re-run the referendum is a fair or acceptable thing to do, not only because it would be anti-democratic but also because it would exacerbate the *resentment* that many Brexiteers expressed with their votes (and that is implied in the widespread observation, including among Leavers, that a vote for Brexit was a 'protest' vote). I also do not think that my own views are less of a valid object of analysis than those of any others, including Leavers'. I am now (albeit ambivalently and reluctantly) in favour of 'soft Brexit', which I see as a possible compromise between Leave and Remain positions. Yet I know that this position is unacceptable to some Leavers (who want Brexit to be 'hard') and even to some Remainers (who don't want Brexit at all and who think, or maybe dream, that it is reversible). As I have said, what is often not resolved by adoption of an assertive political position (and maybe even a compromised one) is conflict. It thus seems to me, for these reasons and for many of the other reasons given earlier, that a psychoanalytic analysis, rather than a straightforward political argument, might be the best way to approach the field of conflict that is Brexit.

Symptoms

Certain features of the referendum lent it the characters of a psychical symptom rather than a decision and thus left it open to psychoanalysis. The referendum question was put in for/against terms: 'Should the United Kingdom remain a member of the European Union?' This cast a complex and conflicting set of issues – to do with political union, peace, sovereignty, immigration, economic stability and national dependence and independence – as a single, decidable issue. Yet it's now clear that this question could never have settled the conflicts that the referendum bought up. This is why, for example, pro-EU politicians often claim that people who voted for Brexit didn't also vote to become poorer. They are pointing out that the referendum didn't include any question as to whether Britain should remain in the Single Market or the Customs Union, where Leavers infer or presume that it did. This is only one of very many issues that the referendum didn't resolve. In other words, the referendum was a *symptom* (and was *symptomatic*) of many conflicts and was – and is – *overdetermined* by them.

Freud uses the terms 'symptomatic' and 'overdetermined' to describe both the hysterical symptom and the dream, both of which are ambiguous and inarticulate representations of acute conflicts, ones that are characterised not only by being complex and unresolved but also by involving repressed content. The hysteric, typically, suffers from repressed conflicts caused by traumatic memories (Freud and Breuer, 1984). The dreamer is often beset by conflicts relating to her or his wishes or desires, which are repressed in her or his waking life but indirectly expressed in dreams (Freud, 1976). The hysterical symptom (for example paralysis) and the dream are thus both distorted signs of a conflict, of which the patient is the sufferer but of which s/he is also – mostly or fully – unaware. Referendum voters were forced, or allowed, to see their Brexit vote as a single, conscious choice that could be settled by answering one question. Yet it was precisely the couching of the Brexit vote thus that allowed the mass of conflicts that underlay it to be avoided or buried, that is in one way or another repressed. A key and indeed defining characteristic of unconscious content, according to Freud, is that it *is* repressed (Freud, 1984a: 147). This repression can be full (in the case of repression *per se*) or consciously denied (in the case of 'negation', when the repressed content appears in consciousness but is felt or claimed *not* to be true) or tacitly admitted but also dismissed as insignificant (in the case of 'disavowal': 'I'm not a racist but . . .' is a classic example) or imagined to be in someone else and thereby disowned (in the case of 'projection'). Yet despite (and partly because of) its expulsion from consciousness, repression can and does often return in a different and disturbing form – for example that of the hysterical symptom. *When* it returns, it often does so with a vengeance (Freud, 1984b). It's arguable that this is why the Brexit referendum – or rather its result – was such a shock (although perhaps it was more of a shock for some and a pleasure for others).

The conflicts and repressions among British voters about Brexit were active before, during and after the referendum. Voters' choices – and their justifications for them – often took positions that suppressed or denied or projected or otherwise hid or disavowed the mass of tensions that the vote *didn't* properly address. More precisely, their stated views, calculations, wishes and decisions often contradicted or obfuscated other ones that they secretly refused but felt or knew and would have to acknowledge as desirable or true if they were admitted. Leavers said that their choice was to do with sovereignty, not immigration, or they said that it was to do with immigration but that this view involved no prejudice. The first of these statements is a negation of anti-immigration views; the second is a disavowal of the prejudices that might be attached to them. In both cases Leavers were arguably not seeing or acknowledging their own attitudes, for fear of having to admit that they might be prejudicial. For their part, Remainers accused leavers of racism, which allowed them to disavow immigration as an issue. Yet although immigration is a net benefit to the UK economy (as Leavers often pointed out) it does cause downward pressure on some wage levels and does put a strain on public service resources (the NHS, Social Services, housing, etc.) in some communities, exactly as some Leavers have claimed (House of Lords

Report). Each side identified – but also projected – ignorance and prejudice into the other.

Recognition

Identifying the forms of denial, evasion and forgetting which have characterised pre- and post-referendum conflicts doesn't completely resolve them. It might, however, begin to lessen them, as long as both sides in all conflicts can begin to *recognise* the positions they are or have been taking up, both individually and in relation to each other. Acknowledging that such positions *have* been taken up, along with understanding their unconscious implications, is the start of achieving something that the French psychoanalyst Jacques Lacan, following a Russian philosopher named Alexandre Kojève (himself following Hegel), describes as *mutual recognition*.

From his philosophical antecedents, Lacan borrows the idea that the self, in its primitive form, is only formed at all by what it opposes itself to. The animal 'self' (including the 'human animal') only attains selfhood via another animal. It first encounters this other animal as potential sustenance, as food, which it needs to stay alive. It thus gets its first sense of itself *as needing* another. This animal-related argument (which is also an evolutionary one) can be made in relation to another primitive: the human child (at which point the argument also becomes psychoanalytic and developmental). The child needs another human being to reflect its sense of self. This is most obviously the mother (Lacan's account here resembles Melanie Klein's).

Yet this discovery of self is not a stable one. In all cases (animal and/or human, evolutionary and/or developmental) the self in question is only apparent via an *other*, which it needs, or at least wishes, to consume (if not literally, then with love or hate). Yet if it does consume this other, it destroys the means by which it appears at all – as a self – and hence loses its identity *per se*. The rudimentary self is only sustained by a tense opposition, instructed by a primitive wish or need, which, if it is acted on, is auto-destructive and eliminates the means by which the self can be constituted at all (Lacan, 2005: 48, 931; Kojève, 1980: 3–4, 13, 15; Murray, 2016: 143–4).

Apart from indicating why identity politics in general is imbued with a sort of childish aggressivity, this Lacanian account of human behaviour begins to suggest why Leavers and Remainers are so at odds. The identity of each is sustained by an opposition to the other that is both fragile and potentially violent, even murderous.

How can this deathly standoff be overcome? According to Lacan's early view (and Hegel's late one) this can only happen by way of mutual recognition. Each being must cease seeing the other as either the means of satisfaction or the threat of extinction, which means stepping out of the death grip that both beings are locked in. In order to get out of the inter-animal and inter-human cycle of need, self-assertion and destruction, one must cease to view the other as only existing to justify one and must accept that one can be seen in other ways than one wants to be seen. This means giving up one's wished-for and narcissistic sense of self and allowing for a more negotiated one. It also means hoping and allowing that the other can do the same. The project requires a willingness to understand both the self and the other on other terms than one's own. This requires three further things: relinquishment of a fantasised identity, confrontation with a 'real' situation and symbolisation of a reasonable and mutual aim (Lacan, 2005: 98; Murray, 2016: 154–6).

How is *this* done, and how can the scenario described and its resolution be related to Brexit? To better understand this, it's worth knowing that Lacan speaks of three categories, or dimensions, of being, which correspond with the three requirements mentioned earlier. They are categories in terms of which human experience and development can be understood. Lacan calls them the 'Symbolic', the 'Imaginary' and the 'Real'. As well as being generally descriptive of human being, the categories describe the different positions that people can take up in response to apparently unresolvable psychical conflicts or dilemmas.

'Imaginary' forms of thinking are ones that are desirable but unrealistic because, for example, they include a contradiction or its converse: a tautology. Thus, according to the EU in general and Michel Barnier (the chief EU negotiator), membership of the Single Market cannot be combined with non-EU immigration controls (this is because of the principle of Freedom of Movement, enshrined in

Maastricht and previous treaties). Yet at different times, both Conservative and Labour politicians (including the leader of the former party) have indicated that such controls can be implemented (Elgot, 2017). Barnier and the EU have also stated clearly that a European country cannot have the same trade advantages outside of the Customs Union as within it (Browne, 2017). Nevertheless, the British Brexit negotiators have presented a position paper suggesting that a different customs agreement might be agreed that has the benefits of the customs union but isn't it (Roberts, 2017). Both the wish for unique British immigration controls and a customs union that is both inside and outside the EU are imaginary constructions *par excellence*.

'Real' forms of thinking – and action – 'act out' ideal wishes in a pathological way, all the time being incapable of making pragmatic compromises that might involve a loss but achieve an acceptable resolution. It's arguable that David Cameron's decision to call a referendum on EU membership was just this. He hoped to unite his party and the country over Europe and only ended up demonstrating how divided it is. His assertion that a plebiscite might deliver a reasoned and agreed democratic decision and his eventual resignation when this error was realised can be seen as having acted out an ideal and impossible wish 'in the Real'.

'Symbolic' forms of thinking are ones that do recognise fantasies and contradictions and can symbolise them as such. They are, in many ways, the goal of Lacanian psychoanalysis. A properly symbolised understanding of Brexit would involve a recognition that Single Market membership and immigration controls *are* incompatible; that one cannot be within and without the Single Market and the Customs Union at the same time. Symbolic formulations would also acknowledge that such aims are impossible and ideal and cannot be implemented without revision or loss. Non-membership of the single market and/or the customs union would necessitate a diminution of both GDP and wealth. Membership would mean loss of immigration controls. Symbolic articulations would acknowledge that both membership and non-membership of the EU involve a cost. Symbolic pronouncements are rare amongst both government and opposition ministers but can sometimes be heard by dissenters in both parties (Chukka Umunna and Ken Clarke are examples).

Resolution

From a psychoanalytic point of view a Symbolic approach to the problem of Brexit would obviously be the recommended one. Yet as I intimated at the beginning of this chapter, this is easier said than done. Psychoanalysis is not easy or cheap, and it tends to take a long time. If there is to be a satisfactory resolution to the problem of Brexit, it seems unlikely that it will come before the official deadline for Britain's exit from the EU. Ultimately history will decide how Brexit plays out, and retrospectively that may not so much look like agreement or choice so much as eventuality or fate.

Bibliography

Browne, R. *UK Cannot Leave Single Market and Keep All Its Benefits, EU Chief Negotiator Says* (CNBC, 6 July 2017). Available at: www.cnbc.com/2017/07/06/uk-cannot-leave-single-market-and-keep-all-its-benefits-eu-chief-negotiator.html

Butler, J. (1999). *Gender Trouble*. London: Routledge, 1990.

Elgot, J. (2017). Labour Would Leave Single Market, Says Jeremy Corbyn. *The Guardian*, 23 July 2017.

Emmerson, C. *Brexit and the UK's Public Finances* (Institute for Fiscal Studies Report 116, May 2016).

Financial Times. (2015a). Labour's Pains: 8 Areas Where the Party Is Divided, 29 September 2015.

Financial Times. (2015b). CBI Pushes to Stay in Single Market Until Brexit Deal Sealed, 6 July 2017.

Freud, S. (1976). *The Interpretation of Dreams*, trans. James Strachey. Harmondsworth: Penguin, 1900.

'The Unconscious' (1984), trans. James Strachey in *On Metapsychology, the Theory of Psychoanalysis*. Harmondsworth: Penguin, 1915.

'Beyond the Pleasure Principle' (1984), trans. James Strachey in *On Metapsychology*. Harmondsworth, Penguin, 1920.

Freud, S. and Breuer, J. (1984). *Studies on Hysteria*. Strachey. Harmondsworth: Penguin, 1895.

Gillborn, D. (2015). Intersectionality, Critical Race Theory, and the Primacy of Racism. *Qualitative Enquiry*, 21 (3).

Greer, G. (2009). *The Female Eunuch*. London: Harper Collins, 1970.

Grigg, R. (1999). *The Early Psychoanalytic Controversies*. London: Rebus Press.

House of Lords Select Committee on Economic Affairs. (2008). *The Economic Impact of Immigration*. London: The Stationery Office Limited.

Hymovitz, K.S. Can Democrats Make Nice with 'The Deplorables'? *National Review*, 14 July 2017.

Kojève, A. (1980). *Introduction to the Reading of Hegel*. ed. Allen Bloom, trans. James H. Nichols, Jr. Ithaca: Cornell University Press, 1969.

Lacan, J. (2005). *Écrits, The First Complete Edition in English* (EC), trans. Bruce Fink. New York: Norton, 1966.

Marcuse, H. (1991). *One-Dimensional Man*. London: Routledge, 1964.

Morgan, D. How Psychoanalysis Can Help Us Make Sense of Brexit. *LSE Weblog*. Available at: http://blogs.lse.ac.uk/politicsandpolicy/how-psychoanalysis-can-help-us-make-sense-of-brexit/

Murray, M. (2016). *Jacques Lacan: A Critical Introduction*. London: Pluto.

Nagle, A. (2017). *Kill All Normies: Online Culture Wars From 4Chan and Tumblr to Trump and the Alt-Right*. Winchester, UK: Zer0, 2017.

Nietzsche, F. (1989). *On The Genealogy of Morals*, trans. Walter Kaufman. New York: Vintage, 1887.

Roberts, D. UK Will 'Mirror' Much of EU Customs System for Brexit, Plans Reveal. *The Guardian*, 15 August, 2017.

Sartre, J.P. (1996). *Being and Nothingness*, trans. Hazel. E. Barnes. London: Routledge, 1943.

Williams, J.C. (2016). What So Many People Don't Get About the U.S. Working Class. *Harvard Business Review*, 10 November 2016.

Žižek, S. (1989). *The Sublime Object of Ideology*. London: Verso.

13

BREXIT AND THE IMAGINATION

Gabriel Josipovici

The world we live in, as Wallace Stevens never tired of saying, is the world of our imagination. The world of the happy man is different from the world of the unhappy man, as Wittgenstein put it. But the world we imagine also shapes the world we leave to our children. Imagine a mean and angry world and you create a mean and angry world. Imagine an open and generous world and there is more chance that this is what will be passed on to your children.

How we imagine the world is in part the result of our histories. That is why any account of how I see Britain and the world at this moment has to start with where I come from.

I was born in Nice in 1940 to Jewish parents born in Egypt, who had come to France to study and then settled there, in Vence. We survived, though my parents separated during the war, and at the end of it my mother returned to Egypt with me. Since I only spoke French she sent me to the French *lycée* but was horrified by the excess of homework even a five-year-old was getting, and so she took me out and sent me to an English school instead. She herself had had an English nanny when she was small, although her Russian-Jewish father and Italian-Jewish mother spoke French at home, and she and my aunt were brought up bilingual and had always had a love of

English literature. After primary school I went to the local English school, Victoria College, Cairo, so that when, from the age of fourteen or so, we discussed my future, university in England figured largely. Thus it was that at fifteen, in the late summer of 1956, two months before the Suez crisis turned into that brief and shameful war, we found ourselves docking at Folkestone. My mother had decided there was no future for either of us in Egypt and, much against the advice of her sister and her friends, sold the property she had there, spirited out the money and hoped to settle, with me, in England. I had a letter from the school I was going to attend for a year, in order, we hoped, to do well enough in my A-levels to obtain a State Scholarship to an English university, so I was ushered through customs without a problem, but my mother was only given month's visa, in order to see me settled (I had obtained a place as a day-boy in a school where my headmaster in Egypt had previously been head), and told that if she wished to stay she could apply to the Home Office. So there we were, on 13 September 1956, on a train to Gloucester, where my former history teacher, who was now teaching at the Cathedral school, had kindly offered to put us up till we could find somewhere to live. A year later, my mother had, after much difficulty, obtained residence for a year and was then granted another year, though not allowed to work, and I had obtained the State Scholarship and a place for the following year at an Oxford college. We decided to move to London and rented an unfurnished flat in Putney at £10 a month 'plus furniture and fittings', as things were done in those days. It looked as if we could start to think of ourselves as permanently settled in England, and indeed five years later we applied for and were granted British nationality. A year or two after that I was offered a post at the newly formed University of Sussex, where I remained till I took early retirement in 1998.

I describe all this because how I subsequently came to view Britain's entry into the EU and the result of the recent Brexit referendum is inevitably conditioned by my prior relationship to this country, and if I have anything to contribute to an examination of what has happened it will be not despite of but because of the relative uniqueness of my personal history. Indeed, it will form part and parcel of that history, and for that reason I need to go on talking in this personal vein.

Oxford was everything I could have wished for. I had inspiring teachers and made important friendships, notably with the composer Gordon Crosse, the music scholar at my college, and the philosopher John Mepham, who was reading biochemistry at Magdalen. But it was only when I got to the University of Sussex that I began, at long last, I realised, to feel truly at home. Oxford, I now saw, though it had provided me with exactly what I wanted, was still, through its college system, basically an Anglican institution and a fairly hierarchical one at that. Sussex, the first of the new universities of the sixties, was aggressively secular (its rather anodyne motto, 'Be Still and Know', only the truncated first half of the Psalmist's phrase, 'Be still and know that the Lord is God') and wonderfully democratic. The Founding Fathers, Asa Briggs, David Daiches, Martin Wight, would eagerly attend seminars presented by the most junior members not in order to monitor them but to learn, and Daiches insisted the senior members of the English Subject Group teach the first-year courses, because, he said, it's those students who need the most experienced teachers. But what made it feel so comfortable for me was the fact that I was teaching in the School of European Studies, and what made me feel so proud, in the years that followed, was that I was part of a group that included a pupil of Georg Lukacs and two academics, Edouard Goldstucker, former Rector of Charles University in Prague, and Zev Barbu, a Romanian sociologist of religion, who had been imprisoned by both the Nazis and the Communists.

Growing up in a multi-lingual society in Egypt, with a mother and aunt steeped in French and English literature and for whom no aspect of culture, Eastern or Western, was out of bounds (my aunt was obsessed with Sufism and had an ongoing and alas never-realised project to find the links between Coleridge on the poetic process and Jung on alchemy), I had found it mildly ridiculous to be studying English literature at Oxford divorced from European literature and culture at large and had, fortunately, found tutors ready to put up with my naïve attempts to bring Hölderlin to bear on Keats and Proust on Wordsworth. At Sussex I was encouraged to teach a course on Homer, Virgil and Dante and one on European modernism from Marx and Kierkegaard to Freud, Thomas Mann and Sartre. We were forever thinking up new courses, and, with an Anglican colleague,

Stephen Medcalf, I started a course on the Bible and English literature (at Oxford we had always been told that it was impossible to
understand English literature before 1900 without a sound grasp of
the Bible, but no-one thought to inculcate that), and both Stephen
and I attended classes on Biblical Hebrew given by a new colleague,
Michael Wadsworth, an Anglican priest and a semiticist who had
recently completed an Oxford thesis under Geza Vermes.

I had come to understand, at Oxford and then at Sussex, that there
was no use pretending to be English. I was European, born in France,
enamoured of Dante and Eliot, beholden, as a writer of fiction, to the
struggles of Kafka and Thomas Mann. But a return to Egypt, the result
of winning a travelling award, the Somerset Maugham Prize, for my
first collection of stories and short plays, *Mobius the Stripper* (1974),
and my immersion in the Hebrew Bible in recent years had made me
realise that I differed from my English friends, however strong their
European interests, by the fact that I had roots in the Middle East. The
Bible had begun to fascinate me partly as the repository of stories
about people I felt to be aunts and uncles and partly because of the
extraordinary directness of its style, the way it told its stories through
a mixture of pared-down narration and dialogue, leaving us to work
out the motives and desires of the speakers. This form of writing was
what I had long admired in the writing of Marguerite Duras and
which I had employed since writing my first novel, *The Inventory*, and
it was startling to find it there, perfectly wrought, in stories set down
at least two and a half thousand years ago.

In other words, settling into the University of Sussex as it was in
the sixties and seventies I felt that I had at last truly come home. In
those optimistic days we all of us felt that redrawing the map of learning, as the Founding Fathers put it, could have a genuine influence
on the direction the country and its culture was going. We would
help a generation of students to realise that England was part of a
bigger whole and that its fortunes were intimately connected with
those of Europe, of America (there was a school of American studies) and of Asia and Africa (there was a school of Asian and African
studies). Britain's joining the EU in 1972 merely confirmed us in
our sense that we were on the right track. New links with European
institutions, both in the sciences and in the humanities, reinforced

the interdisciplinary thinking that was at the heart of the University, and the influx of European students on Erasmus scholarships, from Greece, Italy, Spain, Belgium, Holland, Germany and France, seemed like the logical extension of what we and, we felt, the whole country was moving towards.

The arrival of Thatcher in Downing Street was a bitter blow. She stood for everything we felt we had been trying to move away from. The grocer's daughter from Grantham was determined to prove Napoleon right: the English were a nation of shopkeepers – culture, and especially European culture, was dangerously un-English. Jewish Nigel Lawson might have a house in France, but that was only in order to bask in the sun and drink some fine wines. The spirit of meanness and antagonism to all things foreign and all things intellectual and spiritual, which had been a part of the makeup of the English since the Reformation, was encouraged to thrive rather than being allowed – as we had hoped – to slowly wither. In retrospect, the roots of Brexit lie there, in the appalling Thatcher years – in the spirit it encouraged, in its vision of the world and, ironically, in its disastrous embrace of neoliberal economic policies, which created both the hatred of anything un-English and the desperate conditions which led in the nineties to the creation of UKIP and the growing confidence of UKIP-lite Tory MPs, and in the end to the referendum and its result.

Some years ago, in the wake of the enlargement of the EU to twenty-eight members, I was invited by Rob Rieman, the founder and driving force behind the Amsterdam think tank the Nexus Institute, to take part in an unusual seminar. I had done one or two things for Rob, and he rang me one day with a proposition. Holland is the current Chair of the EU, he explained to me, and I have been asked by the prime minister's office if I would put together a series of seminars under the general rubric of the enlarged EU and the future of education, at the end of which I would report back a summary of our conclusions. He went on to explain that he had replied that he would enjoy that very much but was not prepared to do it unless he could get a commitment from each country that they would send someone to the seminars from each Department of Education or of Development. This had now been given, and he was at the stage of planning. He wondered if I would take part in a seminar to be held in Berlin on the topic. I explained to him that though I thought it was a great idea, I was not an educationalist and could not see that I would have anything to contribute. On the contrary, said Rob, we are inviting historians, social scientists, lawyers, students of international relations, and we would very much like you to take part. Have you any thoughts at all on the subject?

I'd need to think about it, I hedged. No, Rob said, give me some thoughts now. I had been reading Michelle Brown's wonderful book, *The Lindisfarne Gospels: Society, Spirituality and the Scribe* (Brown, 2010), and had been struck by the way, as she described it, the isolated community of monks on the north-east coast of England in the eighth century had in fact been part of a vast Christian community, with links not just to Iona in Scotland and the Irish houses but also to Trier, Cologne, Rome, Byzantium, Syria and Egypt. And I recalled a radio programme I had recently heard in which the mayors of (I think) Barcelona and Milan, Lille and Hamburg talked about the links they wanted to forge with each other rather than always go through their respective central governments and capitals. Partly to tease Rob I said: I suppose I could talk about medieval monasticism as a model for the educational future of the enlarged EU. This would imply that links should be forged not between country and country but between city and city, with the concomitant emphasis on what the cities have in common and pride in civic achievements rather than fear of what separates them and the desire to put up borders. To my surprise Rob said, 'Yes, yes, Gabriel. That is good, that is a very good proposal. You will talk for twenty minutes. I will send you all the details on email'.

So I found myself in Berlin with a fascinating group of people, including representatives from the education departments of, if not all twenty-eight countries, at least a good proportion of them, putting forward my provocative thesis. To my surprise I found it fitted in with the kind of thinking many of those taking part were keen to explore.

Sadly, no British representatives will be present at future seminars of this kind. And if Le Pen and Orban and Beppe Grillo have their way, there will be no future, educational or otherwise, for the EU.

When I think about what has happened all over the world in the past few years, the populists and dictators who have come to power by fair means or foul in Egypt, Syria, Russia, America, Turkey and elsewhere, I am forced to conclude that the bulk of my life was passed in a world which seemed to have suffered so appallingly through two world wars that it wanted to put all that behind it and see if a future free of war and repression could be created. Optimism was the order of the day, as one ex-colony after another shook off the yoke of colonial oppression and the rich Western powers looked back on the Nazi years and swore, 'Never again'. But it seems as if we were too optimistic. As the horrors of the war receded, as indigenous dictators took over in the place of the colonial powers, it has become clear that greed and fear are always present and can be activated by the unscrupulous at any time. With the spectre of a totalitarian takeover of the world looming, the hero of Borges's 'Tlön, Uqbar, Orbis Tertius' retreats to the country to immerse himself in what he describes as 'an uncertain Quevedian translation (which I do not intend to publish)' of Sir Thomas Browne's *Urne Burial*. This makes a fine ending to a chilling story, but it is too passive for my liking. Those of us who do not believe that the only spirit is the spirit of fear, meanness and greed need to keep speaking out not to denounce it but to present readers and listeners (if there are any left) with a vision of other possibilities. Those possibilities are embedded in our universities, and these need to find the will to go on articulating them. Otherwise the country I came to with such high hopes more than half a century ago will indeed become a nation of shopkeepers and nothing more.

Bibliography

Brown, M. (2003). *The Lindisfarne Gospels: Society, Spirituality and the Scribe*. London: The British Library.

Josipovici, G. (1974). *Mobius the Stripper: Stories and Short Plays*. London: Victor Gollancz.

14

THE LOST NOMAD OF EUROPE

Eva Aldea

"Why is it so difficult to imagine a post-nationalist Europe?" asks Rosi Braidotti in a piece written just after Trump's election victory (Braidotti, 2016). She is reflecting on the events of that year revealing a rise in right-wing populism beyond the imagination of those who believed that the world was becoming a more open place. Five years earlier, Braidotti had described the European Union as a laboratory in which a new model of non-national citizenship could be developed based on the idea of the nomadic subject which "actively constructs itself in a complex and internally contradictory set of social relations" (Braidotti, 2011).

The nomadic subject rests on Deleuze and Guattari's distinction between the nomadic and the sedentary. The terms are not predicated on the actual movement of a subject but on its relationship to place. A sedentary subject is rooted in a specific territory, its identity defined by origins. If he or she moves to another territory they become a migrant. A nomadic subject, in contrast, whether they move or not, relates to land as a route rather than a root. The nomad's identity is affected and influenced by their journey, physical or not, but it is not defined by a particular place. It is important to note that the sedentary subject tends to connect to fellow subjects in a hierarchical or filial way, branching out from the roots firmly planted in the land, while the nomadic subject favours the famous rhizomatic structure of the network, rootless and global. To me this is key: the ability to make continual and multiple connections is what makes a nomad, not physical movement as such. It is this openness to connections that allows a subject to "actively construct itself" in complex ways, continually.

Moving from being a sedentary subject to a nomadic one is not easy, however. Braidotti warned that fear, anxiety and nostalgia were part of the process of "dis-identification from established, nation-bound points of reference" but suggested that a praxis of material situatedness, of thinking locally and taking accountability for collective and private history could be the pathway to overcoming what she saw at the time as "the staggering absence of . . . a European imaginary" (Braidotti, 2011).

Brexit made it clear that fear, anxiety and nostalgia had won the day in Britain. It has always been obvious that the British imaginary space has never been fully aligned with that of the continent, but nevertheless for many of us the referendum result came as a shock. Why did so many people reject years of established cooperation and exchange for an uncertain future promise of sovereignty and border control? What does Brexit mean for the European Union as a project for a different kind of relationship to citizenship and place? What hope does the nomadic subject have of surviving in a Britain that goes it alone?

Since Braidotti's nomadic theory specifically calls for a local, situated perspective, I will attempt to answer these questions from such a position. The two main aspects of my own point of view are my national background and my education. My nationality is one of circumstance, and my sense of national belonging is only partially related to the passport in my pocket. My education is closely imbricated with my mixed-up national heritage and directly connected to the place I currently reside in. My family were deeply affected by the last century's wars in Europe, actual and cold. My Polish mother met my Romanian father on holiday at the Black Sea. Their first language of communication was, of course, English. Both had had a long education, partially in English, she in medicine, he in fine arts. For a time they lived in Romania, but my free-thinking papa fell foul of the authorities, and they moved to Poland, where I was born. A baby concentrated their minds on attempting to make a better life on the other side of the Iron Curtain, and they sought asylum in Sweden. After five stateless years, we gained Swedish citizenship. However, my parents remained committed Anglophiles as well as prolific readers. To them, English represented freedom, the Anglo-Saxon West had liberated Europe once, and in their youth Radio Free Europe promised it would do so again. Britain in particular, where the exile government of Poland resided for fifty years, was, in their imaginations, the seat of democracy and justice. The stories they read with most joy and relish, and that they passed on to me, were mostly written by Brits. I realise now that those were often stories in which migration was not an act of loss but of adventure and conquest. Not unproblematically, our own familial narrative of movement was always couched in such terms, making me eager for my own journeys.

I had just reached voting age when Sweden held a referendum on whether to join the European Union or not in November 1994. I voted yes, crossed my fingers, and in less than a year I took up my place to study English literature at a university in the United Kingdom. My tuition fees were paid by the Local Education Authority, just like every other British student's fees, under the principle of equal treatment of citizens of EU member states and nationals.

More than twenty years later, I call London my home. What Brexit means for my status here, I, like millions of other EU citizens residing in the UK, have no idea. My situation is further complicated by a recent spell of residence in Singapore. It all comes down to "exercising my treaty rights" as citizen of an EU member state. By moving from one member state to another, this exercise starts, contingent on work, study, self-employment or self-sufficiency. Contrary to popular belief, without fulfilling these conditions, a citizen of one European member state can only reside in another freely for three months.

Permanent residency status in another EU state must be applied for and is only due after five continuous years of exercising treaty rights. I was not even aware that this status existed or needed formal application during my first almost twenty years in the UK. Brexit was only a whisper, dismissed as an impossibility, in those days. Now, after a couple of years abroad, I am in a situation in which I have started exercising my treaty rights again, but the UK will leave the Union before my five continuous years are completed.

Whatever my personal status ends up becoming, this anecdote highlights a point about citizenship of the European Union that is key. Despite Braidotti's best wishes it is not a post-national citizenship. Far from it.

When she designates it a laboratory for the nomadic subject, Braidotti stresses that the European Union has its origins in the defeat of fascism and Nazism in World War II and at its heart a movement towards antinationalism (Braidotti, 2011). However, the Union also grew out of an economic cooperation centred on national self-interest first (Closa Montero, 2001). The political structures of the Union reflect this duality, and the question of citizenship is a case in point. While freedom of movement of people is one of the four pillars of union membership (together with goods, services and capital – notably all economic activities), it is predicated on *national* and not pan-European citizenship. You only gain the right of movement across borders through your national belonging. You cannot gain European citizenship without gaining citizenship of a member state. You belong to a nation first.

At the same time, the rights conferred by this citizenship are protected by the European Union rather than by the member states and thus only kick in if you exercise your treaty rights by moving across a European national border (Lehning, 2001). The most famous example is perhaps the residency rights of a non-EU spouse to a citizen of an EU state. While your citizenship in a particular EU member state may not allow your spouse residency, if you and your beloved live in *another* EU country for a consecutive period, your non-EU spouse acquires the rights of permanent residency in that EU state, and therefore all other EU states, under European Union Law.

This means that at the heart of the European project lies a notion of citizenship that is contradictory and one which complicates the creation of a nomadic subjectivity on at least two counts. EU citizenship, to be fully enjoyed, requires both national belonging and physical movement away from your nation. It thus fosters a sedentary subjectivity in its approach to citizenship at the same time as denying those who stay in place full participation. It differentiates those who move from those who stay. It gives privileges to migrants that are not necessarily conferred on nationals, driving a wedge through the centre of any sense of European belonging.

This is why it is so hard to imagine a post-nationalist Europe, because if you are not a migrant, there is less reason to become a nomad in the European context. The European laboratory has worked great for us who have been forced or have chosen to move across borders, those of us who have already been invested in the nomadic way of life.

That I identify with the nomadic subject is no surprise. To me it makes more sense – I have never felt that I belonged to a nation. In Sweden I was an immigrant kid, back in Poland, the girl who grew up in the West. Romania remained a land of myth and horrors. It is in my active choice of abode that I feel most at home, and I would like to think that I have added some of the better British traits to my "contradictory set of social relations". However, my home is London, and it would be deluded to think this is a representative part of this nation. London is a nomadic node, a point on the journey of millions; it welcomes those who pass through and those who wish to stay. In its very structure as a modern metropolis London entertains contradictions and enables or perhaps enforces connections. Connections again are crucial: to the nomadic subjectivity but also to why Britain voted leave. Remember, none of the votes cast in the referendum were by those who, like me, call the United Kingdom home but belong, on paper, elsewhere.

Much has been made of why Britain voted the way it did. Age, class and the city–country divide were the clear fault lines between leave and remain voters. It is now common knowledge that the older, the poorer and those outside the large cities tended to vote leave, while the younger, richer and more urban voted remain.

However, a closer look reveals something more interesting behind these demographics. The most significant statistical indicator for vote was not income, age or place but level of education. A report by the Joseph Rowntree Foundation notes that 75% of those lacking qualifications voted leave, but only 27% of those with the highest level of education did so, a larger spread than for any other variable

(Goodwin and Heath, 2017). Clearly education is directly correlated with age, class and community, but it is in the education that the crux lies, not in the lack of money or specific location.

One way of interpreting this data is through the usual idea of the "winners and losers" of globalisation. Education brings with it the skills necessary to flourish in a late capitalist global economy. There has been a lot of talk of those "left behind" by globalisation. However, Goodwin and Heath also note that educational attainment correlates with social attitudes – people with high levels of education tend to be more socially liberal and more open to immigration. Why is this so?

Partly it seems to do with life opportunities and a sense of control. Studies have shown how perceived lack of control over one's life and surroundings correlates with more conservative attitudes and even ethnocentrism (Agroskin, 2010). Clearly economic situation, individual and communal, as well as education are central to a sense of control.

Partly, however, it is also a matter of socialization, that is, of connections. Simply put, people meet other people in education, face to face or through their ideas. Education is one of the most important, if not the most important, opportunities for networking an individual has. It opens up avenues partly due to skills gained and partly, as we in Britain are painfully aware of, through the connections you make. Yet it isn't the "Old Boys' Club" I am interested in here, but simply the number of interactions a person makes through education. Good education exposes you to other people and other views. It is through education, the exchange of ideas, knowledge and language, that people can become nomads – even without moving.

The Demos report on the rise of right-wing populism in Europe "Nothing to Fear but Fear Itself?" makes a striking observation about the referendum voters and is worth considering at length:

> Our analysis finds that those who had socialised with someone who lives in a different town or city in the last six months were 9 percentage points less likely to vote Leave than those who had not. Similarly, those who had socialised with someone from a different part of Britain in the last six months were

10 percentage points less likely to vote to leave than those who had not. Those who had socialised with someone who lives in a different country in the last six months were 15 percentage points less likely to vote to leave than those who had not. Crucially, this is the case controlling for all of our demographic and local area variables – including income, age, whether rural or urban, and local deprivation.

(Gaston and Harrison-Evans, 2017)

I am not denying that economic prospects are an important factor here but suggesting that it isn't money-making capabilities per se that are crucial but the opportunities for human interaction and exchange that such capabilities often, but not always, correlate with. Cities, in particular university cities, despite often including a large proportion of less-well-off people, tended to vote remain. But even more than urbanization, education is key: it allows for those non-physical journeys that open minds and connect people.

The tragedy is that Brexit is likely to shut down opportunities for connections. David Runciman sees the divide between remainers and leavers as one between those who live in a networked world and those who don't. He points out that Brexit will do little to change that:

People who are rooted in particular places, who work in industries that produce physical goods, and whose essential social interactions do not happen online are the ones who wanted Out. They have glimpsed a future in which people like them are increasingly at the mercy of forces beyond their power to control. And they are right.

(Runciman, 2016)

Brexit will not return a sense of control to these groups. Runciman notes that there are few institutions that have stood up to global conglomerates like the EU, citing the case of Google. Add to that the various workers' rights and protections, and yes, the reviled human rights. Finally, consider the loss of opportunities for education and socialisation. Whether Brexit is couched as an opening up for Britain onto the global market or as a return to its own national concerns, it is unlikely to bring benefit to those outside the "networked world".

This is a tragedy indeed, and however it plays out for Britain, it is one that the European Union needs to consider. If antipathy towards the Union in Britain was driven by the lack of connections and education, similar sentiment is felt across the continent, and with similar causes, as noted in the Demos Report. If the European Union as a post-national project is to succeed, it will need to foster the sense of belonging in a nomadic rather than a sedentary sense. Currently it does not, and Brexit is a clear signal that things are awry. A large issue lies with the way that European citizenship is conceived.

However, if Europe is not, after all, the laboratory in which the nomadic subject emerges, it does not mean that the nomadic subject is lost. It is surely even more important in a post-Brexit Britain in particular, whatever shape that may take, to create a society in which people are able to connect to as many of their fellow humans as possible. A strong education system, available to all, is at the heart of such a society. It is what allows a subject to journey and explore, even if she or he does not possess the means, the inclination or the opportunity to travel. It will be crucial for both Britain and Europe.

Bibliography

Agroskin, D., and Jonas, E. (2010). Out of control: how and why does perceived lack of control lead to ethnocentrism? *Review of Psychology*, 17 (2). Available at: http://hrcak.srce.hr/file/105207 [Accessed 3 September 2017].

Braidotti, R. (2011). *Nomadic Theory: The Portable Rosi Braidotti*. New York: Columbia University Press.

Braidotti, R. (2016). *Don't Agonize, Organize. E-Flux Conversations*. Available at: https://conversations.e-flux.com/t/rosi-braidotti-don-t-agonize-organize/5294 [Accessed 2 September 2017].

Closa Montero, C. (2001). Between EU Constitution and Individuals' Self: European Citizenship. *Law and Philosophy*, 20 (3), pp. 345–71.

Gaston, S., and Harrison-Evans, P. (2017). *Nothing to Fear but Fear Itself? Demos*. Available at: www.demos.co.uk/wp-content/uploads/2017/04/DEMJ5104_nothing_to_fear_report_140217_WEBv2.pdf [Accessed 5 September 2017].

Goodwin, M., and Heath, O. (2016). Brexit Vote Explained: Poverty, Low Skills and Lack of Opportunities. *Joseph Rowntree Foundation*. Available at: www.jrf.org.uk/report/brexit-vote-explained-poverty-low-skills-and-lack-opportunities [Accessed 4 September 2017].

Lehning, P.B. (2001). European Citizenship: Towards a European Identity. *Law and Philosophy*, 20 (3), pp. 239–82.

Runciman, D. (2016). A Win for "Proper People"? Brexit as a Rejection of the Networked World? *Juncture*, 23 (1), pp. 4–7.

15

RESEARCHING BRITAIN AND EUROPE, THEN AND NOW

Ann-Marie Einhaus

Writing on Britain's relationship to Europe is of great personal importance to me. Originally from Germany, I have been living in the UK since 2007, and like many others in my position, I feel profoundly European. But as my current research constantly reminds me, close ties between European nations are by no means something we can take for granted. I have been working on literary and cultural responses to the First World War for years, and recently my work has turned to British and German magazines in the inter-war period and Second World War. The literary past of the early twentieth century thus acts as a constant reminder to me of how hard won positive European relations in the present are and how fragile trans-European collaboration is. This short chapter reflects on the parallels between the early twentieth century and the present with regard to British engagement with European cultural identity.

My research work centres on British and German literary periodicals between roughly 1910 and 1945, specifically on debates around and definitions of European cultural identity in this period. As Mark Hewitson and Matthew D'Auria have argued, during the inter-war period:

> Defining and understanding the "European soul" became
> central in all cultural and intellectual milieux; far from being

mere intellectual quarrels, such debates stemmed, on the contrary, from the immediate need to banish the risk of a new war
and, more fundamentally, from the urge to avoid the complete
destruction of European civilization.

(Hewitson and D'Auria, 2012, 2015: 1)

Though I first embarked on this research before the EU referendum was held, the referendum has caused this research to feel ever
more relevant as the Brexit negotiations are unfolding. The concerns
that exercised the pens and typewriters of British contributors to literary periodicals during and between the two world wars often recall
present-day concerns. Like in the 1920s and 1930s, present-day anxieties over Britain's place in Europe and the state of the European
Union are tied up with fears about future peace and prosperity.

Just like contemporary newspapers and magazines, periodicals in
Britain during and between the world wars reflected on Britain's
relationship to Europe constantly. Political developments, particularly
the Treaty of Versailles and its ongoing renegotiations, were rarely out
of the papers and were given considerable space even in periodicals
whose remit was largely cultural or literary. The emerging League
of Nations was hotly debated in the periodical press between the
wars. Some, such as the writers and journalists Vera Brittain and Wini-
fred Holtby, saw the League of Nations as a guarantor of a peaceful
future – perhaps flawed, certainly in its failure to represent women
on an equal footing with men (as some of their regular contributions
to feminist weekly *Time and Tide* argued; see Brittain, 1929), but nevertheless the best means available. Others, including the controversial
writer, artist and polemicist Wyndham Lewis, saw the League and
its privileging of the winners of the First World War as a possible
cause for future war and/or deplored the role of industry and capital
in forging European ties ahead of political approval (see particularly
Lewis, 1936: 32–3).

While there is much with which I disagree in Lewis's political
thought, I tend to agree with his pronouncement, in *Time and Western
Man* (1927), that 'Western Man, as such, is of course the completest
myth' (quoted in Gasiorek, 2004: 129). If we assume that there is
such a thing as a European spirit, culture or unified identity, we are
always confronted with the problem of generalisation and exclusion:

who do we include in these definitions, and what criteria do we apply? Many scholars before me have pointed out, in Gerard Delanty's words, that 'the idea of a European identity' too often relies on a problematic 'ethno-culturalism' that fails to acknowledge wider links between East and West and between white and non-white peoples and cultures (Delanty, 1995: viii). Neither Christianity nor classical antiquity – both seen to be bonds of tantamount importance by many inter-war commentators, not least T. S. Eliot – are adequate foundations for a contemporary sense of European identity, as such constructions ignore the complex makeup of Europe, its relationship to non-European cultures and the shifting alliances even between what we might call Western European nations.

What I do subscribe to, however, is the idea that literature and culture can help bridge divides and create a sense of European identity with the potential to accommodate greater diversity. The ability of literature, art and music to transcend nationalism and build bridges between different European (and indeed non-European) nations and peoples is a recurring theme in inter-war periodicals, and it surfaces time and again. This belief in social and political rapprochement via shared cultural appreciation resonates just as much today as it did in the 1920s and 1930s. It is a belief exemplified in Mathias Énard's 2015 novel *Boussole*, published in English translation as *Compass* in 2017. *Compass* offers an extended reflection on the links between Europe and the East, based on the central characters' exploration of the centuries-old cross-pollination between Western and Eastern music and literature. It is not surprising that, besides winning the prestigious Prix Goncourt, *Compass* was also awarded the 2017 Buchpreis zur Europäischen Verständigung (Book Prize for Mutual European Understanding), introduced by the city of Leipzig in 1994. In his acceptance speech, Énard (2017) stressed that he wrote his novel to remind his readers of the Eastern origins of Europe and to pitch a narrative of hope against exclusionism and a sense of antagonism between (Western) Europe and the East.

The timeliness of Énard's novel (and its translation into English and German) resonates with my own current research on the significance of literature as a mediator between cultures in inter-war Europe – Énard's novelistic project can be linked to an understanding of literature and culture promoted by canonical writers such as

T. S. Eliot, André Gide and Stefan Zweig, as well as many of their lesser known contemporaries. The feminist British weekly *Time and Tide* – lately the subject of my research – saw literature and culture as crucial mediators between European nations, and its regular contributor, the author, journalist and suffragist Cicely Hamilton, argued in 1924 that art could accomplish what organised peace movements were unlikely to achieve by not acknowledging the gulf between nations but 'ignoring its existence':

> it is no mere coincidence that the artist – the worker whose thoughts and labours cannot be organised and broken to system – has of all men the strongest and widest international influence. The spirit that expresses itself in his work overleaps the barriers of space and race – because it obeys its own laws of the spirit, not the laws framed by potentates and parliaments. The artist has a country but his work – so it be true enough – has none; the love of a hillside or a village street, translated into terms of colour or song, may travel half around the globe.
>
> (Hamilton, 1924: 101–2)

While it is easy to see music and visual art, both broadly non-verbal forms of cultural expression, as transcending cultural boundaries with ease, the transnational potential of literature relies on either translation or the learning of foreign languages. As art critic Clemence Dane pointed out in a 1921 review, faced with the question of what beauty is, 'all the literatures break into a babel of explanation', whereas artists can provide a silent yet eloquent answer (Dane, 1921: 210). To resolve the 'babel of explanation', language learning and (literary) translation were the subject of recurring debates in inter-war periodicals. The idea that the English are particularly bad at learning foreign languages is clearly nothing new, as a *Time and Tide* article in 1925 observed that '[o]f all people the English have perhaps suffered the most heavily from [. . .] dumbness, and only the tactful cleverness of foreigners in learning English has saved us from deserved isolation' ('Review of the Week', 1925: 3). Attempts to persuade native speakers of English to learn other languages continue in the present amidst ever-sinking numbers of students opting to study languages, and the most moving plea for language learning in recent years has come from an author, John Le Carré (the pseudonym of David Cornwell) in an article for the *Guardian* Education section in July 2017. In the perhaps most quoted passage, Le Carré argued that

> The decision to learn a foreign language is to me an act of friendship. It is indeed a holding out of the hand. It's not just a route to negotiation. It's also to get to know you better, to draw closer to you and your culture, your social manners and your way of thinking. And the decision to teach a foreign language is an act of commitment, generosity and mediation.
>
> (Le Carré, 2017)

While *Time and Tide* stressed the importance of language learning as a means of promoting transnational understanding in general terms, language learning was also more specifically seen as essential for the appreciation of foreign literatures. In the opening contribution to the first number of Eliot's *Criterion*, George Saintsbury pointed out, by the bye, the merits of learning foreign languages to enable readers to appreciate foreign literary texts in the original, in talking about a 'man of letters' who 'made himself able to read Dante *in* Italian, and read him; and there was no more disappointment that day or any other thenceforward' (Saintsbury, 1922: 12).

The *Criterion* (and other periodicals) recognised, however, that not everyone would be able to copy Saintsbury's polyglot man of letters and learn multiple languages and offered its readers plenty of foreign literature and criticism in translation. The regular 'Foreign Reviews' of periodicals from abroad in each issue of the *Criterion* further opened up literary and cultural events abroad to a primarily English readership. Across Europe, literary and cultural periodicals were doing the same, and though national tastes might vary, the canonical Great White Males (Cervantes, Dante, Dostoyevsky, Goethe, Molière and Shakespeare, first and foremost) were championed as shared European cultural property. Goethe in particular was regularly invoked as a proponent of European identity. In 1943, in the midst of the Second World War, Stephen Spender argued in the pages of Cyril Connolly's magazine *Horizon* that Germany could only be re-educated by means of its own literary and cultural heritage, first and foremost Goethe and Hölderlin, and deplored the lack of knowledge of German culture in Britain (Spender, 1943: 273–80).

Literature, then, was seen as a negotiator between peoples and cultures even in times of extreme crisis. But even well before the start of the Second World War, the International Federation of University Women had got together to compile a list 'of the books which it thought most characteristic of its national life and spirit and ideals' for each of the twenty-three participating countries. On this undertaking, *Time and Tide* commented:

> It has been suggested that nobody can learn to understand another country through its literature. Books? What are books? How can they explain the hot, electric, exciting climate of the Transvaal; the enervating, moist, rich, malarial atmosphere of a Peruvian forest town; the harsh, bracing ardours of a Scandinavian landscape? [. . .] What does Jane Austen tell us of the industrial revolution and the expanding empire which made England what she was at the beginning of the nineteenth century? Even if nationality were to be explained by geography, race or political and economic organisation, we could hope at least to learn something of the characteristics and effects of these influences through books; but in truth literature has much more than information to offer us about life. [. . .] A literature does not only reveal what the nation is; it provides one of the influences which have made it become so. Plato banished drama from his Republic, knowing that letters not only copy life, but that life copies letters.
>
> ('Life and Literature', 1928: 888)

This is a view that many of us, I feel, are still happy to share today – literature may never have prevented war when push came to shove, but it has certainly been building many of the bridges that have prepared the way for peace. And perhaps literature can also help us reconcile our differences in the present: reading Adam Thorpe's novel *Missing Fay* (2017), touted as one of the first 'BrexLit' novels besides Ali Smith's *Autumn* (2016), it did strike me that novels such as Thorpe's have the capacity to make us understand one another a little better. Some of his characters hold views abhorrent to most pro-Europeans; others – like Romanian immigrant Cosmina – embody the trans-European mobility that British citizens may be on the verge

of losing.Yet Thorpe manages to imbue all of them alike with humanity and invites us to consider their lives and convictions as complex
and worthy of our careful attention. If there is a way of learning from
the rifts of the past, my current research makes me hope that literature
can point the way.

Bibliography

Brittain,Vera. (1929). Feminism at Geneva: II Future Possibilities. *Time and Tide*, 10.5 (1 February 1929), pp. 116–7.

Dane,Clemence.(1921).Nationality in Art. *Time and Tide*, 2.9 (4 March 1921), pp. 208–10.

Delanty, Gerard. (1995). *Inventing Europe: Idea, Identity, Reality*. Basingstoke: Palgrave Macmillan.

Énard, Mathias. (2017). *Dankesrede anlässlich der Verleihung des Leipziger Buchpreises zur Europäischen Verständigung*. Available (in German) at: www.leipzig.de/fileadmin/mediendatenbank/leipzig-de/Stadt/02.4_Dez4_Kultur/41_Kulturamt/Literatur_und_Buchkunst/LBEV/Dankesrede_Mathias_Enard.pdf

Gasiorek, Andrzej. (2004). *Wyndham Lewis and Modernism*. London: Northcote House in association with the British Council.

Hamilton, Cicely. (1924).Art and Internationalism. *Time and Tide*, 5.5 (1 February 1924), pp. 101–2.

Hewitson, Mark and Matthew D'Auria. (eds.) (2015). *Europe in Crisis: Intellectuals and the European Idea, 1917–1957*. New York: Berghahn.

Le Carré,John.Why We Should Learn German. *The Guardian*, 2 July 2017.Available at: www.theguardian.com/education/2017/jul/02/why-we-should-learn-german-john-le-carre

Lewis,Wyndham. (1927). *Time and Western Man*. London: Chatto and Windus.

Lewis,Wyndham. (1936). *Left Wings Over Europe: Or, How to Make a War About Nothing*. London: Jonathan Cape.

Life and Literature. *Time and Tide*, 9.39 (28 September), pp. 887–8.

Review of the Week: The Study of Foreign Languages. *Time and Tide*, 6.1 (2 January 1925), p. 3.

Saintsbury, George. (1922). Dullness. *The Criterion*, 1.1 (October 1922), pp. 1–15.

Smith,Ali. (2016). *Autumn*. London: Hamish Hamilton.

Spender, Stephen. (1943). Hölderlin, Goethe and Germany. *Horizon* 8.46 (October 1943), pp. 273–80.

Thorpe,Adam. (2017). *Missing Fay*. London: Jonathan Cape.

16

BREXIT AND THE GERMAN QUESTION

Simon Glendinning

I

Consider three very intuitive thoughts. First, that the most decisive considerations for UK citizens who voted to leave the European Union were framed in terms of freedom – freedom as a political concept. If any slogan gave voice to Leavers it was "Take back control". Second, and not very distantly related, is an assumption bordering on plain fact that the European Union, however closely identified with the faceless bureaucracy of "Brussels", is dominated by Germany as a de-facto quasi-hegemonic power. And third, that France is caught up in all of this – caught up in it not least because it had initially blocked the UK becoming a member in the first place, and also because its principal motivation for pressing for the development of a transnational organization in Europe after the Second World War was to pacify Germany. These are all recent geopolitical features of the European landscape and concern the sort of things one might read about in an op-ed piece about what is going on in Europe today.

In Europe. It is such a familiar (if vague) territorial outline that it is hard sometimes to remember how bizarre it is that there should be any such outline at all. A little promontory on the western edge of a great landmass: it became "Europe". How did it come to be there? Historians can be more or less one dimensional, more or less mono-genealogical, but part of the business of the historian of Europe is to see how that territorial outline settled where it has (in so far as it has) by tracing the sequence of world-historical events which have brought it (and, for "we, the Europeans", us) where it (and this "we") are today. And in the classic European discourse of Europe's history there really is only one sequence to follow. This (the only) history is: Greek-Roman-Christian-Modern. Nothing could be more European than this history of Europe.

Greek-Roman-Christian-Modern. But surely that (roughly) *is* the history of Europe. Right. Europe has produced itself, called itself to be, by making it so that this history will have been its history.

And yet this European history is not one. This history of Europe's becoming is also the history of its (becoming) nation-states. And these nation-states have each had their own relating of the classic sequence in relation to their own becoming and have done so as ways of relating themselves to themselves as in some way also European. In what follows I want to step back to a time in Europe's history when the Germanic peoples were, for the first time and relatively late in the day, configuring into a national shape. Philosophically this was the time of Nietzsche, and I will take a point of departure from him in order to rush forward again to our own time.

II

In Nietzsche's writings "Europe" comes to name an "unexhausted" promise of its own exhausted past. And this passage to its own "beyond" will make its way, he suggests, through the mechanism of a new hidden hand, a new cunning of reason that belongs within the tidal wave of what he calls "the democratic movement in Europe" that unfolds out of the French Revolution (Nietzsche, 1973: 153). It is into this wave that Nietzsche sends an untimely message in a bottle and a call to the future of a certain friendship of "we good Europeans".

Why Europeans? Why the emphasis on "good Europeans"? In his insistent opposition to the growing nationalist appeal in Germany to "we good Germans", why wouldn't Nietzsche say, simply, "we good *whoevers*"? One might want to excuse Nietzsche by referring to the "context" of his times: the world was not so big then; the horizon for his thinking was European because his world was. But that is nonsense. Nietzsche's work is peppered with non-European references, and often, typically even, with great admiration. Nevertheless, while he asks "What Europe owes the Jews?" (Nietzsche, 1973: 161), he does not stop to ask "What Europe owes the non-European in general?" nor even just the non-European migrants into Europe. Nietzsche certainly thinks that the now-exhausted Europe has been a site of "great things" (Nietzsche, 1973: 13) – but he does not think that Europe has a monopoly on that at all: Asia and Egypt are mentioned in the same breath. So why the limit to thinking the newly cosmopolitan "plant 'Man'" of the future to the indefinite but definitively European *milieu*? Is it white racism? Eurocentric parochialism? Modest pragmatism? My suspicion is that it is none of those. It is above all . . . German.

The German question ("What is Germany?") casts a profoundly determining shadow over Nietzsche's reflections on Europe. I will only discuss that a little here. However, it deserves something more ambitious, and my hypothesis would be that when Germany thinks itself, it thinks itself in an essentially European horizon, a European horizon that it invents and projects as the context of its own "spiritual" destiny. Germany will not have been alone in this, nor even the first to do so. Indeed, as I have indicated, no European people has ever been able entirely to do otherwise: there is, we might say, an ongoing agon of mainly national projections internal to Europe's cultural identity.

Nevertheless, there is, I think, a peculiar intimacy between the German question and the European question, or at least a distinctive shaping of both in that relation. We know how difficult it is to comprehend how the horrors of National Socialism could possibly belong within German history except as an absolute aberration. But with the invitation to think Europe as a German thing, I do not mean this to imply that we must always be on our guard against what Jürgen Habermas has called a "fatal" temptation for Germany to "succumb to power fantasies" of achieving "'semi-hegemonic status'" in Europe.

(All references to Habermas here are to his online article, "Democracy, Solidarity and The European Crisis", www.socialeurope. eu/2013/05/democracy-solidarity-and-the-european-crisis/.) No, the European horizon is just as visible in Habermas's own call for Germany finally to give up those fantasies as some kind of repentance for its indulging them. Habermas may make a more welcome gesture when he says "that it is in our [German] national interest to permanently avoid" them, since not doing so leads only to "catastrophe". But it is still the same programme: German national interests and German destiny are conceived, I want to suggest, as inseparably connected to a particular European future. Not only that it will have one (I'll come back to that idea too) but that properly having one is critically bound up with the realisation, led by Germany, of a political union among its peoples. Habermas's call for rapid steps to be taken towards the formation of a "supranational democracy" at the European level, and the crossing of "the red line of the classical understanding of [national] sovereignty" that this would entail, is fully part of this German story, as is his insistence that "the German government holds the key to the fate of the European Union in its hand". These intertwined fates and fatalities belong, I think, to "the German question", making of it at once entangled with what Habermas calls "the European question".

"Europe" may be something of a German thing. But of course it is not only a German thing. Not only has it never long remained an uncontested German thing – other becoming-Europeans will have their own ideas. However, as the French philosopher Phillipe Lacoue-Labarthe has stressed, the German way of styling "Europe as a whole" is something whose development was "essentially induced by the French one" (Lacoue-Labarthe, 2007: 79). There is a fascinating tête-à-tête between France and Germany here, what Lacoue-Labarthe calls "a mimetic rivalry" that is played out in relation to the question of "the imitation of the Ancients" (Lacoue-Labarth, 1990: 90). With both rivals conceiving Greek antiquity as the point of origin of a movement of world history which unfolds into Europe's modernity, Lacoue-Labarthe identifies two distinctive models of self-identification, French and German respectively, that are forged through the appropriation of that heritage *and through that the future of Europe*. France, on the one hand, returns to Greece through "Latinity": the Roman and Renaissance imitation. The Germanic world, on the other hand, "situated beyond the *limes*" of Latinity, is faced with the choice, in Alfred Bäumler's words, "to be either the anti-Roman power of Europe or not to be" (Lacoue-Labarth, 1990: 91). Germany finds its voice in this struggle over the appropriation of the Greeks, aspiring to create itself thereby as "the creator of a Europe that will be more than a Roman colony" – and to do so through the inheritance of "an altogether different Greece" (Lacoue-Labarthe, 1990: 91). This other imitation finds its decisive expression in Winckelmann's famous invocation to the Germans to imitate the Ancients "in order to make ourselves inimitable in turn". In this "*Kulturkampf*" with French neoclassicism and republicanism (Greek-Roman-Christian-revolutionary), it became necessary for Germany

> to 'invent' a Greece which had up to that point remained unimitated . . . which would allegedly be at the foundation of Greece itself . . . What the German imitation is seeking in Greece is the model – and therefore the possibility – of a pure emergence, of a pure originality: a model of self-formation
>
> (Lacoue-Labarthe, 2007: 79)

One might begin to summarise all of this by recalling the Delphic Oracle's reply to Zeno: "Take on the colour of the dead" – which Zeno interpreted as "study the ancients"; repeat them. And then we have two models: either the Latin model, which is *do what they did* in the sense of becoming *like* them in your ways (democratic self-government), or the German model, which is *do what they did* in the sense of becoming yourself in *your own* ways (autochthonous).

In his discussion of the German sword in the tree called "Nothung" that cuts through Wagner's *Ring* cycle, Stephen Mulhall invites us to follow something of Nietzsche's claim to see "the Wagnerian representation of Wotan's overthrow . . . as itself the refounding of a new, non-Christian [ie. non-Latin, SG] culture that might run counter to the philistinism of contemporary *Germany* by reconnecting *Europe* to its sources in Greek culture" (Mulhall, 2013: 22, my emphasis). Mulhall speaks here about Germany/Europe and its genealogy not in geopolitical terms but geophilosophical terms: through its Greek philosophical origin. Germany, attaining itself in this appropriative way – through the authentic repetition of the inimitable rather than the mere imitation of the classics – would enable Europe too to attain to "the innermost course of its history" which, as Heidegger will insist, was "originally 'philosophical'" (Heidegger, 1956: 31). Nietzsche came to think that "late Wagner" lost his way and began to "preach *the road to Rome*" in his *Parsifal* (Nietzsche, 1973: 171–2). "Is this still German?" asks Nietzsche pointedly, and with barely disguised disgust, in a rhyme that closes the "Peoples and Fatherlands" chapter of *Beyond Good and Evil*. In the *Querelle des Anciens et des Modernes* played out in this Franco-German duet it barely makes a difference whether the German "key" is sounded through an affirmation of the Germanization of Europe (through a union that would overturn Latinity) or the Europeanization of Germany (through the authentic repetition of the originary, non-Latin, source of Europe). What matters is the rivalry with (now mostly French) Latinity over the meaning of the historical sequence that is Europe's history.

Only it is not a duet. Geophilosophically speaking there is an invariable, if sometimes deliberately set aside or omitted, third hand in this drama of the modern geopolitical in the form of that most semi-detached of European states: Britain (what Nietzsche, like most who do recall it, calls "England"). Always on the verge of another European Brexit of one kind or another, always ready to oppose itself to a "Continental Europe" that is itself (primarily) the divided German/French Europe, Britain too will have its say. I cited Mulhall's remarks on the sword in the tree called "Nothung" a moment ago in part to help get this into view: for he goes on to note that the British Arthurian legend embodied in the (not actually the) sword-in-the-stone called "Excalibur" represents a myth of British national identity "that is historically constructed (and repeatedly reconstructed) in opposition to the very aspects of Northern European culture . . . with which [Wagner] proposes to reconstruct German life and values" – and hence, we might now say, with which he proposes to reconstruct European life and values (Mulhall, 2013: 22). Britain has never been wholly cut off from (what it calls) the Continent, nor always – in fact, rarely – omitted in considerations of European life and values.

It remains the case, however, that the philosophy of modern Europe has often exhibited a rather binary aspect: it is a French and German battle over who will be (or will have been) the "creator of a Europe" (Lacoue-Labarthe, 1990: 91).

III

Nietzsche is a notable exception here: his own experimental "synthesis" of the "European of the future" (Nietzsche, 1973: 170) is more or less entirely composed of a Germano-Franco-Britannic trio, although with a significant debt to Europe's Jews. However, with the exception of one (crucial) moment that we will come back to, this synthesis is constructed mostly by leaving everything "English" *out*.

I will examine Nietzsche's take (down) on the English at the end of this chapter, but it is tempting to imagine an exemplary Britain in the "mimetic rivalry" we have been following here. Unlike Germany, Britain had been mostly Romanised. But there was a decisive break with Rome. And it came (not with a religious revolution but) with the demand of an English king not to be dictated to by an overweening and corrupt alien power: the Papacy. (He wanted a divorce.) One might wonder if the modern "English" model of liberty, or freedom as a political concept, has its own corresponding and commendable form: not as "sovereignty" (of "the people") and not a fantasy of "autochthony" (of "the people") either but as "non-domination" (of *whoever*). With respect to the mimetic *agon* this would also imply a third way: that one can learn from the ancients – or indeed other moderns – but without thereby feeling oneself obliged to imitate them. Indeed.

When I come back to Nietzsche on the "English" I will also have something more to say about domination. As I indicated at the start, for Nietzsche the movement of political democratisation in Europe that unfolds from the French Revolution holds within its formation the possibility for the creation of a new European configuration beyond petty nationalisms: equality for *all* cannot finally be radically (or arbitrarily) restricted to "we French" or "we Germans" or "we English". As we have seen, Nietzsche sees the trajectory of this movement as the emergence of a new kind of "Man" whose identity is most radically marked by its national-self-overcoming: "good Europeans".

Such Europeans are not mono-cultural but in themselves distinctively multi-cultural and "supra-national". Nations may seem to fade into the background here. However, in the construction of this new European humanity, Germany, the nation Nietzsche regards as the most stupidly nationalistic (because so promisingly European) of the silly European nations, remains, *exemplary* for the good Europeans to come:

> The German soul is above all manifold, of diverse origins, more put together and superimposed than actually constructed: the reason for that is its source [viz] a large number of souls. As a people of the most tremendous mixture and mingling of races, with perhaps even a preponderance of pre-Aryan elements, a "people of the middle" in every sense, the Germans are more incomprehensible, more comprehensive, more full of contradictions . . . than other peoples are.
>
> (Nietzsche, 1973: 155)

As a "thinker who has the future of Europe on his conscience" (Nietzsche, 1973: 163) this "German" characteristic is central to Nietzsche's constructive task, which is precisely a matter of selective-inheritance ("breeding") from the old European "stock". And while he takes Germany to be presently the main carrier of nationalist sickness – exemplary too, therefore, in its failure to be more boldly European, that is, more boldly German ("Is this still German?") – he takes this multi-sourced German soul-characteristic as capable of giving rise to a built-in capacity for what he calls "development": its capacity to exist as a movement of becoming, and in the case under construction of becoming European, where that is precisely not being European (as such) at all, or being such only in the sense of being in a condition that has always belonged to Germany: of always holding open "the question" of what it is: of, always eluding "definition" (Nietzsche, 1973: 155). This is the first and most compelling "ruling concept" in his affirmation of what he calls the "Germanization of all Europe" (Nietzsche, 1973: 156). It would lie not in making Europeans more comprehensible, less comprehensive and less contradictory, but retaining those "German" characteristics as part of its new synthesis. Nevertheless, at issue for this multiplicity of souls is a Europe that, in the movement of democratisation, "*wants to become one*" (Nietzsche, 1973: 169).

Nietzsche sees here the possibility of Europe acquiring a new "*single will*": a supra-national *European* "single will" that would largely displace the "outmoded feelings" of national belonging (Nietzsche, 1973: 152). Nietzsche recognised that even "good Europeans" (himself, for example) would occasionally lapse into old and outmoded "atavistic attacks" of "fatherlandishness", but they would be short-lived and they would be quickly "restored" to their "good Europeanism" (Nietzsche, 1973: 152).

IV

As I have indicated, Nietzsche's Europe of the future is not exclusively German – or, rather, it remains German through and through only because the German soul is already many. And, as I have stressed, Nietzsche does look beyond Germany in his "new synthesis" that constructs experimentally "the European of the future" (Nietzsche, 1973: 170). Those new European supra-nationals who have got over the stupid nationalism of Europe today, will most resemble, Nietzsche suggests, "such men as Napoleon, Goethe, Beethoven, Stendhal, Heinrich Heine, Schopenhauer . . ., Richard Wagner . . ., writers from French late romanticism of the same period (especially Delacroix)" (Nietzsche, 1973: 170). A good mix of German and French figures there; vying for domination in the mimetic agon. Nietzsche will often refer to such individuals as "European events" rather than national ones (Nietzsche, 1973: 159). These are figures "like Goethe, like Hegel, like Heinrich Heine, [and] Schopenhauer" (Nietzsche, 1990: 79), all of whom avoided, for the most part, exclusive identification with a "fatherland" (Nietzsche, 1973: 170) – and in this case who were all German. Indeed, Nietzsche suggests that there is a greater chance of greatness that is due to the Germans than the French in view of the fact that "we . . . are still closer to barbarism than the French" (Nietzsche, 1973: 171).

The French get a pretty good run for their money nevertheless and have "three claims" to superiority in spiritual culture over any other Europeans, and, Nietzsche stresses, they too "understand things that an Englishman will never understand" (Nietzsche, 1973: 168). For the most part, and once again, the *agon* over the future of Europe is a primarily French and German affair.

But the English will appear in Nietzsche's synthesis too – sort of. It is an unlikely event since no English figures figure as European events – or rather they only appear when what is at issue is, for example, the low point of European "feeling", the low point where "the same European destiny that in Beethoven knows how to sing found its way into words", and "into words" that Nietzsche clearly finds utterly unmusical: "Rousseau, Schiller, Shelley, Byron" (Nietzsche, 1973: 159; see also Nietzsche, 1973: 165). On the face of it, then, England is not a great contributor to this new Europe. The English are, Nietzsche thinks, "a race of former Puritans" (Nietzsche, 1973: 139) who are clever enough to make Sundays so "boring" that people look forward to going back to work on Monday (Nietzsche, 1973: 94). We (and I say "we" here deliberately) are "clumsy" and "ponderous", our literature is "impossible" (even Shakespeare takes a hit; Nietzsche, 1973: 134), and our special vice is "cant" (i.e. whinging and whining – and he's right about that, especially about ourselves) (Nietzsche, 1973: 138–9). We cannot "dance", indeed Englishwomen, despite being "the most beautiful doves and swans" on earth can hardly "walk" (Nietzsche, 1973: 165). We are marked by our "profound averageness" (Nietzsche, 1973: 166), and the English utilitarians are "herd animals" who, preaching "one morality for all", are fundamentally detrimental to the "higher men". Indeed, the utilitarian's so-called "happiness of the greatest number" is anyway, in reality, simply the happiness of England. In short, the English contribution is absolutely minimal: "they are no philosophical race" ("it was against Hume that Kant rose up"), and "what is lacking in England" is "real power of spirituality" and "real depth of spiritual insight" (Nietzsche, 1973: 164–5).

There is a certain exemplary representativity of everything awful about modern Europe . . . in the English. For Nietzsche the "profound averageness" of the English is precisely what "the *German* spirit has risen against in profound disgust" (Nietzsche, 1973: 97). And as we have seen, what should be preserved from the German spirit is best understood as, precisely, its potential for becoming the leading spirit of the new "good European".

V

But wait! While it seems to Nietzsche that no Englishman has ever been a "European event", he seems also to think, amazingly, that, nevertheless, it would be "useful for such [English] spirits to dominate for a while" (Nietzsche, 1973: 165). Ha! What a turn-up for the books, especially when a Brexit pattern is already in view. I will exploit this.

Nietzsche's reasons for giving the English a temporary priority in dominating the movement towards the new Europe are basically practical and pragmatic: working towards a new Europeanism will be safer in the hands of "mediocre spirits" instead of the "exalted spirits" of the French and German type, who have a tendency to "fly off", not keeping to the "rules" (Nietzsche, 1973: 165–6). English "narrowness, aridity and industriousness" is thus better suited to "dominate" in our time "for a while", even though we are utterly incapable of "being able . . . to *be* something new" (Nietzsche, 1973: 166).

Well, thank you. But having been given the floor by Nietzsche (for now), I would like to suggest immediately and in closing that what Europe needs today, tomorrow and any day thereafter really is not the "German" ideal of unity through (anyone's) domination. Let's call that the German interpretation of "ever closer union": the one that conceives it on a becoming-increasingly-more-federalist model, a model in which the nations of Europe become merely "implementing authorities" of a European supra-national government (Habermas). Instead, I would urge a (genuinely) more modest proposal: where "ever closer union" simply means cultivating conditions in which war between the nations of Europe becomes increasingly less likely. We Europeans (since you don't mind an Englishman speaking in this name) are, I think, a unity only of the singularly different: we can be drawn together as *one* (spiritually) precisely because we are not one (spirit). *We are the one that is not one.*

We Europeans, we are in trouble again now, in our today. Not simply because of some "purely external" threat from outside us but in a paralyzing uncertainty regarding the kind of unity we want to make of ourselves. In this chapter I have focused on one troubling thing that a perhaps still recognizably "German" spirit within us is now increasingly desiring for ourselves: the unity of a "single will". The "English" spirit in Europe (even if no longer in the EU) simply holds fast to Nietzsche's acknowledgment of "manifold souls". What made us a "we" really worthy of the name – what made it worth speaking about "we, the Europeans" all together as one and all distinctively European – is, as J.S. Mill put it, our "individuality": the "singularity" of the people and peoples within the diverse nations of Europe, and their "unlikeness" one to another (Mill, 2015: 66). And there we "English" spirits want to *stick*. Yet today, Mill says – Mill in his today which is very close to Nietzsche's and also not so very far from our own – today this modest union is weakened by forces which imagine it would be strengthened by a more radically assimilating, amalgamating "we":

> What has hitherto preserved Europe from [becoming stationary]? Not any superior excellence in the [European family], which, when it exists, exists as the effect not as the cause; but their remarkable diversity of character and culture. Individuals, classes, nations, have been extremely unlike each other: they have struck out a great variety of paths, each leading to something valuable; and although at every period those who travelled in different paths have been extremely intolerant of one another, and each would have thought it an excellent thing if all the rest could have been compelled to travel his road, their attempts to thwart each other's development have rarely had any permanent success, and each has in time endured to receive the good which the others have offered. Europe is, in my judgement, wholly indebted to this plurality of paths for its progressive and many-sided development.
>
> (Mill, 2015: 67)

While Mill does not explore the idea directly, the creation of a European Union that wants both to preserve and secure the diversity of Europe's nation states and to reduce their extreme intolerance of one another is surely something he would welcome. So his text offers a timely warning for the present generation of European enthusiasts: that its courageous efforts to achieve "ever closer union between the peoples [sic] of Europe" carries inside itself the threat of wanting the plurality invoked here finally to be eliminated as a politically salient feature of Europe's politics – a final overcoming of what Habermas sees as the debilitating effects of "national particularisms" in European politics – as if the ideal *telos* of European integration would be the creation of a "European people" that really *is* one because it really is *one*.

In Mill's view, by contrast, and I think we still need to heed this, the best and most European of Europeans today are those who come to "see that it is good that there should be differences" (Mill, 2015: 68). The alternative is a nightmare of a distinctively European form of history-ending "stationariness": the levelling demand for uniformity that, often enough in the form of a profoundly hollowed-out appeal to "democratic feeling", betrays Europe because it "proscribes singularity" (Mill, 2015: 66). For sure, what we need, what many of us singularly will, is indeed a united Europe of states. But this is not a call for an international state or "supranational democracy" but, rather, for a transformation of the fractious nation states of Europe into co-operative member states of their union, a union that would not itself have the dominating power like that of a state. In the referendum the majority of UK citizens who voted said "No" to what they were increasingly framing as a project of supranational power, preferring what looks like non-domination to a promise of economic stability that many were not seeing anyway.

Bibliography

Habermas, Jürgen. *Democracy, Solidarity and The European Crisis*. Available at: www.socialeurope.eu/2013/05/democracy-solidarity-and-the-european-crisis/

Heidegger, Martin. (1956). *What is Philosophy?* Lanham: Rowman & Littlefield.

———. (1990). *Heidegger, Art and Politics*. Oxford: Wiley-Blackwell.

Lacoue-Labarthe, Phillipe. (2007). *Heidegger and the Politics of Poetry*. Urbana, IL: University of Illinois Press.

Mill, J.S. (2015). *On Liberty, Utilitarianism and Other Essays*. Oxford: Oxford University Press.

Mulhall, Stephen. (2013). *The Self and Its Shadows*. Oxford: Oxford University Press.

Nietzsche, Friedrich. (1973). *Beyond Good and Evil*. Harmondsworth: Penguin Classics.

———. (1990). *Twilight of the Idols*. Harmondsworth: Penguin Classics.

17

BREXIT

Thinking and resistance

Thomas Docherty

1 Brexit means Brexit

'Brexit means Brexit'. What, we might reasonably ask, does that mean in fact? What might it mean to say it? On one hand, the statement says nothing; at the same time, in saying nothing, it speaks in an ostensibly definitive fashion, as if it is stating something profoundly meaningful and doing so absolutely and definitively. It proposes a *truth* that is utterly self-evident: after all, how could Brexit mean anything other than the meaning of Brexit? It has all the truth and complete certainty of a mathematical equation, reflected in the linguistic structure of a pleonasm or rhetorical *anadiplosis*. At the same time, the semantic content of that truth remains entirely enigmatic and covert. In a striking rhetorical paradox, the formulation states truth and meaning in the clearest possible linguistic manner while simultaneously occluding truth and meaning completely. The fact that such a trite and banal statement carries the enormous political weight that it does requires examination and explanation.

The referendum vote that led to Theresa May's Pauline conversion to the Brexit cause and to her uttering the phrase – a conversion that was coterminous with her becoming Prime Minister, without any election, on 11 July 2016 – took place in a particular and peculiar historical atmosphere. The prevailing mood that shaped the rhetoric of the Leave campaign throughout the previous year was that of resentment, *ressentiment*, a sense of generalised grievance. T.S. Eliot's description of his post-war poem, *The Waste Land* of 1922 – 'the relief of a personal and wholly insignificant grouse against life' – captures well the mood of a population living in 2016 through the long ongoing aftermath of the post-2008 financial crisis and its various social and political legacies.

The resentment in question in 2016 was captured almost entirely in and by the Leave campaign's key slogan, 'take back control'; and the key word in that slogan is 'back'. In encouraging people to *re*-claim something, the slogan alleged – indirectly but clearly – that someone had improperly taken something away from us. In the context, the criminal perpetrator of this wrong was identified with spectacular but politically convenient imprecision as 'the EU'. Now was the moment, our once-in-a-lifetime opportunity, we were told, to redress the wrong, to secure retribution, to judge and ascribe guilt definitively to those who have got away with doing us over. In so doing, we would distinguish ourselves from such criminality and re-claim autonomous control – above all control of 'our own' laws and 'our own' geographical borders. Those borders, of course, remain themselves subject to disputes and wars that have been silently waged for decades and more (witness Ireland or Gibraltar as the most obvious examples) and that continue to have a percussive effect, like the ghost of Hamlet's father, under and across the land; but this was not to be the moment for attending to such detail. Control of our own laws was equally crucial: the judgement that would inform our vote was to be a reassertion of autonomy, quite literally (from the Greek roots of the word) giving ourselves the law, being a law unto ourselves.

Six months after her 'Brexit means Brexit' statement, in her Lancaster House speech of 17 January 2017, May had had time to reflect. Beyond the first enthusiastic flush of apostasy, she now gave a definitive semantic content to Brexit. 'Brexit', she said, 'must mean control of the number of people who come to Britain from Europe'. The very formulation is telling: it presupposes that Britain is already distinct from Europe, not part of it, and that Europe is 'foreign' or alien to those who will identify as 'British'. Yet she also stated in this same speech that while we were leaving the EU, we were not leaving Europe. What lies behind the speech, it seems clear, is a deeply ingrained claim for a very British exceptionalism. It is with that sense of being a particular exception to the general law that we find the source of the resentment that dominated the campaign. Why was our special and exceptional status not being fully acknowledged? Indeed, exceptionalism is a defining historical feature of UK participation in the EU. We demanded special opt-out clauses from any number of policies: the Charter of Fundamental Rights, the Social Chapter, the Euro, European work-time directive, Schengen. This exceptionalism, however, was not a celebration of cultural difference and diversity; instead it was an assertion and a determination of a supposed superiority of 'the British' over the rest of Europe.

The fundamental allegation of the Leave campaign was that the EU was what Donald Trump would call 'a loser' and that we were being held back from fulfilling our potential by our affiliation with it. In the paper that gave May her claim that 'no deal is better than a bad deal', the 'Leave Means Leave' group (their name echoes and reinforces the banality of 'Brexit means Brexit'), describes the Single Market as 'the world's least successful economic zone' (Tice, 2016: 3). Boris Johnson – for the paradigmatic example – reveals the source of this kind of thinking.

Just over a year before the campaign opened, Johnson had published a biography of Churchill, and his account starts from an observation about the 1939–45 war, according to which the distinction between Britain and the countries of Europe is clear: 'The most important geostrategic consideration of May 1940 was that Britain – the British Empire – was alone' (Johnson, 2014: 9). This is a position that would be vaunted by the Leave campaign time and again during the debates. It makes clear that the sense of exceptionalism – our particular standing ourselves alone and apart – has its own historical source in the 1939–45 war, a source whose relevance will become clear in the account that follows here.

2 Justice or revenge

In Lancaster House, May argued that the logic of Brexit necessitated our leaving the economics of the Single Market and, intrinsically linked to that, our leaving also the jurisdiction of the European Court of Justice. The Leave campaign falsely alleged that laws were being imposed upon the UK from Brussels, as if Britain had never been present at any of the governmental meetings regarding the passing of those laws. It was in this context that Johnson made his claim that the EU was 'pursuing a similar goal to Hitler in trying to create a powerful superstate'. Interviewed by *The Telegraph* on 15 May 2016, he invoked Churchill and encouraged us to emulate Churchill's wartime defiance not just of Hitler but of all that was happening across Europe and to 'set the country free and save the EU from itself by voting to leave' (Johnson, 2016).

Charged rhetoric such as this – which was commonplace in the Leave campaign's case – makes it apposite to consider in this context some more detail regarding the normative account of justice and of law that derived from the 1939–45 war and its European aftermath. In his historical memoir, *East West Street*, the barrister and academic Philippe Sands gives an account of the Nuremberg Trials of 1945–46. In the procedures and norms that governed that court, there was a crucial and determining distinction made between the proper operations of justice and the distortions and self-defeatism of a negativity that is based in a self-obsessed nationalist 'autonomy'. The point to underscore in this – and the point most relevant to the Brexit case – is that Sands demonstrates that a system of justice worthy of the name of civilization depended upon acceptance of the fact that national laws have to be endorsed by international law, especially with regard to all laws pertaining to human rights.

Sands quotes Robert H. Jackson, the American Supreme Court judge at the trials, whose opening speech argued a specific case:

> That four great nations, flushed with victory and stung with injury, *stay the hand of vengeance* and voluntarily submit their captive enemies to the *judgement of the law* is one of the most significant tributes that Power has ever paid to reason
>
> (stress added; Sands, 2016: 288)

Legal constraint – justice, not vengeful retribution – is itself a force for civilization and for the restraint that reason imposes on otherwise unrestricted brute power; and the entire burden of Sands's memoir is advanced towards the compelling thesis – and nothing makes this more compelling than the particular case in question, that of the Holocaust – that individual states must themselves be subject to international laws.

At issue in Nuremberg was a fundamental opposition. On one hand, brute political power, often enforced by state violence, is set against the primacy of rationality itself. The very legitimacy of state power can rest only upon that power's answerability to reason – to the strength of thought and of intellect – rather than on the physical force of the body. These are high stakes, and they are, in fact, as relevant to the ostensibly less charged dimensions of the Brexit debate as they were in the post-war Europe of Nuremberg.

By contrast with the logic of Nuremberg, however, Brexit means abandoning commitment to that very international system of law, at least insofar as that is vested in the European Court of Justice (ECJ). Of course, the relevance of the post-war Nuremberg trial to Brexit could never be easily acknowledged; and in its place, there is, within the UK, a very precise and seemingly less dramatic origin for this sentiment in the political crisis that immediately preceded Brexit. On the morning of 19 September 2014, the result of the referendum on Scottish independence, held the day before, was known: Scotland had voted against seceding from the UK. David Cameron, the then Prime Minister, immediately made a speech that was shocking to Scottish ears, because he used the occasion to declare English independence. Having welcomed the Scottish decision to remain within the UK, he said that

> I have long believed that a crucial part missing from this national discussion is England. We have heard the voice of Scotland – and now the millions of voices of England must also be heard. The question of English votes for English laws . . . [subsequently known as EVEL] requires a decisive answer
>
> (Cameron, 2014)

People who would become leading Brexiteers rowed in behind: Bernard Jenkin supported EVEL; Labour's Frank Field urged Labour to avoid being seen as 'anti-English' and to answer 'the English question'; Graham Brady, Chair of the Tory 1922 Committee, suggested there might be 'English-only days' in Parliament; and Nigel Farage described Scotland as an irritatingly noisy tail that wagged the supposedly silenced English dog, adding 'We must have English MPs voting on English only matters' (Farage, 2014).

EVEL – English votes for English laws – is at the very core of Brexit and informs the 'decision' to secede from the ECJ; and its source lies in a speech that stirred up a sense of resentment among the English whose troubles – it was alleged – stem from the fact that they were supposedly not making their own laws, while the Scots, Welsh and Irish had all 'taken control' of their lives. Cameron's ill-judged speech essentially gave voice and respectability to the idea that the ethnic English were right to feel resentful at their own alleged lack of control of their political lives, notwithstanding the dominance of the English voice in Westminster, the political centre from which other jurisdictions were granted devolved responsibilities.

The demand for legal autonomy might, of course, seem eminently reasonable; and it was certainly made to appear so during the campaign. Yet Philippe Sands also reveals that such a view is precisely what the Nazis used to justify their own atrocities and to excuse themselves from responsibility for any crime. A key aspect of their defence was that what they were doing was not criminal because it was not against their own internal and national Nazi laws. Such laws allowed for the excesses of a perversion of all forms of justice. The Nazi defendants were 'obeying the law' as well as just 'obeying orders'. Against this, the prosecution in Nuremberg argued successfully that both the human rights of individuals and the rights of specific groups of people (Jews, Poles, Romani, homosexuals, the disabled and so on) must transcend whatever laws any particular state might establish as 'their own laws'. In the case of Brexit, the demand for legal autonomy is related firmly to the resentments associated with the fact that Europe, the world – even Scotland – all fail to recognize the truly exceptional status of the English and of England. The Brexiteers' claim for legal autonomy has this troubling precedent, and the relevance of the precedent derives from the Brexiteers' rhetorical appeals to the wartime spirit.

Reasonable readers will have already thrown their heads into their hands at the references here to the Nazis: in any argument, the first person to refer to Hitler has lost the debate. Yet in this instance, the comparisons are utterly apposite, because the Leave campaign rested a good deal of their case on nostalgia for the specifically national ethos associated with the war of 1939–45. The many 'vox pop' interviews that peppered the mainstream media made endless Johnsonian references to the war, to the spirit of plucky and stubborn resistance against Nazi Europe and to a completely imaginary 'good old days' when Britain stood alone and proud, its people waving their own blue passports as markers of a distinct imperial identity and making the best of our privations. In many cases, the Britain in question was identified – misidentified – specifically as England. The predominant tone of the vox pop was a rehearsing of Shakespeare's John of Gaunt, the character who – having claimed that 'they breathe truth that breathe their words in pain' – goes on to speak nostalgically of England as 'this scepter'd isle'. The England in question then as now is *always* a Paradise or Eden that is *lost*; and, as with Gaunt, it is often mistakenly described as an island. England, of course, is not an island; and nor even is Britain, that archipelago with its outposts elsewhere around the globe.

Justice, we might say, exists in order to preclude the sentiments of revenge and vengeance that dominate the Shakespearean image of British history. Justice – as Shakespeare himself saw – exists to rein in a political power that rests its case in physical force with its scant attention to reasoned debate or to rationality itself. Justice helps to regulate – to place under agreed law – the sentiments felt by the victim of a wrongdoing and her or his desire to do vengeful wrong in turn to the perpetrator of the initial crime. It is marked by grace and not resentment.

By contrast, the spirit of revenge, grounded in resentments real or imaginatively stirred up, runs counter to civilization itself. Revenge, in fact, has its own intrinsic and perversely inflationary economy; and it is against the extension of the perversities of a desire for revenge that justice works. You take my eye. Revenge says that I must take yours. However, that does not suffice, for while it offers an ostensible balance of wrongs, it fails to address the fact of your initial motivation for taking my eye in the first place. Revenge depends upon the resentment that I feel at this inability to correct the simple fact of history, the fact that you gratuitously acted as you did in the first place. I must therefore do more than 'take back' your eye. I must add a further action, one that will seek to redress that initial historical motivation: the desire behind your action, a desire for which I myself bear no responsibility. I demand, therefore, your eye and more. You are now also feeling wronged. Escalation of hostilities ensues in a potentially rabid and uncontrolled inflation of violence; and this is a brief if crude account of a post-Versailles Europe after 1918. Justice is what intervenes to ask both parties to subscribe to an agreed law that will transcend individual desires.

To step outside such a court of justice – as May and the Brexiteers say we must do – is to invite the indulgence of revenge, with all that that entails: a specific kind of inflation and an inability to avoid resentful hostility against the forces of history or simply against 'all the stuff that has happened recently'. There is no doubt that the Leave vote was essentially constituted by that general resentment at the hand that history has been dealing many people: the financial crisis that has wrecked whole economies; an austerity culture rooted in a long period of the systematic transfer of common wealth into private hands; the political failure to deal with advanced technologies that are decreasing the need for human labour and thus extending unemployment; the demeaning of labour as such, as more and more industries exclude the workforce from production and ask the customer to 'do it yourself' or to assemble an entire 'flat-pack' life; the sense that many people have that they have lost out in a 'competitive environment' and in a general culture of socio-economic competition to which they never willingly or personally chose to sign up; the constantly widening distance between the wealthy and the poor that follows from competition; general inequality of opportunity and even of biological existence; the sense that there are elites in various spheres of power and influence who care little for those outside; and many rank historical eventualities besides.

The Leave vote for Brexit determinedly indulged these resentments, with a rhetoric that was determinedly banal and thoughtless, to win the referendum. The consequences are anything but banal:

they are actually a matter of life and death. The Brexit vote was a vote against reason, against *thinking*, against everything intellectual because 'the people of this country have had enough of experts'; and it came close to being a celebration of violence, carrying eerie echoes of the language and politics of 1930s Europe. On 18 May 2016, Nigel Farage told the BBC that 'it's legitimate to say that if people feel they have lost control completely – and we have lost control . . . then violence is the next step' (Farage, 2016a). When the violence erupted directly, just a month later on 16 June with the murder of Labour MP Jo Cox, shame led the political class – and the general public – into a conspiracy of pious silence before normal service was resumed, supposedly purged. In that silence, it was as if the country and its political class were trying to ensure that the reverberations of 1930s Nazism and far-right ideology could be regarded as irrelevant. We would not be permitted to realize that Brexit would in any way carry the brutalities of the earlier period into our everyday life of the present time. Brexit, apparently and ostensibly, would be different from all that.

It is time to break that pious silence. We need to be aware of what Brexit means.

3 On truth and lies in a political sense

It was in the wake of the controversies over her *Eichmann in Jerusalem* that Hannah Arendt pointed out that 'no one, as far as I know, has ever counted truth among the political virtues. Lies have always been regarded as necessary and justifiable tools not only of the politician's or the demagogue's but also of the statesman's trade' (Arendt, 2006: 223). Political lying not only has a long and distinguished history, it also has its own protocols and fundamentally agreed modus operandi. The politician will perhaps refuse to acknowledge the empirical facts of any case, preferring to present that case through the prism of their own ideological preferences. The task of the voter is to descry, through that perverted presentation of the facts of the *particular* case, the *general* political trajectory that determines the politician's language and to decide whether to assent to that general direction of political travel or to desist from it. In all cases, however, and on all sides, there is an at least tacit acknowledgment that the facts of the case actually exist in the material and historical realm.

Something different happened in 2016 – both in Brexit and in Donald Trump's 'Brexit plus' election as US president that same year. In the usual case, we expect that we can measure and judge political claims against empirical realities; and we then choose whether to support it or not. In 2016, this structure was reversed. Trump's lies, like those of the Brexiteers, were so pervasive that they had a different point and purpose. The point was to break down entirely any idea that linguistic claims can be tested against empirical realities. Trump, like Farage, Gove, Johnson and the rest, had no problem at all with endlessly repeating lies that were proven to have no legitimate epistemological claim upon reality at all, be it the largest crowd ever at a presidential inauguration or a fictional £350 million a week for the National Health Service (a lie again repeated by Boris Johnson in September of 2017: Sir David Norgrove, Chair of the UK Statistics Authority publically declared that he was 'surprised and disappointed').

In a famous rhetorical chiasmus, Salena Zeto noted what was at issue with Trump. She wrote in *The Atlantic* on 23 September 2016 that when he makes obviously false claims, 'the press takes him literally, but not seriously; his supporters take him seriously, but not literally' (Zeto, 2016). His supporters were not interested in whether what he said could be measured in terms of its accuracy or otherwise in relation to material and historical facts. Instead, they wanted to hear someone who was 'on their side'. That requires an entirely different metric. Empirical truth telling gives way entirely to the demand for the politician's sincerity and authenticity, an authenticity that is given precisely by its distance from all the ethical norms of truth telling and all the more usual demands for a political realism.

How does a politician demonstrate such sincerity and authenticity? First, she or he will endlessly repeat their claims – especially those that test the very demands for truth telling and realism that 'normal' politicians acknowledge. In other words: lie in the most obvious manner possible and challenge 'normal' politicians to question your case. Second, this new politician will depart as much as possible from norms of political rhetoric. Argument is replaced by spurious insult, the more outrageous the better, because that will be understood as the politician authentically telling it like it is instead of observing niceties and courtesies, instead of 'playing the game', refusing to accept the taboos of 'political correctness' or diplomacy. Now, to break the taboo is seen precisely as speaking the truth that taboos have allegedly eradicated from public speech.

Brexit worked in the same way. In the final instance, of course – and at the extremes – verbal abuse veers towards physical abuse and violence. Trump physically imitates a disabled reporter. Then, yet more extreme, Thomas Mair murders Jo Cox, shouting 'Britain First' and 'death to traitors'. That is the direction of travel for the Brexiteer. No respectable Brexiteer would believe this, of course, and would respond by saying that I am lying here. But the question now is: how does the anti-Brexiteer respond to such a charge at this point? How does reasonable political argument over Brexit actually become possible?

4 Rhetorical Brexit and the assault upon meaning

A key issue throughout 2016 was focused on the position of 'elites'. At least since 2008, it became understood that the world is organized around structured and determined inequality. Such a political structure breeds resentment as a normative dominant social mood. This is all the more so when we realize that the political class as a whole appears to have become fully invested in inequality. The logic of market fundamentalism and its attendant demand for competitiveness breeds an anarchic neo-Hobbesian war of all against all. Those who lose out – the 99% or at least the majority who, by definition, cannot become 'elite' – are said to lack aspiration, to be responsible for their own poverty, their own failings. They deserve their lot.

It is little wonder that a focus on the elites should embody that very resentment that is structural to the Brexit referendum vote. 'The people' – the 99% – have been wronged; and it is, above all, the political class – those who endorse the marketised and competitive self as a social and political norm – that has wronged them. As a result, it is the political outsider who will now gain support, gaining and even embodying the vox pop, the voice of the people. The scene is set for the rise of the demagogue, who will gain the support of the people by demonstrating their affiliation with the people and their suffering. It is a perversion of Bill Clinton's famous statement that 'I feel your pain'.

The Brexiteers, like Trump, gained a reputation for authenticity precisely by distancing themselves from their own elite position. Johnson's chummy would-be street patois, Gove's attack on experts, Farage's beer-swilling – all of this is designed to secure affiliation of 'the people' by being authentic. As Farage put it, the result was for 'the real people, for the ordinary people, for the decent people' (Farage, 2016b).

In this rhetorical game, the key to victory is distancing oneself from the elites and their social norms. Sincerity and authenticity become measured by the deviation from the norms of political discourse, the distancing of the speaker from the game of rhetorical engagement. It follows that the more outrageous the rhetoric, the more the politician is seen to be telling it like it is (even – and especially – if he is lying). This is why Trump's vote went up every time he insulted someone or said something scandalous. In the same way, it is why the Brexit vote went up every time Boris Johnson and others rehearsed – with as much vehemence as was needed – the lies that we would all be better off, that £350 million a week would come back to the NHS, that nations outside the EU were just gagging to do trade deals with us that would benefit us even as it might harm them, and so on. The point was not to tell the truth but to speak a language that rebelled against the intellectual demand for truth itself. Rely on your physical gut. 'The people of this country have had enough of experts'.

It is impossible to argue against this kind of rhetoric. First, you can't use reason, for that is precisely what is being abandoned and regarded as elitist, the imposition of a thinking (available exclusively to the 'knowledgeable' elites) or intellectual point of view that might restrain the revenge-seeking vengeful body. Second, if you realize that the strength of 'BrexiTrump' lies in insults, say, and then you too start to insult, you become merely a weak *imitation* of sincerity and thus insincere. You undo precisely what you meant to do.

The assault upon truth is part of a more general assault on reason itself and on the intellectual as elitist. The great worry here is that thinking itself is increasingly seen as elitist and thus to be disavowed. We have seen before – in the Europe of the 1930s and in many neo-fascist states since – where this leads. Arendt noted that the 'banality of evil' in Eichmann's case derived from his 'quite authentic inability to think' (Arendt, 2003: 159), for example. In another specific case, on 25 June 1946, David Maxwell Fyfe faced Konstantin von Neurath, who had been Hitler's first foreign minister, in the Nuremberg court. Von Neurath had proposed that Czechoslovakia could be 'Germanized' by expelling Czechs and, above all, by destroying the Czech intelligentsia as a whole. As reported in *East West Street*,

> "What you wanted to do," Maxwell Fyfe told von Neurath, "was to get rid of the teachers and writers and singers of Czechoslovakia, whom you call the intelligentsia, the people who would hand down the history and traditions of the Czech people to other generations." That was genocide.
>
> (Sands, 2016: 337)

A campaign that is driven by the banality of a thoughtless slogan and that endorses gut feeling instead of the thinking of experts or of intellectuals who might know something has a dangerous precedent.

5 A culture of persecution

In 1946, Britain objected to the idea that membership of the emergent League of Nations should be tied to a 'commitment to bestow equal treatment on racial and national minorities'. As Sands reminds us, 'Britain objected to any depletion of sovereignty – the right to treat others as it wished – or international oversight. It took this position even if the price was more "injustice and oppression"' (Sands, 2016: 72).

This looks uncannily prescient of our own moment, especially in the light of proposed legislation regarding the rights of EU nationals in the UK after Brexit. We are witnessing an assault on the idea that all people might be equal in terms of their rights. The whole post-Brexit debate regarding immigration is organised around giving a priority to those who are regarded as *echt* English. English exceptionalism comes down to this: a sense of the superiority of the English national character over any and all other peoples and races.

This is all an assault upon the intellect, which, by definition, cannot be 'national'. The intellect – thinking – is what takes us beyond our own body, our own physical self. It is the intellect that opens us to foreignness, to things previously undreamt of in our philosophies. Brexit is a steely closing of that and every other door. Its domestic character is exemplified most fully by the assault on our universities, as they are increasingly forced to betray their commitment to the intellect and to operate instead as businesses, essentially as shell companies for the production of structural social inequality.

It is utterly incumbent on us to resist this entire trajectory. If we do not, we will be partly responsible for the tragic and not farcical repetitions of history toward which it is steadily taking us. Fascism is on the march, very visibly across Europe and elsewhere; and if the intellectuals have nothing to say or do about that, then we become complicit in it.

But Nazism? Brexiteers are clearly not Nazis. Of course. It is, however, worth remembering that most Nazis did not start out as Nazis. They failed to resist a language and a political trajectory and thus became complicit in its disastrous outcomes. Principal among those outcomes was the scapegoating of groups, underpinned by a scapegoating of rational thought and a politicisation of the institutions in which rational thinking – and oppositional criticism – should have been encouraged. As Arendt reminds us:

> the extermination of Jews was preceded by a very gradual sequence of anti-Jewish measures, each of which was accepted with the argument that refusal to cooperate would make things worse – until a stage was reached where nothing worse could possibly have happened

> (Arendt, 2003: 37)

The structure of Brexit, especially since the actual vote, is similar: it is a fulfilment of the banal thoughtlessness of 'there is no alternative'.

Those of us who see where this road is leading have a duty to think, to respond as fully as possible to the Brexit warning that if you dare to think or be different in any way, you are a traitor, an enemy of the people. This is all the more pressing for those of us engaged in the study of linguistic meaning and the undercurrents of rhetoric.

What, then, does Brexit mean? In the words of the French resistance fighter and philosopher Jacques Lusseyran, it means this: '*penser, 'c'est résister*' (Garcin, 2016: 79). Brexit is a call to resistance and to a resistance grounded in the university as the site of thinking as such.

Warwick, September 2017

Bibliography

Arendt, Hannah. (2003). *Responsibility and Judgment*. New York: Schocken Books.

Arendt, Hannah. (2006). *Between Past and Future*. London: Penguin.

Cameron, David. (2014). Available at: www.gov.uk/government/news/scottish-independence-referendum-statement-by-the-prime-minister

Farage, Nigel. (2014). Available at: www.bbc.co.uk/news/uk-politics-29271763

Farage, Nigel. (2016a). Available at: www.theguardian.com/politics/2016/may/18/nigel-farage-shades-enoch-powell-chuka-umunna

Farage, Nigel. (2016b). Available at: www.theguardian.com/commentisfree/2016/jun/24/nigel-farage-ugliness-bullet-fired

Garcin, Jérôme. (2016). *Le Voyant*. Paris: Gallimard.

Johnson, Boris. (2014). *The Churchill Factor*. London: Hodder & Stoughton.

Johnson, Boris. (2016). *Telegraph*. Available at: www.telegraph.co.uk/news/2016/05/14/boris-johnson-the-eu-wants-a-superstate-just-as-hitler-did/

Sands, Philippe. (2016). *East West Street*. London: Weidenfeld & Nicolson.

Tice, Richard. (2016). *Why the EU's Single Market Is Failing Britain*. Available at: www.leavemeansleave.eu/research/eus-single-market-failing-britain/

Zeto, Salena. (2016). Available at: www.theatlantic.com/politics/archive/2016/09/trump-makes-his-case-in-pittsburgh/501335/

EPILOGUE

The immigrant at Port Selda

George Szirtes

[Editor's note: this is a lecture given at the at the symposium, *The legacy of Brexit and citizenship in times of uncertainty*, held at the University of Southampton in the summer of 2016. I've retained its spoken form.]

Thank you very much for inviting me to give this keynote talk. I must confess I have no qualification for doing it, am not directly affected (for now) and am keenly aware of speaking to those who do. I can only speak in my character as an unwitting child refugee to these shores, a poet and translator, and as an occasional writer of articles in the press, on, among other things, the issue of Brexit: about the campaign itself, the impact of the campaign and its likely future impact.

On that last, of course, I can only speculate. We are not out yet, we don't know anything about the terms of disengagement, and we have no clear idea of how this or that set of terms may impact our lives.

I did in fact campaign for Remain, but my role and experience was very minor. In asking Leavers why they intended to vote as they did the two answers I repeatedly got were: 'So *they* won't tell us what to do any more' and, 'Things were better before'. These words will be familiar to most people here and seemed to me to be perfectly rational responses to the two major arguments of the Leave campaign regarding sovereignty and free movement of people. The way those arguments were presented elicited precisely these responses.

As I have already said, I am not qualified to address those questions because I am not an expert in any of the relevant areas and because I am, by birth, *parti pris* on one side of the question, in that I am a foreigner and therefore one of those factors in things somehow being better before my arrival.

I don't want to caricature the Leave campaign. I don't want to call those who voted differently from me stupid, or simple, or racist. Life is far more complicated, and I did have some intelligent conversations with people who wanted to leave the EU, particularly those on the Chomskyite left of the political spectrum, whose arguments centred on globalisation, capitalism and high finance as expressed, occasionally, in terms of sovereignty.

I don't want to caricature the Leave campaign, but the day after the referendum there was an incident in Norwich, a city that had voted to remain in a region that had voted to leave, in which a small Romanian supermarket was firebombed. Students at the university from which I had retired immediately set up an appeal to raise £500. By the next morning it had raised over £20,000, so the field was not altogether lost. Despite what we are continually told about the clear will of 'the people' there were enough people willing to raise money for a minor indirectly demonised enterprise.

I don't think demonisation is too harsh a word, in that Leave rhetoric deliberately called forth certain demons. Leave rhetoric quite consciously opened the trapdoors where such demons were hiding. It legitimised them. It called forth the firebombers. It called forth those who immediately set upon elderly widows of French and German birth who had lived in the country for decades and taunted them by asking when they were going home. It called forth the teenagers on the Manchester tram who demanded a black American get off it. It called forth the murderer of Jo Cox.

By the time that happened a certain madness had set in. All the Leavers rushed to distance themselves from the murder, of course. This was nothing to do with them. None of those xenophobic incidents, and there have been and continue to be plenty of others, had anything to do with them. It was nothing to do with their presentation of sinister foreigners in Brussels and sinister gangs of Albanians hanging round Dover and Boston, or with the sinister cheap labour of mushroom pickers and chicken packers who were taking much-coveted jobs from true Brits. No! they protested. That was not what they meant. They had nothing to do with encouraging the taxi driver we met who had moved from Kings Lynn because there were too many Lithuanians and Poles there, foreigners whose rather marvellous supermarket down a side street was, as he put it, 'taking the place over'.

Perhaps I could go back in time and take a more personal line in order to think about what it is that might make one properly British or, more problematically, a foreigner.

2

My family of four, along with some 200,000 others, that is one-fiftieth of the population, left Hungary in the months following the defeat of the 1956 Revolution. I am not entirely sure why we left. My parents had taken no part in the fighting and were unlikely to be arrested in its repercussions. My father, as the leader of a department within the Ministry of Building, would have been exposed in the revolution itself, as much as a Jew as a member of the apparatus, but I think he would have stayed. It was my mother who insisted we leave.

Why did she do so? I don't think it was for ideological reasons. Neither my mother nor my father hoped to feel more comfortable among free-market liberal capitalists than in a restored post-Stalinist state. They were both of the left, my middle-class mother further to the left than my working-class father who actually worked in a ministry. Ideology would, if anything, have kept them at home. They lived quite well in the given context and weren't economic migrants.

The truth is that my mother was afraid, not so much for herself as for us, her children. She had survived two concentration camps; my father had survived forced labour. They had history gnawing at their nerves. Neither of them could have demonstrated that their lives were in immediate danger. Instead they took the dangerous impromptu risk of walking out of the country at night in a wholly arbitrary party of a dozen or so, across the Austrian border, arriving there with one suitcase of clothes and nothing more. At that stage I had just three words of English – A.A. Milne's AND, BUT, SO as read in my bilingual copy of *Now We Are Six*. We also had a bilingual edition of Milne's *Winnie the Pooh*. In this poem based on the memory of crossing the Hungarian-Austrian border by night, Milne's characters – the owl and the ass in the Hundred-Acre Wood – serve as forms of familiarity.

My father carries me across a field

My father carries me across a field.
It's night and there are trenches filled with snow.
Thick mud. We're careful to remain concealed

From something frightening I don't yet know.
And then I walk and there is space between
The four of us. We go where we have to go.

Did I dream it all, this ghostly scene,
The hundred-acre wood where the owl blinked
And the ass spoke? Where I am cosy and clean

In bed, but we are floating, our arms linked
Over the landscape? My father moves ahead
Of me, like some strange, almost extinct

Species, and I follow him in dread
Across the field towards my own extinction.
Spirits everywhere are drifting over blasted

Terrain. The winter cold makes no distinction
Between them and us. My father looks round
And smiles then turns away. We have no function

In this place but keep moving, without sound,
Lost figures who leave only a blank page
Behind them, and the dark and frozen ground

They pass across as they might cross a stage.

We might well have been moving into extinction. My parents would never again be what they had been and what they might have become. Once in Austria the process of unbecoming became relatively easy. Refugee services were waiting for us, both in Austria and, a few days, later in Britain, after we had been offered a flight there. Reception was efficient and kindly. We were regarded as victim-heroes of a failed but heroic Uprising against the Cold War enemy. Sentiment was with us.

So was our historical baggage. In Metro, the longest poem of my career, there are a couple of verses in which I try to sum up what we had left behind in Budapest. The physical city described in it stands in for history: the empire of the living becomes the empire of the dead.

[Metro 2 2/3]

The empire underground: the tunneling
Begins. The earth gives up her worms and shards,
Old coins, components, ordnance, bone and glass,
Nails, muscle, hair, flesh, shrivelled bits of string,
Shoe leather, buttons, jewels, instruments.
And out of these come voices, words,
Stenches and scents,
And finally desire, pulled like a tooth.
It's that or constancy that leads us down
To find a history which feels like truth.

That baggage of old coins, components, bits of lace and so forth is the kind of thing any refugee brings with them. It is an emblem of the real baggage of those who leave without much deliberation or calculation simply because of what appears as a pressing necessity. The children and teenagers in the jungle at Calais carry something similar. They bring their foreignness with them to squat in the mud of an alien port.

England was not our intended destination. That was Australia where my father had a cousin: we had no one in England. But Australia rejected us because of my mother's health, so we had to remain. Altogether some 28,000 Hungarians chose to remain in the UK.

What did we offer our kindly hosts?

My father had some English before we came. The rest of us – my mother, brother and I – had none. The English my father possessed made him useful in helping to process other refugees, which is what he did while we spent four months along with those others in various off-season boarding houses in or near Margate, attending English classes. My father interpreted for fellow refugees, who were sent off to jobs in Wolverhampton or Luton or wherever their skill and experience would come in handy. My father's particular skill lay in plumbing, heating and ventilation at managerial level, so they found him a first job in London and, remarkably enough, enabled us to put down a deposit on a first house there. Starting from zero that was nothing short of a miracle, a remarkable act of generosity that was enough to make life-long anglophiles of us all. Meanwhile my mother, a press photographer, found work in a photographer's studio and shop in Oxford Street.

Having settled in we set about assimilating. First of all we were to speak English, not Hungarian, at home. We would never go back; very few people in the world spoke Hungarian so the language would be redundant and only slow down the rate at which we, the children, learned English and made a go of school. Budapest was no longer home. My father anglicised the pronunciation of his name to Surtees, as in the racing driver, even altering the spelling for strictly work purposes when visiting building sites to make life easier for foremen and site managers. His face and accent did not accord with the adopted name of course, and the accent was thick.

But it was a reasonable, relaxed ambience. By the time we began our English school careers there were other immigrant issues to think about. The Notting Hill Riots of 1958 for example and, ten years later, Enoch Powell's 'rivers of blood' speech. Then, just four years after that, in the wake of Idi Amin, came the Ugandan Asians. We might have been foreign but at least we were white.

And because we were white and less conspicuous we did not experience the resentment that met West Indians or Asians. We took the mild if diffident benevolence of England for granted. We had melted in hadn't we? And the country into which we had melted was a stable, powerful force in the world, a safe place, ever less powerful now perhaps, ever less imperial, but still safe.

In 1984 I returned to Hungary for the first time as an adult. And kept returning. In 1989 my family and I spent almost the whole year there watching the state fall apart. Ten years later, after several books I changed publishers for the second time, and my work to that date was sorted into two distinct volumes: *The Budapest File* (2000) dealing with work that had a Hungarian interest (by which time I had written a good deal on that) and one titled *An English Apocalypse* (2001), that dealt with settling in England and simply being here. In this way my work – and self – was neatly divided for public consumption.

An English Apocalypse was chiefly written in Ireland while I was a fellow at TCD, Dublin, and contained many memories of the seventies but also registered what I sensed was a mounting crisis in English identity and self-confidence. There were five apocalypses at the end of the sequence. This is one of them.

Death by deluge

I have seen roads come to a full stop in mid-
sentence as if their meaning had fallen off
the world. And this is what happened, what meaning did

that day in August. The North Sea had been rough
and rising and the bells of Dunwich rang
through all of Suffolk. One wipe of its cuff

down cliffs and in they went, leaving birds to hang
puzzled in the air, their nests gone. Enormous
tides ran from Southend to Cromer. They swung

north and south at once, as if with a clear purpose,
thrusting through Lincolnshire, and at a rush
drowning Sleaford, Newark, leaving no house

uncovered. Nothing remained of The Wash
but water. Peterborough, Ely, March, and Cambridge
were followed by Royston, Stevenage, the lush

grass of Shaw's Corner. Not a single ridge
remained. The Thames Valley filled to the brim
and London Clay swallowed Wapping and Greenwich.

Then west, roaring and boiling. A rapid skim
of Hampshire and Dorset, then the peninsula:
Paignton, Plymouth, Lyme, Land's End. A slim

line of high hills held out but all was water-colour,
the pure English medium, intended for sky, cloud, and sea.
Less earth than you could shift with a spatula.

Something important began in the seventies that more-or-less coincided with the time of Britain's EU entry: a process that involved the fuel crisis, the three-day week, the winter of discontent, and the rise of Margaret Thatcher, which was followed by the destruction of old mass industries that had sustained stable communities and provided social cohesion. Britain had become the sick man of Europe. And despite an economic recovery through the later eighties and nineties, the cohesion had vanished. The economic body was no longer sick, but the social soul was.

Somebody had to be blamed for all this, and the EU was the easiest scapegoat. If Britain was falling apart by 2001 in the way *An English Apocalypse* suggested that can't have been Britain's fault, can it? Who took away our pounds and ounces, our twelve pence to the shilling and our pride? Our image of sinister, faceless foreign bureaucrats – so beloved by the right-wing press – conjured our own long resentful demons. The foreigners kept coming. They were after our jobs, after our benefits, after our houses, changing our ways of life, the ground of our very being. These foreigners were not all the result of the EU's free movement policy, more to do with globalisation beyond Europe, with the disasters of wars or famine, with Britain's own colonial history.

The concerns associated with large numbers of immigrants were masked by what people – and increasingly the popular press – called 'political correctness' (Political Correctness Gone Mad), by which they meant the control of language and manners, and in some cases of law, of the means of even beginning to address the concerns. That was seen as repression and, in some ways, for the best of reasons, so it was.

What I am suggesting is that that which was successfully suppressed after Notting Hill in 1958 was inarticulate and still struggling for manoeuvre in 2016 when it finally found an outlet in the referendum campaign. The end of empire had found its cry. Hence the fury. Hence the demons.

Two or three years ago I was chairing a small literary festival in the small Norfolk town where we live. In order to publicise the event we decided to read poems in the marketplace on market day. That was fun. Somebody there decided to read John Betjeman's 'A Subaltern's Love Song', which begins: 'Miss Joan Hunter Dunn, Miss Joan Hunter Dunn/furnished and burnished by Aldershot sun . . .', a poem that wonderfully conjures an England of the 1930s. After the event the sweetest and nicest person on the committee said to me, 'I don't suppose you will ever fully understand that poem, George'.

Maybe he is right. Maybe, even to the nicest of men, a foreigner can never be truly of the atavistic tribe. That wouldn't be peculiar to the English, of course: that is, I suspect, a general truth about specific historical moments when tribes come under pressure. Maybe the English tribe is at such a point and has decided to wash its hands of foreigners. I started out by saying that I am not, for now, directly affected by Brexit and the tide of emotion it has loosed. But the conversation with the genuinely nice man who pointed out that I could never truly understand the heart of Englishness in the Betjeman poem – and he may be right, of course – is a salutary reminder that, in subtle ways, I remain a foreigner. Maybe the door to Brexit is the door out for some of us.

I will finish with a short poem titled 'Port Selda'. There is a much loved popular poem by the Anglo-Welsh poet Edward Thomas titled 'Adlestrop'. In Thomas's poem of 1917, it is a sunny day during the war when his train makes a brief unscheduled stop at a tiny station, Adlestrop, by an empty platform where no one gets in or out. It seems quiet there until suddenly the poet hears 'all the birds of Oxfordshire and Gloucestershire'. What we know, as readers, is that the poet himself was very soon to die in the war. For many people this poem represents a sense of England at war, England as the elegiac quiet place sensed as if by accident.

My title, 'Port Selda', is in fact the word Adlestrop spelled backwards. It is about the beauty of the country and the inevitability of rejection. Many of us are at Port Selda now.

The immigrant at Port Selda

I got off at Port Selda and looked out for the harbour
but it was quiet, nothing smelled of the sea,
all I saw was a station by a well-kept arbour
with a notice pinned to a tree.

It said: *Welcome to Port Selda, you who will never be
our collective unconscious nor of our race.
This is the one true genealogical tree
and this the notice you will not deface.*

It was beautiful there. It was Friday in late
autumn and all the birds of the county sang
their hearts out. I noted down the date.
The sun was shining and the church-bells rang.

INDEX